Emile Durkheim and
the Reformation of Sociology

EMILE DURKHEIM
and the
REFORMATION OF
SOCIOLOGY

Stjepan G. Meštrović

Rowman & Littlefield
PUBLISHERS

ROWMAN & LITTLEFIELD PUBLISHERS, INC.

Published in the United States of America
by Rowman & Littlefield Publishers, Inc.
4720 Boston Way, Lanham, Maryland 20706

British Cataloging in Publication Information Available

Library of Congress Cataloging-in-Publication Data

Meštrović, Stjepan Gabriel.
Emile Durkheim and the reformation of sociology /
Stjepan G. Meštrović.
p. cm.
Includes bibliographical references and index.
1. Durkheim, Emile, 1858–1917. 2. Sociologists—
France—Biography. 3. Sociology—History. I. Title.
HM22.F8D854 1993
301'.092—dc20 93–16886 CIP
[B]

ISBN 0–8476–7602–1 (cloth : alk. paper)
ISBN 0–8476–7867–9 (pbk. : alk. paper)

Printed in the United States of America

For my brother Domagoj, my father Tvrtko,
and my grandfather Ivan, who all died too soon

Contents

Preface to the Paperback Edition

W HY SHOULD A POSTMODERN READER of the 1990s be interested in a book on Emile Durkheim and his sociology? Hasn't sociology moved beyond Durkheim's works and theories, most of which were published in the 1890s? Hasn't enough already been written about Durkheim? These are questions that the critical reader ought to ask as he or she picks up this book.

My reply is that the present *fin de siècle* finds sociology in a crisis of relevance every bit as acute as it was about a century ago,[1] when Durkheim "almost single-handedly first established sociology as an independent academic discipline"[2] and tried to relate sociology to the pressing social problems and issues of his age. The world today is again in such dire straits that it needs the Durkheimian insights that it never appreciated fully enough during the past century: Nationalism, socialism, capitalism, communism, and fundamentalism—the leading "isms" that Durkheim tried to apprehend sociologically—are still causing turmoil in the world. As for all those books on Durkheim, with the notable exception of Harry Alpert's 1939 classic, *Emile Durkheim and His Sociology*, most of them perpetuate the erroneous interpretation that Durkheim was a positivist. Nowadays, postmodernism, not positivism, is the buzzword in academia, yet very few persons can understand what postmodernism stands for. In short, both sociology and the world seem to have lost their bearings, and Durkheim's sociology, more than any other, can help to restore balance.

Durkheim presents food for thought in this, our troubled *fin de siècle*, because he cuts through erroneous standardized clichés and stereotypes concerning the role of sociology and its conceptual arsenal for forging a liberal democratic world order. Perhaps the most disastrous error and cliché has been, and continues to be, that Auguste

Comte was the father of sociology. Closely related is the stereotype that sociology is a child of the Enlightenment, and that Durkheim was a disciple of Comte.[3] These are disastrous errors because the end of the twentieth century has called in question more deeply than ever before the Enlightenment legacy of progress and faith in the establishment of liberal democracy solely on the basis of rationalism. The postmodernists, especially, have linked the Enlightenment legacy to terror and totalitarianism.[4] In particular, Marxism and communism are modernist doctrines derived from the Enlightenment, such that the recent fall of communism in the former Soviet Union and Eastern Europe has called into question the viability of the rest of the so-called modernist project.[5] Because twentieth century sociology had wed itself to Marxist, functionalist, positivist and other modernist doctrines derived from the Enlightenment—and not Durkheim's *fin de siècle* version of sociology—it is implicated in the demise and controversy that surrounds these doctrines.

Consider the Durkheimian problem that Harry Alpert (1961: 13) cited as most controversial, namely, the relationship between the collective consciousness and collective representations. This is still a problem, even for postmodern intellectuals. I devote many pages in this book to an explication of these two central Durkheimian concepts. Without the notion of a collective consciousness, sociology loses its *raison d'être*, and the layperson lacks a vocabulary that enables one to speak of cultural differences in the world. This is because the collective consciousness is like a nation's unique, albeit composite, personality. If a collective consciousness does not exist, then one must assume a Marxist, functionalist, or some other modernist vision of the world in which nationalism does not count and individualism is derived solely from the individual. Yet, the failure of communism to stamp out nationalism should make intellectuals question, finally, the viability of the Enlightenment delusion that the social world consists solely of individuals. The capitalist world that supposedly "won" the Cold War with its narcissistic ethic of consumerism may also have reached its limits in the so-called West. In any event, nationalism and ethnic identity have become noisier than ever in the post-Cold War era, and cannot be ignored.

Durkheim's concept of the collective representation is equally crucial. Representationalism assumes that the world does not consist of brute facts, readily and directly accessible to the knower. In this form, representationalism has been accepted by philosophers at least since Immanuel Kant. But Durkheim adds a new twist, that the Kantian mental categories used by the individual to make sense of the world are not derived exclusively from the individual. Instead, they are derived, in large measure, from the collectivity, ranging from culture to other varieties of the collective consciousness. This Durkheimian insight is every bit as momentous as Kant's, and, in fact, complements Kant's exclusively psychological formulation of how knowledge of the world is derived. It is vital for the revivification of sociology and for enabling individuals to communicate with each other cross-culturally. Yet contemporary communication theory perpetuates the Enlightenment delusion of a universal ground for discourse that exists independently of culture.

Contemporary intellectuals in diverse fields still cling to the outmoded, naive, and counter-sociological idea that individualism is derived from the individual. In chapter 8 especially, but throughout this book, I strive to convince the reader that Durkheim was more correct to claim that individualism is actually a collective phenomenon: the high regard for the individual that is taken for granted in modern societies is supported by collective representations and other "moral forces" emanating from a nation's collective consciousness. The consequence of this insight is that philosophical and sociological ideas cannot be addressed without taking into account national purpose. Against the Marxists and other modernists who sought to eliminate all nationalism, Durkheim ([1925] 1961) sought to distinguish "good" from "bad" nationalism, and to nurture the former while attempting to find ways to restrain the latter. With the end of the Cold War, nationalism has become the most important driving force behind world events, yet most Western intellectuals still tend to cling to Marxist or positivistic assumptions which tend to support the view that all nationalism is dangerous or antithetical to individualism. Durkheim would have one consider the apparent paradox that only a healthy, moral form of nationalism can nurture a healthy, moral form of individualism, distinct from narcissism, egoism, and anomic forms of individualism.[6]

Despite Durkheim's efforts, the notion of collective consciousness still sounds strange to the Western, modernist ear, and in the late twentieth century, it is likely to be labeled as being a "politically incorrect" concept. This is because this Durkheimian concept assumes cultural *differences*—that each nation's collective consciousness is something like a unique personality—whereas the prevailing postmodernist cliché in the present *fin de siècle* is that humanity has reached "the end of difference," which means that all individuals are supposedly the same regardless of culture.[7] If humanity had finally reached the "end of culture"[8] as well as "the end of history,"[9] why do travellers still perceive differences and problems in communication when they travel to countries other than their own? Moreover, all this apocalyptic discourse leads straight to the notion of the "end of sociology,"[10] for it negates the *raison d'être* for sociology as a discipline distinct from psychology. Here again, intellectuals in the present *fin de siècle* blithely repeat the prejudices that Durkheim had attempted to transcend during the *fin de siècle* in which he lived.

Durkheim's Continued Relevance

Why was Durkheim so sensitive to the idea of collective consciousness or collective personality? And why are his insights still important today? One reply to the first question points to Durkheim's Jewish heritage, and in particular, his family's rabbinical background, both of which accentuated the importance of tradition and of the collectivity despite modernity. Another answer lies in the widespread influence of Arthur Schopenhauer's philosophy during the previous *fin de siècle* (Ellenberger 1970, Magee 1983, Simmel [1907] 1986). Schopenhauer challenged Kant's focus on the lonely individual as the seat of an *a priorism* and rationalism whose origins were left unexplained. Schopenhauer argued that the will to life was the ground or referent for rationality. Even though he did not argue explicitly for the notion of society, it was a short step for Durkheim to complete the step that society might be a manifestation of the will to life that serves as the ground or referent for various cultural phenomena, ranging from language and religion to civilization itself. And this is still important because the notion of the will to life puts the struggle for existence at the center of all arguments. Most of the non-Western world still struggles for existence in an open and dramatic way, and one of Durkheim's ([1893] 1933) most important arguments was that modernity itself merely softens and attenuates, but cannot eliminate, this same, primitive and primal struggle for existence.

Some reviewers have tried mistakenly to attribute to me the unprovable claim that Schopenhauer influenced Durkheim directly. Let me note here that I never made such a claim and that in any event, according to Durkheim's grandson, Etienne Halphen, all of Durkheim's notes and unpublished papers were lost during the Nazi era, so that one shall never know for certain who influenced Durkheim. My argument is much more straightforward, and perhaps more important: Evidence abounds from philosophers, historians, and artists that Schopenhauer was *the* philosophical superstar of the previous *fin de siècle* in Europe. Durkheim had no choice but to confront Schopenhauer's vast influence on the conceptual vocabulary of his age, a vocabulary that includes Sigmund Freud's concept of the unconscious, Henri Bergson's *l'élan vital*, Georg Simmel's concept of life, and Charles Darwin's focus on the struggle for existence, among many others. A closely related and interesting theme for future investigation might be why so many of the leading intellectuals from the previous turn of the century who developed Schopenhauer's conceptual apparatus were Jewish.[11] To this end, I offer the analysis of Freud's and Durkheim's views on religion in chapter 6 as an illustration of what is distinctive about this discourse.

In reality, once one abandons the fruitless search for direct influences upon Durkheim, one is in a position to appreciate the obvious anti-Enlightenment strands in Durkheim's sociology that have been neglected for much too long. Consider the concept of anomie, misconstrued by the functionalists as the nonexistent "normlessness." In chapters 4 and 5, I demonstrate that Durkheim never wrote of anomie as normlessness, but as a state of collective evil or derangement characterized by a painful state of infinite desires that are never satiated. Here again, Durkheim's Jewish and particularly rabbinical heritage probably played a role in sensitizing him to the idea that society itself could be evil: anomie becomes the secular counterpart to the religious notion of sin (Meštrović 1985a). Yet these religious and traditional dimensions to anomie also meshed, again, with the popularity of Schopenhauer's own notion of the infinitely striving will that makes the enlightened person suffer more, not less, than his or her ancestors.

The most important yet neglected social problem today is that of anomie: "Anomie, according to Durkheim, is the most pervasive discontent with which modern civilization is beset" according to Harry Alpert (1961:24).[12] This problem goes beyond the structural-functionalist misinterpretation of anomie as a pathological distortion that lies at the periphery of society and affects only its deviants. Rather, in Durkheim's original intent, anomie afflicts society at its core. And an anomic society hides its collective sickness from itself. As such, the remedy for anomie requires radical social restructuring which can occur only after the neurotic society achieves collective insight into its affliction. One has only to think of the dramatic social problems in today's postmodern societies, from violence to the near extinction of the family, to appreciate the relevance of Durkheim's conceptualization of anomie as collective derangement over the insipid and useless functionalist notion of "normlessness."

The power and importance of Durkheim's concept of *institutional anomie*—again, a condition that affects modern and by extension, postmodern society at its core, not just its periphery—applies also to the societies that have just emerged from the oppressive yoke of communism (and that might well return to communism in a counter-revolutionary wave that will shock the world).[13] Following the dramatic collapse of the Berlin Wall in 1989, Western economists began to export consumer-based capitalism to nations that are still reeling from the collective pathology engendered by the communist experiment. Durkheim's writings lead one to predict that the introduction of infinite consumption—already problematic in the West—to nations whose societal institutions such as the family, professional groups, and religion have been weakened by communism is an invitation to rampant anomie.

In calling on sociologists to reexamine and reappreciate their heritage through Durkheim, that most sociological of sociologists, I echo Harry Alpert's fear that contemporary sociology has already become "the 20th century's dismal science, just as economics became the dismal science of the 19th".[14] Alpert continues:

> For a number of years sociology has been suffering from a progressive degeneration of the critical faculty, with its energies increasingly devoted on the empirical level to niggling descriptions of social minutiae and on the theoretical level to bland apologetics for things as they are. As a discipline, therefore, sociology badly needs to recover its bearings, and one way to accomplish this is by going back to the beginning and finding out what went wrong. Going back to the beginning means, to a considerable extent, going back to Durkheim.

Why Durkheim?

Several colleagues have questioned why I chose the reformation of sociology, not society, as the focus of this book, and why Durkheim was singled out as sociology's most important reformer. Why should sociologists consider making Durkheim's sociology the centerpiece of sociology's renewal, as opposed to the legacies of Karl Marx, Max Weber, George Herbert Mead, Talcott Parsons, or any number of other intellectual traditions? The most obvious reason is that these other traditions have been central to many intellectual movements in the twentieth century, and they have failed to avert sociology's present crisis of relevance or to make good on their grand promises for establishing the good society. Marxism, functionalism, Weberian "value-free" science, and symbolic interactionism, among other popular sociological movements, eclipsed completely the legacy of Durkheim's followers. In sum, these other sociologies have had their chance, and have failed overall, whereas Durkheim's sociology was never apprehended correctly, and was never given a fair hearing.

The less obvious reason for throwing one's lot with Durkheim is that these other sociological traditions are less sociological at their core. No other sociologist has matched Durkheim's insistence that in order to exist, sociology must have its own subject matter, namely, society. And for society to be a subject unique to sociology, society must be conceived as a phenomenon *sui generis*, distinct from the sum of individuals who comprise it. This centerpiece of Durkheimian sociology has been largely rejected by subsequent sociologists (Alpert 1961), yet the proposed alternatives have not resolved the dilemma of why sociology should be taken seriously if it does not have its own, unique subject matter. Thus, contemporary sociology has deteriorated into a no-man's land, a hopeless hodge podge of concepts that resembles psychology, anthropology, economics and the other social sciences, but that cannot claim its own right to exist independently of these other sciences.

It is not my intention here to delve further into the implications of Durkheim's conceptualization of society relative to other theorists and theories—that is accomplished in the pages of this book. But I should offer one clear illustration of why Durkheim should be taken seriously. Consider the Marxist concept of alienation, which stresses the human person's sense of estrangement from his or her self due to the fact that one has been reduced to being treated as a cog in the machinery of modern living. Marx's proposed solution is to restore the human person back to his or her self. But this is a psychological solution to a devastating social problem that begs the question: What is the source or referent or ground for the psychological category of "human dignity?" Marx, along with the functionalists and other modernists, assumes that individualism is derived from the individual, whereas Durkheim claimed that it cannot be self-begotten, and must be derived from society. Given the failure of the Marxist experiment in communist lands, and the problems with modernity cited by the postmodernists, Durkheim's argument ought to be given a fair hearing at long last.

The present book is structured so that it addresses Durkheim's most basic concepts, the nuts and bolts of sociology, so to speak: collective consciousness, collective representations, anomie, society, social fact, and the individual. I do not use the word postmodernism in this book as I have in subsequent elaborations of my argument, and that is probably a good thing. Postmodernism is a buzzword that serves to confuse more than to clarify contemporary discourse. Yet the present discussion of Durkheim's basic concepts is useful in cutting through some of the confusion in the postmodern discourse. I would like to point out some of the key elements in this power of Durkheim's sociology to continue to clarify and explain issues so late into the twentieth century.

Since this book has been published, the world has witnessed the dramatic collapse of communism in Eastern Europe and the former Soviet Union. Yet the aftershock and unforeseen consequences of this grand *event* proved to be more far-reaching than most people could imagine, and this will continue to be true well into the next century. Most intellectuals and commentators responded to this dramatic event solely as an event, not as a *social fact*, as taught by Durkheim. "Facts versus events" (pp. 88-91) is a key opposition in Durkheim's writings. If Durkheim is right that the collapse of communism is a social fact, then it resulted from long-standing social fissures and forces that led to the events that continue to preoccupy intellectuals in the present *fin de siècle*.

Thus, I emphasize in the present book Durkheim's disdain for Marxism, and his prediction in *Le Socialisme* ([1928] 1978) that social-ist doctrines, including communism, were destined to fail. One should consider that when Durkheim made these predictions, most intellectuals were predicting that socialism would "win" over capital-ism, and that twentieth century intellectuals took Marx much more seriously than Durkheim. The much touted New World Order of the present *fin de siècle* is a faint echo of the heralded, *socialist* New World Order of the previous *fin de siècle*.[15] Durkheim's courage and foresight in defying the opinions of his contemporaries need to be appreciat-ed. But in addition, Durkheim had warned that without moral regula-tion, capitalism would fail every bit as miserably as socialism and com-munism, because all three doctrines are erected on the incorrect premise that economic self-interest can promote moral integration in society.

Durkheim's ominous prediction reverberates with the deep-seated cynicism that followed quickly on the heels of the collective Western euphoria at the interpretation that capitalism had "won" the race with communism. At the present time, the citizens of capitalist nations are weary of all the economic scandals, recessions, injustices, and hardships caused by so-called victorious capitalism. True, no one knows what system might replace capitalism. But all over the world, people are searching for a new faith. Alas, capitalism does not and cannot inspire faith, because it is predicated on selfishness and is merely expedient and useful.

In suggesting that Durkheim's sociology serves as the basis for sociology's revivification so that it will be in a position to help societies chart a new, just, and moral course, I do not mean to imply that Durk-heim had the last word in sociology, that he should not be criticized, or that his sociology cannot be improved. Rather, I mean that his soci-ology needs to be used as the springboard for further thinking, and that since his death, sociology has struggled to survive in an arrested stage of development. The sociology that Durkheim fashioned about a century ago is now in real danger of becoming extinct, and radical measures are needed to revive it. In their attempts to respond to this crisis of relevance, even struggle for existence, sociologists will no doubt try to revive the many other non-Durkheimian traditions that were absorbed by sociology, and some will even try to preserve the *status quo.* My central point is that these other sociological traditions are not up to the task of revivification without the bedrock that only Durkheim's sociology can provide. Without the Durkheimian vocabulary of social facts, collective consciousness, and society as a phenomenon *sui generis*, sociology cannot exist as sociology.

Finally, the Durkheimian projects of social renewal seem to be more, not less, relevant in our troubled *fin de siècle*: Rationalism still needs to be renovated, not abandoned, because the postmodern revolution is threatening to overthrow the reign of reason that has been the hallmark of Western culture at least since the Enlightenment. Anomie needs to be apprehended in its original, Durkheimian meaning as the "infinity of desires," not the fictitious "normlessness" promoted by the functionalists, because the mere imposition of norms has done nothing to contain the tyranny of passions that are an integral aspects of postmodern social life. The planet is quickly running out of resources that make anomic consumerism possible or practical. The intellectual anomie that Durkheim has warned against needs to be recognized in the compartmentalization, waste, fraud, and increasing irrelevance of the academic establishment in enabling humans to survive. Durkheim conceived of sociology as the "science of morality," but this phrase still conjures up oppressive images of imposing someone else's system of morality upon us and our children. Yet without a system of morality, is it any wonder that crime and violence have reached epidemic proportions in the world? Durkheim's original insight in this regard still seems relevant: By virtue of its existence, every society is a moral system, such that without morality, there can be no society as such, only the isolated individual. And the isolated individual is the enemy of civilization, in Durkheim's typically *fin de siècle* assessment.

Finally, Durkheim's distinction between two forms of individualism, one moral and benign, which bestows dignity upon the human person, and the other cancerous and dangerous, which leads to narcissism, needs to be taken seriously. Otherwise, humanity will not free itself from the limitations of being forced to choose between an illusory freedom from all social restraints promulgated by liberals that leads only to narcissism,[16] versus the nostalgic return to oppressive traditions touted by conservatives.[17] The cataclysmic changes and crises in all aspects of contemporary society, from corrupt political institutions to the disintegration of the family, call for new insights and solutions. I contend that Durkheim's original sociology offers a powerful basis for such a renewal, and that the full import of his ideas has not been appreciated despite a century's worth of elaboration upon his ideas. This is because he was always apprehended through a prism inimical to his intentions, whether the prism was Marxist, functionalist, positivist, or otherwise modernist and non-Durkheimian. In the pages that follow, I attempt to offer a genuinely Durkheimian Durkheim.

Notes

1. See Meštrović, Stjepan G., *The Coming Fin de Siècle: An Application of Durkheim's Sociology to Modernity and Postmodernism* (London: Routledge, 1991).

2. Alpert, Harry, "The Second Inventory of Sociology," *The New York Times Book Review* 15 July 1973:21.

3. Anyone who questions Alpert's argument should read the severe criticisms of Comte as well as Henri de Saint-Simon in Durkheim, Emile, *Socialism and Saint-Simon* (Yellow Springs, Ohio: Antioch Press [1928] 1958).

4. Lyotard, Jean-Francois, *The Postmodern Condition* (Minneapolis: The University of Minnesota Press, 1984).

5. Bauman, Zygmunt, *Intimations of Postmodernity* (London: Routledge, 1992).

6. Many intellectuals have been preoccupied with these problems associated with Western intellectuals, including Riesman, David, *The Lonely Crowd* (New Haven, Conn.: Yale University Press, 1950); Bellah, Robert N. *Habits of the Heart* (Berkeley: University of California Press, 1985); Lasch, Christopher, *The Culture of Narcissism* (New York: W.W. Norton, 1979); Bloom, Allan, *The Closing of the American Mind* (New York: Simon & Schuster, 1987), among others.

7. See Rosenau, Pauline, *Postmodernism and the Social Sciences* (Princeton: Princeton University Press, 1992); Baudrillard, Jean, *America* (London: Verso, 1986); Fukuyama, Francis, *The End of History and the Last Man* (New York: Free Press, 1992), among many others.

8. Baudrillard, Jean, *America* (London: Verso, 1986).

9. Fukuyama, Francis, *The End of History and the Last Man* (New York: Free Press, 1992).

10. See Kantrowitz, Barbara, "Sociology's Lonely Crowd," *Newsweek*, 3 February 1992:55. See also the editorial entitled "Accounting for the Declining Fortunes of Sociology," *The Chronicle of Higher Education*, 16 September 1992:B3.

11. Zygmunt Bauman touches on some aspects of this question in his *Modernity and Ambivalence* (Ithaca, NY: Cornell University Press, 1990), but without touching directly on Schopenhauer's philosophy. Nevertheless, his discussion of Freud, Simmel, and Kafka in this context is first-rate.

12. Note the close similarity to Freud's ([1930] 1961) emphasis on the theme of civilization and its discontents, which is not peculiar to either Freud or Durkheim, but typical of intellectual discourse in the previous *fin de siècle*.

13. Obviously, I lack the space in this essay to pursue this important theme. The interested reader should consult Meštrović, Stjepan G., *The Road From Paradise* (Lexington, KY: University Press of Kentucky, 1993); Meštrović, Stjepan G., *The Barbaric Temperament* (London: Routledge, 1993); and Meštrović, Stjepan G., *Postmodernism and Postcommunism* (London: Routledge, 1993).

14. Harry Alpert, "The Second Founder of Sociology," *New York Times Book Review*, 15 July 1973:21.

15. Wells, H.G., *The New America: The New World* (London: Cresset, 1935).

16. Lasch, Christopher, *The Culture of Narcissism* (New York: W.W. Norton, 1979).

17. Bloom, Allan, *The Closing of the American Mind* (New York: Simon & Schuster, 1987).

Preface and Acknowledgments

T HE RESEARCH FOR THIS BOOK was supported by a fellowship from the National Endowment for the Humanities which enabled me to leave my teaching duties and travel to France to search for the historical and personal Durkheim. I am grateful to Philippe Besnard at the Maison des Sciences de l'Homme in Paris for his help in locating persons and texts, as well as for sharing his ideas. Durkheim's grandson, Etienne Halphen, was also extremely gracious and allowed himself to be interviewed at length on several occasions, formally and informally, and has continued to correspond with me since my return to the United States. Descendants of Durkheim's followers were also helpful regarding interviews or information, among them Pierre Halbwachs, Pierre Mauss, Gerard Hubert, Francette Léon, and Marie Mauss. The curator at the Musée Landowski, Michèle Agis-Garcin, and the curator at the Musée Bouchard, Marie Bouchard, were also very helpful.

I appreciate the assistance of Rabbi H. Elkaim and the entire staff of the records department in the city hall in Epinal, Durkheim's birthplace. I would also like to thank the Grand Rabbin de la Moselle, Jacques Ouaknin, for granting me an interview in Metz. In the United States, I was assisted in obtaining library materials by our fine reference staff at Lander College: Ann Hare, Susan Going, Betty Williams, and Mary Beth Fecko.

With regard to interpreting the data thus obtained, I extend my deepest appreciation to David Riesman. While I am solely responsible for the interpretations put forth in this book I want to indicate the great extent of his intellectual influence upon me. In particular, he suggested the distinction between the two types of individualism that I develop herein; he suggested that I pursue the question of how much sociology existed in Durkheim's time; he referred me to specific readings and texts; and he put me in touch with persons whose comments were helpful in formulating my arguments. These persons include his son, Paul Riesman, whom I met in Paris, and Mustafa Emirbayer, a doctoral candidate at Harvard University, who critiqued the earliest draft of Chapter 1. My correspondence with Professor Riesman concerning his *Lonely Crowd,* Bloom's *Closing of the American Mind,* and innumerable other topics was also helpful in my formulating various insights that went into this book.

For the most part, this work was written in April 1987. Still, seeds for various arguments had been planted prior to that magical springtime, and I gratefully acknowledge the help of others in this regard. The idea of representationalism developed from my 1982 doctoral dissertation and the guidance of Barry Glassner. We remain friends to this day, and I continue to benefit from his intellectual stimulation. The theme of representationlism developed through an essay published in *Current Perspectives in Social Theory* (see Meštrović 1985c) to its finally being wedded to Schopenhauer's philosophy as a result of my research in France. As an undergraduate at Harvard University, I rebelled at Merton's notion of anomie as "normlessness." No doubt my graduate training in theological studies at Harvard Divinity School enabled me to seize upon the moral implications of *anomie* as Durkheim used the term, which was brought out in essays published by the *Journal for the Scientific Study of Religion* (Meštrović 1985a) and *Social Problems* (Meštrović and Brown 1985). Helen Brown was very helpful in my explorations of the meanings of anomie as *dérèglement* and in helping me compare French and English versions of Durkheim's writings. Conversations with Robert W. Daly and Guy Martin were also inspirational. But again, my discovery of the importance of Schopenhauer's philosophy to Durkheim recast all these previous efforts into a new light. Professor Riesman's comments on individualism, linked with my interest in Schopenhauer, resulted in my essay on political anomie in *Research in Political Sociology* (Meštrović 1988a). I am grateful to the editors who worked with me in the above-mentioned projects—Scott McNall, Donald Capps, James D. Orcutt, and Richard Braungart—and to Richard Koffler, who carefully read and considered this book for publication. Thanks also to Janet S. Johnston and Mary D. Simmons for editing this manuscript.

The issue of translation must be addressed briefly. Having been raised on Serbo-Croatian, and with the American version of English as a second language, I am aware of the differences in thinking that a language can make in a nonabstract, personalized sense. Simply put, Yugoslavia "feels" profoundly different from America to me, and France "feels" closer to Yugoslavia than to America. In any case, in this book I alternate between English (American or British) and French translations, depending upon my intuitive sense for the text. Where several English versions exist—as in George Simpson's (1933) versus W.D. Halls's (1984) translations of Durkheim's (1893) *Division of Labor*—I use different translations for different passages, and sometimes resort to the original French version. I do not believe that Halls's translation is superior to Simpson's in every respect and lament the fact that Halls decided to drop the original introduction to *Division of Labor* (included as an appendix in Simpson's translation, pp. 411–35) without a word of explanation. When Simpson's translation becomes obsolete, how many future generations of sociologists will know that this important introduction—in which Durkheim battles Kant, Guyau, and the utilitarians in relation to the scientific study of morality—has been lost? My bibliography includes the French editions for most of the works I cite, so the reader who finds certain translations problematic is free to turn to these originals.

I have included my translation of passages from the text of Jean-Claude Filloux's relatively straightforward interview with Henri Durkheim. This text was given to me by Philippe Besnard and, to the best of my knowledge, has never been published in its entirety. The passages from Durkheim's (1908) debate on the unconscious are also my own translation; the reader is encouraged to read the original version in French. I should add that Lukes (1982, pp. 211–28) includes selections from this text translated by W. D. Halls, but his choice of passages does not indicate breaks in the text, and I found some of Halls's translations problematic. For example, Halls's translations of Durkheim's *agent* into the English "participant" and *conscience* into "consciousness" play into the hands of those who wish to criticize Durkheim for minimizing the psychological role of the human agent.

Finally, no account of my intellectual indebtedness in writing this book can omit why I was struck so powerfully by the connection between Durkheim and the sculptor Paul Landowski. My grandfather Ivan Meštrović and my father, Tvrtko Meštrović, were both sculptors. Both died when I was five years old—my father tragically—and left me with questions for which I have found answers in an intellectual domain and context far removed from them: Durkheim, sociology, and German philosophy. My explorations through the wilderness of sociology have always been filtered through my concerns with art and questions that are often labeled as "humanistic." I would like to think that my father and his father would have been proud of me.

CHAPTER 1

Introduction

A FEW DAYS before I was scheduled to leave France, Durkheim's grandson, the son of Durkheim's daughter, Marie, called me. Etienne Halphen said that his grandfather had been friends with the famous French sculptor Paul Landowski and had posed for Landowski's statue of John Calvin (Landowski's best-known work is the massive statue of Christ overlooking Rio de Janeiro). The Calvin statue became part of the famous group of statues in Geneva entitled "La Réformation" (described in Bouchard 1983). I was struck by the news, and M. Halphen supplied part of the reason: "Imagine my grandfather, a Jew, posing for John Calvin!" Indeed. Durkheim denigrates art and esthetics in his writings, warning, in a Calvinist vein, that all esthetic appreciation is an invitation to immorality because it focuses on pleasure, not seriousness, duty, nor discipline. So Durkheim's posing for a statue, and especially one of John Calvin, is extraordinary.

But Landowski was not just a sculptor. He regarded himself as a philosopher and, according to the curator at the Landowski museum in Paris, Landowski's friends were almost exclusively philosophers. It is often overlooked that despite Durkheim's fame as a sociologist, he was trained in philosophy and is still regarded as a philosopher in France. And Durkheim's favorite philosopher seems to have been, not Auguste Comte, whom he belittles frequently, but Arthur Schopenhauer.

André Lalande, Durkheim's colleague in the French Philosophical Society, remarked, upon the occasion of the 100th anniversary of Durkheim's birth, that Durkheim was so enamored of Schopenhauer that his students nicknamed him "Schopen" (Lalande 1960, p. 23). Nor is this unusual, despite the fact that Lalande's insight has been almost completely overlooked by contemporary sociologists, for Arthur Schopenhauer's philosophy, not Comte's positivism, seems to have constituted the starting point for much, if not most, turn-of-the-century thought (see Baillot 1927; Durant 1961; Ellenberger 1970; Goodwin 1967; Hamlyn 1980; Janik and Toulmin 1973; Lèvy 1904; Magee 1983; and Simmel [1907] 1986). The connection between Durkheim and Schopenhauer is highly suggestive and is related to Durkheim's admiration for Calvin. Schopenhauer's pessimism, focus on suffering, and treatment of suicide are passé and acknowledged readily by philosophers, but Durkheim's obsession with suffering and unhappiness tends to be ignored by sociologists.

Why did Durkheim write *Suicide*? Why did he claim in *Division of Labor in Society* that modern forms of social solidarity result in increased unhappiness for individuals? Why did he conclude in *Elementary Forms of the Religious Life* that suffering is the sacrifice individuals must pay to society? Why did he focus on constraint as a force that opposes the egoistic will in his definition of the social fact? Schopenhauer's *The World as Will and Idea* ([1818] 1977) creates a context for answering these questions because suffering, suicide, and pessimism are intimately linked to his philosophy. And Calvin's world-view provides part of the solution to the dilemmas that Schopenhauer posed. If the tyrannical, imperious "will" is the cause of all wickedness and immorality, as Schopenhauer argued, then the "will" must be disciplined, constrained, and harnessed. In Durkheim's sociology, society became the representation of John Calvin's stern God.

What the Calvin-Durkheim connection achieves, most of all, is a representation, an image, a metaphor. Durkheim built his sociology upon the notion of representations, ideas, and symbols, insisting that society is a system of representations. But Schopenhauer had earlier made that claim in *The World as Will and Idea*, which Durkheim ([1887] 1976c) apparently admired. The philosophical starting point for Schopenhauer is that no inquiry should start with the object or the subject—as most inquiries do, especially in contemporary sociology—but with the representation, which encompasses both. The world can never be known as a thing-in-itself; reality can never speak for itself. As Schopenhauer put it in the opening lines of his *The World as Will and Idea* ([1818] 1977):

> "The world is my idea:"—this is a truth which holds good for everything that lives and knows, though man alone can bring it into reflective and abstract consciousness. If he really does this, he has attained to philosophical wisdom. It then becomes clear and certain to him that what he knows is not a sun and an earth, but only an eye that sees a sun, a hand that feels an earth; that the world which surrounds him is there only as idea, i.e., only in relation to something else, the consciousness, which is himself. . . . No truth therefore is more certain, more independent of all others, and less in need of proof than this, that all that exists for

knowledge, and therefore this whole world, is only object in relation to subject, perception of a perceiver, in a word, idea.

Extending Schopenhauer's opening move to this inquiry on Durkheim, one would conclude that one can never know the real Durkheim, only a representation of him, for there is no such thing as the "real" Durkheim. And one cannot start with one's subjective opinions of him, because so much of our knowledge is buried in the unconscious (collective and private). Yet somehow, both poles of *homo duplex* must be mediated. I accept this premise from the outset. The starting point for this inquiry is the representation of Emile Durkheim as the John Calvin of sociology, the reformer who wanted to purify sociology and renovate rationalism. I shall assume also that contemporary sociology, more than ever, is in need of renovation and reform. Finally, I accept Schopenhauer's ([1813] 1899) claim that the most important aspect of an argument is not the logic that supports it, but its starting point.

The other side of the representation, according to Schopenhauer, is the will. The will is that mysterious striving force, spontaneous action and, above all, imperious desire that does its work regardless of the intellect. In fact, it works even when the intellect rests, as in sleep. It works without the intellect, as in plants. The will is stronger than the intellect. What Schopenhauer called the will became Freud's mysterious "Trieb" and was refracted into Freud's conviction that we are all "lived" in addition to the fact that we live. And what of Freud's particularistic understanding of unconscious forces that behave like persons within persons? It has Schopenhauer's mark on it. Indeed, in the middle of one of his lectures, Freud paused and said to his audience: "You may perhaps shrug your shoulders and say: 'That isn't natural science, it's Schopenhauer's philosophy!' But, Ladies and Gentlemen, why should not a bold thinker have guessed something that is afterwards confirmed by sober and painstaking detailed research?" (Freud [1933] 1965, p. 107).

Schopenhauer's will became Georg Simmel's "life," which creates its own channels, victories, and defeats regardless of what humans believe they achieve through conscious effort. Simmel made Schopenhauer's importance to sociology explicit in his *Schopenhauer and Nietzsche* ([1907] 1986), although this remains one of Simmel's least known works. The will became Bergson's "intuition," a part of Bergson's (1970) rebellion against the overly rationalistic conception of human action. The will is a concept that in Durkheim's time influenced philosophers and serious thinkers too numerous to mention, from Nietzsche ([1901] 1968) and his "will to power" to William James ([1896] 1931) and his "will to believe." And it found expression in

Durkheim's sociology. Durkheim's collective conscience is the social will acting upon humans even when they are asleep or otherwise unaware of it. It is the spontaneous action of the division of labor, which human agency did not and could not create. For Durkheim, even representations are partially autonomous and independent of the will of the human agent: they have a will of their own, combining and producing fresh representations of their own accord, something like Freud's free association of ideas. The will is the source of anomie, that bottomless abyss of human desires, as well as the origin of bias in scientific reasoning. But it is also the genesis of all that is orderly and beneficial in social life.

But the will is only the other side of the representation. Schopenhauer refuses to take sides with either pole of the object-subject distinction. The thrust of his philosophy is that it is an error to begin inquiries with either the human subject's perceptions *or* "objective" reality. Rather, the representation mediates object and subject and is always susceptible to the more powerful will. Schopenhauer posits a *homo duplex* within a *homo duplex*. Durkheim reproduced Schopenhauer's epistemology almost exactly. Durkheim, too, rejects both idealism and realism and opts for the middle ground. He makes his position especially clear in his essays "Individual and Collective Representations" (1898) and "The Dualism of Human Nature and Its Social Conditions" (1914), but it is a position ubiquitous to his works. The consequences of this move for his sociology are enormous. Durkheim avoids both the under- and oversocialized versions of society that dominate contemporary sociological theory. Durkheim denies that society is merely the outcome of human agency as well as that humans are strictly determined by society. He attempted to find a fresh solution to this age-old dilemma, although this fact has been missed in most contemporary writings about him. Contemporary sociology is in a state of crisis, polarized into the "objective" quantifiers versus the "subjective" qualitatives, with no reconciliation in sight on the contemporary horizon (Horowitz 1987). Because of its philosophical premises, Durkheim's thought holds the potential for unifying sociology and healing this serious rupture.

That Durkheim's thought holds this potential is not immediately apparent. The representations of Durkheim that have dominated thinking about him since his death do not take account of his "will" nor the "social will" of his milieu. Rather, he has been represented as an advocate of one or the other pole of the object-subject debate, refracted through sociology's crisis. For example, Durkheim has been labeled as the conservative who supposedly regarded the French Revolution with horror. It is alleged that he sought some "objective" state of social order as his penultimate goal, because he allegedly feared the "chaos" of subjectivism. In this regard Parsons (1937) wrongly aligned Durkheim's thought with Hobbes—even though Durkheim ([1892] 1965) criticized Hobbes precisely on this point (see Giddens 1986)! Moreover, this representation of Durkheim as the supreme conservative cannot explain why Durkheim thrived in the Sorbonne of the *belle époque*, which was leaning to the left (Bourgin [1938] 1970; Chastenet 1949; Logue 1983), nor his socialist tendencies, nor his ardent patriotism and loyalty to the principles of the French Republic. The concept of justice was the rallying cry of the French Revolution as well as of the socialist movement in Durkheim's time. And justice, not social order, was the "will" that drove Durkheimian sociology. As Durkheim put it in his *Division of Labor in Society* ([1893] 1933, p. 388): "Just as ancient peoples needed, above all, a common faith to live by, so we need justice." Durkheim was committed to democratic ideals. It is doubtful that he could have survived, much less thrived, at the Sorbonne had he supported "social order" in opposition to justice, had he, in other words, opposed the "social will" of the Third Republic.

Positivist and realist are two more, common representations of Durkheim, both further refractions of "objectivism." But he and his followers denied both representations (see Bouglé 1938; Durkheim [1895] 1982, p. 34; [1928] 1958). Again, one must consider that in Durkheim's time it would have been intellectual suicide to adopt either stance. Schopenhauer was not the only one who attacked positivistic sentiments with his focus on representationalism. The concept of representation—which, to repeat, mediates object and subject—was crucial to the writings of Descartes, Leibniz, Hegel, Kant, Malebranche, Ribot, Renouvier, Herbart, Wundt, Freud, Jung, Bergson, Levy-Bruhl, and a host of other philosophers and precursors of the social sciences in that era (see Lalande [1926] 1980, pp. 920–22). This concept caused an intellectual crisis with regard to the object-subject distinction and the neat division between realism and idealism. Durkheim called his resolution of this crisis "renovated rationalism," a stance that is "midway between the classical empiricism and apriorism" (Durkheim [1912] 1965, p. 31). He used "rationalism" because the world can be known only as representation, never as a thing-in-itself, and "renovated" because rationalism had to reckon with experimental science and the manifestations of the will which were becoming increasingly more free and therefore noisier—the "body" and its "appetites" and "passions." Durkheim continued (ibid.), "Thus renovated, the theory of knowledge seems destined to unite the opposing advantages of the two rival theories, without incurring their inconveniences." To miss this point is to miss the entire point of what Durkheim was trying to achieve with his version of sociology, and what it has to offer to contemporary sociology. Yet it has been missed by many contemporary commentators who write about Durkheim.

"Son of a rabbi" is another powerful symbol that has been used in writing about Durkheim. It is part of the "subjective" version of Durkheim. It is alleged that Durkheim's conception of God and religion is essentially Jewish; that he turned to religion in the first place as the result of some Freudian-like trauma because he would not become a rabbi like his father (Filloux 1977; Lacroix 1981). In other words, his sociology was but a projection of his personal troubles. But M. Halphen said that he has no knowledge of any such trauma, and pointed out that his mother, Durkheim's daughter, abandoned the Jewish faith completely, as did Durkheim. There is no evidence to suggest that Durkheim's turning away from his father's profession was necessarily traumatic. And evidence abounds that the "social will" in Durkheim's time encouraged Jews to abandon their religion and assimilate into the wider culture (Marrus 1971). Finally, anyone who compares the major tenets of the Jewish religion with the broad outlines of Durkheim's thought will find profound differences that overshadow the superficial similarities. The Jewish religion is supposed to be an optimistic, pragmatic religion that denies the existence of Satan, evil, and the necessity of suffering (Ochs 1986). Even Durkheim depicted the Jewish religion in *Suicide* as a religion devoid of despair. But Durkheim raged against pragmatism, especially in his *Pragmatism and Sociology* ([1955] 1983); he insisted that as societies progress, human happiness decreases; and, especially in his late works, he insisted—as I have already mentioned—that human suffering and sorrow are the price one must pay to society. It is far easier to spot the outlines of various versions of Christian will, with all its overtones of pessimism and emphasis upon a wicked world, in Durkheim's thought than evidence of the Jewish world-view. Durkheim, like Schopenhauer, was profoundly pessimistic in his outlook. Yet Lukes (1985, p. 546) writes that Durkheim was, "like so many of his generation prior to 1914, an optimist." In contradistinction to Lukes, I agree with Ellenberger (1970) that Durkheim and many of his colleagues should be regarded as pessimists.

Still another often-used label for Durkheim is that of extreme sociologue. It is alleged that Durkheim abhorred psychology, that he pushed his sociological argument to an extreme, that he denied the human individual any degree of freedom, feeling, or even active participation in society (Lukes 1985). His followers, especially Bouglé (1938), Mauss ([1950] 1979a), and Halbwachs ([1938] 1970), took up charges like these and always denied them. Durkheim's sociology is profoundly interdisciplinary in nature. The topics covered in the famous journal he established, *L'Année sociologique*, testify to that. The socialist tendencies of his followers testify to Durkheimian sociology's extreme sensitivity to the individual's suffering in modern society. One of Durkheim's closest followers, Paul Fauconnet ([1922] 1958, p. 32), went so far as to claim that "one would not be proposing a paradox by giving [Durkheim's] theory the name of individualism."

Not only are most of the existing symbols of Durkheim easy to criticize when one examines the context of Durkheim's historical setting, they are self-defeating with regard to sociology's right to exist as an academic discipline, even to its image. They oppose the "social will" of modern societies, which may explain why sociology is still considered to be something of an ugly word in most countries where it is practiced. For example, the focus on "social order"—alleged at least since Parsons (1937) not to be *a* problem, but *the* problem of sociology—carries an unpleasant, even offensive connotation. It is offensive to the political right as well as to the political left. The dominant ideology in America today is individualism, in its benign as well as its destructive varieties. The social order perspective definitely takes a negative attitude toward individualism. Durkheim never claimed that social order is sociology's main problem. Rather, he referred to justice in this way. It must be kept in mind that the idea of justice was the representation that provided the link among social-ism, the new Sorbonne in Durkheim's time, and the Third Republic (and, if the Jewish religion is to be invoked, one must keep in mind that justice is the dominant value expressed in the Old Testament). Moreover, not all social order characterized by what Parsons termed "normative consensus" is necessarily just. For example, dictatorships and totalitarian governments may produce a high degree of order but score low on justice. As one of Durkheim's most eloquent disci-ples, Célestin Bouglé put it (1938, p. 38):

> But let there be no mistake. Solidarity, interdependence, the weight of tradition, the necessity of connections, that is not the equivalent of overwhelming the individual, or of recommending submission to au-thority, without any reserves or criticism. Otherwise we should have admitted that sociology recognizes the rightness of totalitarian regimes, which pride themselves on suppressing the rights of the human being. Such an admission would have seared Durkheim's lips. He was the first to distinguish two kinds of solidarity, one which standardizes and one which differentiates. The former is compulsive and does not tolerate the liberty of the individual conscience. The latter, on the contrary, grants and fosters it, with the one condition that free personalities should accept the contractual order which permits them, after discussions as equals, to work as collaborators. A solidarity turned toward justice and liberty—such was the vocation of Western civilization in modern times. And sociology was not tardy in justifying this vocation in its own way.

To put it another way, one should expect that an unprejudiced person would regard contemporary sociology's expressed concerns with social order, phrased in terms of normative consensus, as unwholesome, threatening, and at least a little bit bizarre. Would one trust *any* profession that claimed its *main* concern was social *order?* Even the military, the sternest of disciplinarians, and the most conservative politicians do not claim that order is their main concern. Durkheim certainly did not make this self-defeating claim, and efforts to attribute the focus on social order to him only hurt sociology's reputation, even its chances of survival, in an era that is moving, however imperfectly, toward a morality based on individualism and justice.

What good could come to sociology from mislabeling Durkheim as a realist or positivist? If one denies the other pole of *homo duplex*, the lower, desiring, egotistical part—as these doctrines, in their overly rational optimism about human progress, deny it—then how could one explain anomie and the malignant forms of individualism? If the origins of wickedness are not in the imperious, egotistical will, then they must lie in society itself. But why would society produce its own sickness? Even if it did, the individual could do nothing to remedy the situation. Who would be interested in studying a sociology that, at every point, unwittingly denies itself and its right to exist?

Durkheim opposed egoism and narcissism, but not individualism. In many ways, this complex position is like Schopenhauer's treatment of evil in relation to the will to life, as well as John Calvin's effort to transcend "mere" individualism. By this I mean that Schopenhauer understood the spontaneous action of the will as something good, and evil as an abortion of man's rational meddling with that will. And although John Calvin advocated individualism in the sense that he felt that salvation was a private affair between God and man, it was God who was most important in that relationship—not man as the narcissistic bundle of will. Similarly, Durkheim regarded individualism as a collective representation, a force that would impress itself on human minds regardless of their subjective opinions, *as well as* the manifestation of the egotistical will. In other words, Durkheim distinguished between two radically different forms of individualism that correspond roughly to the two poles of *homo duplex*, a collective representation of individualism that battles the narcissistic will. These two antagonistic forms of individualism also correspond roughly to Schopenhauer's opposition between individualism as an "idea" versus "will." Durkheim was in favor of the liberal-democratic ideals that guide modern societies, but he wanted to reform these ideals lest they be consumed by egoism. This may be the secret of his admiration for John Calvin. In any event, it is inconceivable, given the tenets of his sociology, that Durkheim would have opposed the social currents of his time, and even more inconceivable that he could have launched sociology had he opposed them. Durkheim grasped the will of history and its logical outcome in the future—namely, this new "religion of humanity," this new kind of collective, moral individualism–despite the tumult and anomie of his immediate surroundings. He wanted to reform and purify that will, not oppose it. But it is equally inconceivable that contemporary sociology can survive much longer if it continues to align Durkheim with dying systems of thought, and if it continues to adhere to these dying systems. Positivism and realism are dead issues in philosophy, but they still animate—miraculously—a good portion of modern sociological thought.

The State of Sociology at the End of the Nineteenth Century

Was there much sociology to reform in Durkheim's time? It is not common knowledge that Durkheim intended to publish a history of sociology, which he never completed (the notes for this project are lost). Yet he had plenty to say—most of it critical—about Marx, Spencer, Comte, Saint-Simon, and William James, as well as about figures he labels as precursors of sociology: Montesquieu and Rousseau, even Wilhelm Wundt and Johann Herbart. There is evidence to suggest that he was keenly aware of the writings of Simmel, Guyau, Tönnies, Darwin, Weber, and Freud. A host of thinkers who wrote in a sociological vein at the turn of the century are now forgotten or unknown, including Ribot, Hamelin, Espinas, Schaeffle, Renouvier, with whom the Durkheimians dealt in their journal, *L'Année sociologique*. Some of the most obscure and neglected writings of the Durkheimians have to do with intellectual similarities and differences between Durkheim's version of sociology and the sociologies of some of these others, even if some of that sociology goes by the names psychology and anthropology today. Durkheim and his followers tried to show that their version of sociology could solve problems uncovered in these other sociologies.

For example, Célestin Bouglé's (1918) exciting essay on the intellectual affinities and differences between Durkheim and Marx has, to the best of my knowledge, never been cited. The same is true for Bouglé's (1922) effort to synthesize the evolutionism of Darwin, Marx, and Durkheim. Pierre Halbwachs, the son of Durkheim's follower Maurice Halbwachs, informed me that one of his father's aims in *The Collective Memory* ([1950] 1980) was to find a common ground between Durkheim's and Freud's concepts of memory and representation, particularly in relation to Freud's ([1900] 1965) *Interpretation of Dreams*. Maurice Halbwachs (1925) also wrote a Durkheimian analysis of Weber's *Protestant Ethic and the Spirit of Capitalism*, which he also incorporated into many of his other works (for example, see Halbwachs [1912] 1974; [1938] 1964). Durkheim's nephew and collaborator Marcel Mauss ([1950] 1979a), invokes the sociological dimensions of many anthropologists and psychologists in his *Sociology and Psychology*. This is especially evident in his use of the concept of the "total social fact," which invokes the social, psychological, and physiological dimensions of a phenomenon simultaneously, and which, Mauss claims, Durkheim implied with his concept of anomie (discussed in Meštrović 1987). This list could be extended. In general, it must be remembered that the neat divisions of the social sciences into psychology, sociology, anthropology, economics, and so on, did not exist in Durkheim's time. The Durkheimians were acutely aware of the amorphous sociology implied in the writings of a host of writers.

Schopenhauer arrogantly dismissed most previous philosophers, even the mighty Kant and Hegel. Similarly, Durkheim dismissed most previous attempts at sociology. It is a mistake to regard Durkheim as a pupil of Saint-Simon or Auguste Comte, for example. Instead, Mauss (ibid, p. 12) writes that Durkheim was "the pupil of [Wilhelm] Wundt and [Théodule] Ribot, [Alfred] Espinas." Wundt and Ribot are widely regarded as the founding fathers of German and French psychology, respectively. Moreover, both Wundt (1874; 1886; 1887; 1907; 1912) and Ribot (1896) incorporated Schopenhauer's philosophy into their psychologies and apparently had little difficulty incorporating metaphysics into an otherwise thoroughly objective social psychology. Ribot is almost excessive in his praise for Schopenhauer in his *La philosophie de Schopenhauer* (1874). Espinas ([1882] 1977; 1925) incorporated the notion of representationalism as well as metaphysics into a study of animal societies, which Durkheim ([1885] 1978) cited with praise. Durkheim ([1887] 1976a; [1887] 1976c) incorporates the works of Espinas, Wundt, and Ribot into the philosophical context established by Kant *and* Schopenhauer, although these works have yet to be translated into English.

In any case, in his *Socialism and Saint-Simon* ([1928] 1958) Durkheim dethrones Comte as the founder of positivism or sociology and ascribes these honors to Saint-Simon. But Durkheim then proceeds to criticize Saint-Simon for being unscientific, for lapsing into subjectivism, and for establishing his system upon a contradiction: "What caused the failure of Saint-Simonianism is that Saint-Simon and his disciples wanted to get the most from the least, the superior from the inferior, moral rule from economic matter" (ibid., p. 240).

This is a rich passage, for it implies an epistemological as well as a practical mistake. Durkheim criticizes Saint-Simon's version of socialism for assuming, much as classical economic theory assumes, that human desires will regulate themselves of their own accord. Durkheim regards this move as Saint-Simon's failure to provide for a mechanism that will prevent desires from degenerating into anomie. Contrary to Saint-Simon's alleged error, we have seen that for Durkheim, as for Schopenhauer, representationalism is intimately yet antagonistically related to the will, the politics of desire.

Durkheim is no less critical of Marx. He sympathizes with Marx's humanism, but dismisses his system as being unscientific and accuses him of being biased in favor of the suffering of the lower classes at the expense of the suffering of society as a whole. Durkheim is explicit ([1897] 1986, p. 143):

> The malaise from which we are suffering is not rooted in any particular class; it is general over the whole of society. It attacks employers as well as workers, although it manifests itself in different forms in both: as a disturbing, painful agitation for the capitalist, as discontent and irritation for the proleteriat. Thus the problem reaches infinitely beyond the material interests of the two classes concerned. . . . [one should] address, not those feelings of anger that the less-favoured class harbours against the other, but feelings of pity for society, which is suffering in all classes and in all its organs.

In the language of Schopenhauer, Durkheim is accusing Marx of missing both the idea and the will of both capitalism and socialism. Bouglé (1918) caps Durkheim's critique by charging that Marx implied that representations are mere reflectors, epiphenomena, of other realities (consider Marx's treatment of religion, for example). But according to Bouglé (ibid.), Durkheim regards representations as *prisms,* refractions of reality that are themselves realities, not reflectors.

Durkheim ([1893] 1933) is most harsh on Spencer because he perceived Spencer's brand of individualism to be almost entirely subjective—almost pure will. He is kinder to Montesquieu and Rousseau, complementing them for realizing that society and the individual are two distinct phenomena. Still, Durkheim ([1892] 1965, p. 135) faults them for treating the individual as a "natural" phenomenon yet society as "something that is added to nature." With regard to Johann Herbart, recognized today as an important precursor of modern psychology, Durkheim said that because Herbart "admits that mental life reduces itself entirely to representations [he] thus opened the way to the scientific study of psychological phenomena" (in Lukes 1985, pp. 632–34). The inclusion of metaphysics even in the title of Herbart's classic work, *A Textbook in Psychology: An Attempt to Found the Science of Psychology on Experience, Metaphysics, and Mathematics* ([1816] 1904) should be noted. Durkheim studied under

Wundt during the years 1885 and 1886 and described how deeply influenced he was by the experience (Durkheim [1887] 1976a). Like Durkheim, Wundt believed that representations lie on a continuum from the collective to the individual and that the "individual will," although it is contained in a "social will," is necessarily opposed to it (Wundt [1886] 1902, pp. 58–96). Like Durkheim, Wundt (1907) attempted to launch the scientific study of morality. Wundt seems to have foreshadowed many of Durkheim's moves, but never quite launched sociology. It is interesting to note that Durkheim is kinder when writing about Wundt than about most other thinkers.

Durkheim reviewed Ferdinand Tönnies's *Community and Society* ([1887] 1963) in 1889 and specifically noted Schopenhauer's influence upon Tönnies's thesis (Durkheim [1889] 1978, p. 115). Indeed, Tönnies distinguishes between the "natural will" of *Gemeinschaft* and the artificial, "rational" will of *Gesellschaft*. Durkheim ([1899] 1978) agrees with Tönnies's conclusion that modernity is to be characterized as a period in which the "unleashing of the will" predominates, but he disagrees that modern society is "artificial." This dispute over interpreting Schopenhauer may be the real reason why, when Durkheim wrote his classic *Division of Labor in Society* ([1893] 1933) a few years later, he deliberately reversed Tönnies's progression from "natural" to "artificial" groupings into his own "mechanical" versus "organic" solidarity, respectively. There is much at stake in this dispute. Tönnies, like Marx, wanted to return to a previous era that was allegedly more "natural." But Durkheim, like Schopenhauer, believed that the division of labor is fueled by a "will" of its own that develops independent of human reason, because it must. Evil and anomalies in the division of labor are not inherent to this progress of the "will," but stem from the improper tampering with it on the part of human reason, and these anomalies could be repaired. How one interprets this dispute between Tönnies and Durkheim in the context of Schopenhauer's philosophy makes all the difference in how one approaches the phenomenon of individualism in modern times. Yet, contemporary sociologists have not phrased the dispute in the context of Schopenhauer's philosophy.

Similarly, Durkheim ([1887] 1975) took issue with Jean-Marie Guyau's ([1887] 1909) own extension of Schopenhauer's thesis that the future held moral anomie as its ideal, the emancipation of the individual from religious dogmatism. Guyau ([1887] 1962, p. 375) wrote that "We have proposed as the moral ideal what we have called moral anomy—the absence of any fixed moral rule. We believe still more firmly that the ideal toward which every religion ought to tend is religious anomy, the complete enfranchisement of the individual in all religious matters, the redemption of his thought, which is more precious than his life, the suppression of dogmatic faith in every form."

But according to Durkheim ([1893] 1976, p. 282), there could be no such thing as "moral anomie," because anomie as the lack of restraint upon the insatiable "will" is the essence of immorality (see the discussion on this dispute between Durkheim and Guyau by Orru, 1983 and 1987). Nietzsche was influenced by both Schopenhauer and Guyau, and Nietzsche's ([1901] 1968) own version of irreligion and "will to power" is well known. Durkheim ([1955] 1983) took up Nietzsche's brand of individualism as well in *Pragmatism and Sociology*, and criticized it on grounds similar to his attack on Guyau.

In sum, an amorphous sociology seems to have existed in Durkheim's time which more or less implied the notion of society as will and idea. Some authors placed the accent on the will, and others on the idea. But the imperfections in grasping this new way of conceiving society seem to have irritated Durkheim greatly. For him, society is a representation, not the outcome of human agency nor material determinants. It is neither entirely objective nor subjective. And because the representation is a reality sui generis, not a mere reflector, it expresses its will—in part—independent of the will of human agents. Durkheim seems to have been as dogmatic about this new way of perceiving an old problem as Schopenhaeur was about his insights. Compare Schopenhauer's prefaces with the prefaces Durkheim wrote for his works, especially the second prefaces! How misunderstood they both felt; how angrily they expressed their irritation.

Another hint of what Durkheim was trying to renovate and reform is provided by the epistemologies of his followers. First is their obsessive use of the term *representation*. Thus, for Robert Hertz ([1907–1909] 1960), right- and left-handedness are representations, death is a collective representation (not "a brute fact"), and images of saints and heroes are representations (see Hertz 1928). Czarnowski ([1919] 1975) extended Hertz's study of heroes as representations with regard to Saint Patrick. For Hubert and Mauss ([1904] 1972), religion and magic are representations, and so is the notion of sacrifice (Hubert and Mauss [1899] 1964). For Fauconnet (1920), the study of responsibility is a representation. Meillet (1906) studied language as a representation, and Hubert ([1925] 1934) applied Meillet's conception to a reconstruction of the history of the Celts based on linguistic analysis. Halbwachs ([1950] 1980) regarded memory as a representation, a social and individual construction, not "reality." Levy-Bruhl ([1922] 1966) approached the study of the personality and the concept of the self as representations. Bouglé ([1908] 1971) studied the caste system as a representation, and criticized Marxism from the perspective of representationalism (Bouglé 1918). And so on. The works of the Durkheimians are loaded with jabs at other thinkers and researchers who, in treating the same topics, had begun at one or the other pole of the object-subject distinction and thereby failed to grasp, in the view of the Durkheimians, the correct approach to these topics.

Second, the Durkheimians frequently made their own explicit epistemological statements that resonated with Durkheim's. Thus Halbwachs ([1938] 1970) referred to "empirical rationalism" as his epistemology, not one or the other system alone. In *The History of Modern Philosophy in France* (1899), Lucien Levy-Bruhl addressed the reconciliation of rationalism with modern empirical methods such as experimentation. He treated Comte severely, accusing him of an unconscious adherence to metaphysics despite his avowed positivism, and gave Durkheim the place of honor at the end of the book: Durkheim will lead sociology into the promised land with his "science of moral facts," and will resolve and reconcile these debates. Fauconnet (1920) was careful to refer to Durkheim's epistemology as "Durkheimian rationalism," to distinguish it from other forms of rationalism (see Besnard 1983, p. 129; Fauconnet [1922] 1958, pp. 38–39). Bouglé (1938, p. 23) referred specifically to Durkheim's "renovated rationalism." Georges Davy (1922) aimed explicitly at reconciling idealism and realism in his study of law.

Finally, we further understand what Durkheim was trying to reform by considering who and what systems of thought he admired. This is an important point to consider. If he did not align himself with positivism and other "isms" commonly attributed to him—not even naive rationalism—just where did his intellectual affinities lie?

Consider Durkheim's ([1938] 1977) *Evolution of Educational Thought,* a terribly neglected work almost never cited by sociologists. In it, one may find Durkheim's opinion of Western culture as he traces it from Socratic Greece to his own time. In general, he demarcates a hiatus between ancient Greek and Christian cultures. The Greeks, he thought, attributed sacredness to the "real world"—which is why Durkheim thought that science and reason flourished in their culture—but Christianity attributed sacredness to man himself. Durkheim asks (ibid., p. 281), "Why then did Christian civilisation develop in the reverse direction [from the Greeks]? Why was it immediately attracted to man and to things human whereas, by contrast, it exhibited such great and sustained indifference towards the things of the external world?"

It should have caught someone's attention that Durkheim abhorred the Renaissance, which most history books still depict as the flowering of Western civilization following the "Dark Ages." For Durkheim, the Renaissance was an exaggeration of Christian Humanism, a period of anomie, of intellectual and moral crisis: it encouraged a narcissistic and excessive preoccupation with humanism at the expense of the "real world." In Schopenhauer's words, it was a period of excessive will. Durkheim admired the pre-Renaissance Scholastics because of their discipline and rationalism. Similarly, the reader is almost tempted to sigh with relief when Durkheim finishes his attack on the Renaissance and turns finally to the Reformation, which he regarded as the beginning, however imperfect, of mankind's re-discovery of the "real world." But even the Reformation fell short of his expectations. Durkheim expresses the highest admiration for the Jesuits, that "army" who wanted to reform the Reformation! Here Durkheim exposes the deeper meanings of his "renovated rationalism," for the Jesuits essentially wanted to synthesize humanistic and scientific studies. Durkheim was seeking a similar synthesis, and his quest for this synthesis is all the more necessary in contemporary sociology. Let us examine his argument in somewhat more detail.

The Contemporary Crisis in Sociology

A good entry-point to the discussion is Durkheim's analysis of the eighth century distinction between *trivium* and *quadrivium,* which Durkheim depicts as the forerunner of our distinction between the humanities and the study of the real world, respectively. Durkheim was seeking the social origins of what has come to be known as the object-subject debate. He regarded the period between the ninth and the twelfth centuries as an age of reason that synthesized and balanced these two opposing tendencies. Far from regarding this period as the "Dark Ages," he admired it greatly. In general, he thought that Scholasticism sowed the seeds of the Age of Reason, which would blossom in the seventeenth and eighteenth centuries. But several eras of "painful anguish and general anxiety" (Durkheim [1938] 1977, p. 65) had to be endured first. One such period of anomie occurred in the tenth century, but it was brief and did not compare with the anomie of the Renaissance.

In the Renaissance, according to Durkheim (ibid., p. 168), "logic lost its former prestige." It was an era characterized by a horror of all regulation and discipline, which is how he describes anomie elsewhere. The motto of this period was, according to Durkheim (ibid., p. 181), "Do as you wish." This is an arresting phrase, with its seemingly obvious overtones of Schopenhauer and Freud with regard to the primacy of the "wish," as well as its echoes of the more recent "Do your own thing." In fact, Durkheim derives it from Rabelais, whom he treats with contempt. According to Durkheim (ibid.):

The dominant idea in all of Rabelais' works is a horror of everything which means regulation or discipline, or which creates obstacles to the free generation of activity. Everything which hampers, everything which restricts the desires, the needs, the passions of man is an evil. His ideal is a society where nature, liberated from all restraint, can develop in complete freedom. This perfect society is achieved in the famous Abbey of Thélème whose rules are entirely based on this very simple formula: do as you wish. The entire life of the Thélèmites, says Rabelais, "was directed not by laws, statutes or rules, but by their own desires and free-will." They ate, drank and slept when they liked, how they liked and as much as they liked. . . . No vows, of course, since the aim of vows is to fetter and curb the will. Not even any bells or clocks to divide the day into definite sections or prescribed periods devoted to predetermined occupations. Hours are like limits placed on time; time also must flow easily and freely, without any self-awareness, so to speak. At the root of this entire theory is the fundamental postulate of the whole of Rabelaisian philosophy, that nature is good, completely and without reservation or restriction.

Durkheim (ibid., p. 188) cannot accept Rabelais's "insatiable thirst" for "the infinite," because he regards Rabelais as "the spokesman of his age." And, Durkheim (ibid.) adds, "Indeed we shall see that these aspirations are by no means peculiar to him, and that the Renaissance strove to realise this unrealisable ideal." But Durkheim attacked similar tendencies toward the infinite in *all* his major works and with regard to many major thinkers, especially Saint-Simon.

Even the vocabulary Durkheim uses to describe the Renaissance is his vocabulary of anomie: it was a period of "impatience with all limitations," "unbridled passion," lack of "discretion or moderation," "infatuation," "lack of discipline," "insatiable thirst," and "infinite longings" that led to "disarray" and the "enfeeblement of moral feeling" (ibid., pp. 181–88). In general, it was a "monstrous period." The emphasis was upon the literary and aesthetic aspects of life as opposed to the empirical or practical, and Durkheim (ibid., p. 207) apparently believed that "Any culture which is exclusively or essentially aesthetic contains within itself a germ of immorality, or at least of inferior morality." This excess of "egotistical passion" leads to nihilism, Durkheim writes. That is Schopenhauer's thesis in a nutshell. Durkheim (ibid., p. 225) concludes, "Thus the sixteenth century is a period of educational and moral crisis."

"Isn't Protestantism a carry-over from the ills of the Renaissance?" Durkheim (ibid., p. 231) asks. For Durkheim, early Protestantism's version of individualism was still egoistic. This is why he was so full of praise for the Jesuits: they introduced piety and discipline to traditional rationalism in response to the Reformation and thereby reformed both! Durkheim emphasizes that Descartes was trained by the Jesuits and adds that "all the great names of the 17th and 18th centuries were pupils of the Jesuits" (ibid., p. 239). It is curious that Durkheim does not treat Calvin in this discussion. But it is evident that Calvin's aim with regard to the Reformation was also one of introducing piety and discipline.

The result was—according to Durkheim—that in the Age of Reason, the humanities and the study of the real world were synthesized, made into an interdependent alliance; for Durkheim (ibid.), this was the "characteristic of the whole philosophical movement from Bacon and Hobbes to Saint-Simon and Auguste Comte." It gave birth to sociology, which is the scientific study of man, the grandest synthesis of the humanities and science, of the world as will and idea. But this insight was in danger of being lost and corrupted again in Durkheim's time. The Industrial Revolution, like the Renaissance, extended the horizons of mankind's will to infinity, and the result was another period of intellectual and moral anomie.

Thus Durkheim ends the book (ibid., p. 337) on the note that the two poles of knowledge must again be synthesized: "Far from it being the case that between the disciplines which deal with the world of persons and those which deal with the world of things there is a great gulf fixed, the fact is that they mutually imply one another and converge on the same end." Referring back to the Renaissance, he (ibid., p. 341) laments that "the training in logic which had been instituted by the Scholastics was swept away by the Humanist revolution without anything being put in its place." He believed that something similar was occurring in his day, and insisted that "Everything points to the fact that the great gulf which still separates the study of physical nature and the study of human nature is now nothing but a relic which is destined to disappear. The day will soon come, and we must seek to hasten it, when the idea of trying to educate a historian or a linguist without first of all initiating him into the discipline of the natural sciences will appear to be a veritable aberration" (ibid., p. 342).

It seems that that day has still not come; science is still separated by a great gulf from the humanities. Moreover, the social sciences themselves are separated by various epistemological gulfs, some favoring the subject and others the object. Sociology has been polarized into the "objective" quantitative camp and the "subjective" qualitative camp. The quantifiers tend to write in terms of "value-free" methodology, while the qualitative camp writes in terms of cultural relativism, ideology, and subjective meanings. Much has been written in recent years about sociology's intellectual crises, but few solutions have been proposed. The solutions that have been proposed are on the fringes of sociology. They do not have a "totem" to which they can point that can unify these polarized camps. My point is that Durkheim is the perfect "totem" to achieve this contemporary reconciliation. After all, reconciliation was his goal.

The difference between Durkheim's and Comte's and Saint-Simon's portrait of the evolution of reason, which culminated in sociology, is this: whereas Comte and Saint-Simon regarded the progress of reason as a steady march, a straight line—despite "critical epochs" and periods of crisis—Durkheim regarded it as being in constant danger of being snuffed out. He thought of reason itself as being divided by *homo duplex,* with mankind alternating in its worship of one or the other pole of this dualism. Sociology is the grand experiment born from the synthesis of objectivism and subjectivism, of will and idea, but it is in real danger of dying out if this synthesis is not achieved and maintained.

Since Durkheim deals in eras, centuries, and epochs, it is wrong to relegate him to the status of a historical figure, a relic who has nothing of value to say to contemporary times. On the contrary, he is profoundly modern. The problems he recognized at the turn of the twentieth century are still very much with us. We seem to be in a period of intellectual and moral anomie similar to the one that disturbed Durkheim in his day. David Riesman's ([1950] 1970) *Lonely Crowd* and Allan Bloom's (1987) *Closing of the American Mind* are examples of works closer to our time than Durkheim's works, yet concerned with a similar crisis: how can individualism be maintained without succumbing to narcissism? Thus, this book is more than a work in the history of social thought. The representation of Durkheim as reformer and renovator speaks to us today.

CHAPTER 2

Durkheim's Life as Representation

Steven Lukes (1985, pp. 39–43), Durkheim's authoritative biographer, devotes only four and a half pages in a text of more than six hundred pages to Durkheim's childhood. This is surprising, given our post-Freudian knowledge of the importance of character formation in childhood. Moreover Lukes, and students of Durkheim who have followed his lead, seem to imply that Durkheim's character was shaped more by the various "isms" he encountered in Paris than by his childhood in Epinal. Greenberg (1976, p. 624) put the matter well: "Psychologists tell us that the child fathers the man, but how he does so depends a great deal upon his father. This should be an obvious truth in social relations, yet it is one that even sociologists have sometimes neglected. They have assigned Emile Durkheim's paternity much more readily to Auguste Comte, Charles Renouvier, classical rationalism, the age of enlightenment, or a host of German scholars rather than explore the debt due the natural father Moses Durkheim."

This dearth of factual knowledge concerning Durkheim's childhood, or even interest in it, is certainly strange, but some of it can be explained. M. Halphen told me that his mother (Durkheim's daughter Marie) "forgot" all of Durkheim's papers during the Nazi occupation of France. These included drafts of all of Durkheim's lectures, which he apparently revised afresh each time he taught a course. But the details surrounding this great loss to scholarship are peculiar. It does not seem to be the case that the papers were "forgotten" because of haste or fear for life. Rather, according to M. Halphen, the evacuation of the family to the south of France took several months. Everything but the Durkheim papers, which were all stored in one

19

room, was evacuated. Durkheim's daughter literally "forgot" about the existence of the papers until after the war. M. Halphen claims that on their way back to their Paris home, his mother exclaimed something to the effect, "Oh my goodness, I forgot his papers!" and she expressed apprehension that they had been destroyed, (they had). I inquired whether this destruction had occurred because the Nazis had targeted Jewish writing. Not at all, M. Halphen responded. The family that had moved into their house simply did not know the nature or value of the papers, and had thrown them into the garbage (see also the account of how the papers were lost by Halphen 1987).

One is tempted to analyze this unusual case of "forgetting" in the light of Freud's treatment of such forgetting as an instance of repression, but I shall merely mention the possibility. In any event, a scholarly treasure was lost in an unfortunate manner. M. Halphen claims that his mother hardly ever spoke of her father. None of Durkheim's descendants kept diaries, and apparently, none of the descendants or relatives has attempted to write down what knowledge of Durkheim he might have possessed.

But suppose the room full of papers in Marie Halphen's home had survived. That fact in no way would guarantee that our knowledge of Durkheim would have been more complete. Reality does not speak for itself. Durkheim's life would still have to be a representation. The important point to consider is, first, why Durkheim's life has not been approached as a representation, and second, the consequences of considering it as a representation.

Had someone had the interest in the representations of Durkheim even a few decades ago, some important persons who might have had direct knowledge of Durkheim would still have been alive. For example, Durkheim's brother-in-law, Albert Cahen, lived in Epinal until his death in 1962. A prominent physician, Dr. Cahen shared opinions and anecdotes concerning Durkheim with various historians writing about Epinal, especially Robert Javelet (1969) and Jean Bossu (1967, 1982). But these historical studies do not inform any of the sociological works on Durkheim, nor have sociologists interviewed Javelet and Bossu, so that these sources, and probably many others, have not been fully tapped. Other members of Durkheim's family and the family of his in-laws lived to very old age and might have shed light on key questions. Then there are Durkheim's many students. What happened to all their notes and impressions?

Some of Durkheim's prominent friends, like the great philosopher André Lalande and the famous sculptor Paul Landowski, survived into the 1960s. Durkheim and Lalande were colleagues in the French Philosophical Society. Lalande ([1926] 1980) achieved lasting fame with his dictionary of philosophy, which is still in print and is still cited by philosophers. It is noteworthy that Durkheim figures prominently in Lalande's treatment of philosophical terms, especially the terms *conscience, représentation,* and *sacré.* The depth of the friendship between Durkheim and Landowski is indicated by the fact that Landowski sculpted busts of Durkheim as well as of Levy-Bruhl and Mlle. Bouglé (see Isay 1946). I should add, however, that M. Halphen believes that Bouglé brought Durkheim and Landowski together (see Halphen 1987). Landowski (1943) makes a sharp philosophical distinction between rationalist and irrationalist conceptions of art. For the irrationalists (in addition to himself, Landowski lists Rodin, Courbet, Degas, Corot, Manet, Delacroix, and Gericault as part of this Schopenhauerian movement), the work of art is at the same time a creation of the individual and nature, and like nature, does not depend on rules or science, but exists in itself (ibid., pp. 84-86). The artistic movement that Landowski describes rebelled against the rationalist conception of art that Landowski believes was formed in the Renaissance. Landowski (1943) seems to take a stand toward the Renaissance that is very similar to Durkheim's ([1938] 1977), although in a different context. In this rationalist-Renaissance conception of art, at least according to Landowski, nature is perceived to be indifferent to the works of the artist, and art is the result not only of inspiration but of long labor. It would have been intriguing to know what Landowski and Durkheim discussed at their meetings.

The extent of knowledge concerning Durkheim's relationship with Lalande and Landowski that is still buried in the nineteenth century must also be noted. Durkheim contributed extensively at the meetings of the French Philosophical Society, and some of his remarks have been published in the *Bulletin de la Société Française de Philosophie.* Yet even these published remarks, while accessible, are almost completely unknown to (or uncited by) contemporary sociologists. One of the most intriguing, to my mind, is the article entitled "The Unknown and the Unconscious in History," in which Durkheim (1908) makes his conception of the unconscious most explicit. Yet Freud continues to receive all the "credit" or notoreity regarding the unconscious. Another indicator of the knowledge that has been lost is the fate of Landowski's bust of Durkheim. To my surprise, the curator at the Landowski museum as well as officials at the Sorbonne indicated that they did not know what had happened to this bust. When I asked to see a photograph of the bust, I realized that it was the same one that M. Halphen had discussed with me and that was in his possession! It was strange that persons who knew of each other in Paris apparently had never gotten around to discussing important matters concerning Durkheim.

How much material can still be retrieved is an open question.

The curator at the Landowski museum indicated that the Landowski diaries contain many entries regarding Durkheim, but would not make the diaries available for inspection. It was my impression that there exists much hitherto unpublicized correspondence between Durkheim and various followers, but I have not been able to determine its full extent or whereabouts. A descendant of one of Durkheim's followers is in possession of the full correspondence by this follower, which details his ancestor's relationship with Durkheim, but he would not let me examine it because, he said, it was too personal. My point is that contemporary writings on Durkheim give the impression that we now know all that is available about Durkheim, whereas a veritable gold mine of information still seems to exist in France. Yet its full extent may never be known.

Among the important questions that still need to be addressed are the following: Did Durkheim receive rabbinical training? What was his relationship with his father? How did his father respond to his choice not to become a rabbi? What was Durkheim like as a child? How extensive was his admiration for Schopenhauer? What were his favorite and least favorite thinkers, and why? We will never have definitive answers to these questions, which are important because they are steps in reconciling the subjective and objective in Durkheim's life and thought.

Of course, some persons who knew Durkheim, like Georges Davy and Henri Durkheim, have been interviewed. Even so, the information they supplied was shaped by the questions put to them. With the possible exception of Filloux (1977), who asked Henri Durkheim some things about Durkheim's Jewish background, the questions did not focus on Durkheim's childhood.

It is also surprising that the most influential scholars writing about Durkheim have apparently not visited Epinal. "Nothing new can be found," I was told by a well-known Durkheimian scholar when I proposed a visit. The implication seems to be that only "objective" facts are worthwhile. Yet it seems inconceivable that one would write on any thinker with any degree of finality without wanting to experience for one's self the representations that shaped that thinker as a child. But that is precisely what has happened. Most writers have approached Durkheim as if he did not have a childhood, as if no milieu had shaped his childhood.

Several powerful, subjective impressions of Epinal have remained with me. The massive, old cathedral in the center of town literally dominates Epinal. Durkheim grew up and lived within sight of the cathedral; he could not have escaped the tolling of its bells. His father's synagogue was destroyed by the Nazis, but no one knows who succeeded Moïse Durkheim as rabbi, not even the present rabbi of

Epinal. In fact, it was very difficult even to find out where the synagogue once stood. By careful searching in various government offices, I found that a gas station now stands on the site where Durkheim was born. No plaque marks his birthplace, although Epinal is dotted with plaques commemorating other famous native sons.

There are minute details about Durkheim and his family that do not change the facts appreciably, but certainly yield interesting representations. A visit to city hall yielded a fact hitherto overlooked by Durkheim's biographers, and unknown even to M. Halphen: Durkheim had an elder brother named Israël Desiré, who was born at 11 p.m., 5 January 1845, and who died on 17 September 1846. Lukes (1985, p. 39) says there were four children in the family, but apparently five were born. This is admittedly a small discrepancy, but it does raise the possibility that other facts may not be as accurate as one would like. Durkheim's birth certificate indicates that he was born at half-past midnight on 15 April 1858 at the family home at 6 Rue Leopoldbourg, which street was later renamed the Rue Rualmenil. His mother was thirty-eight years old, and his father was fifty. Various birth and death certificates for Durkheim's family indicate that the family was extremely poor, that they changed residences frequently, and that the witnesses who signed the various documents were mostly lower class.

Javelet's (1969) photographs of Epinal at the turn of the century show buildings, streets, and landmarks almost the same as they were in Durkheim's day. Weymuller's (1985) *Histoire d'Epinal* contains photographs of the old synagogue as well as of the newly built College d'Epinal, which Durkheim attended and which still stands. Durkheim's allegiance may have been torn between his father's tradition and the new symbols of the future that were entering Epinal in his youth. Casual interaction with the citizens of Epinal disclosed that part of the enmity for Germany and the defeat in 1871 seems to live still in modern Epinal. It must have been extremely powerful in Durkheim's lifetime for it not to have dissipated. Javelet's (1969) photographs of the German occupation of Epinal, which Durkheim witnessed, reinforce that impression.

The family grave in Epinal's Jewish Cemetery, where Moïse and Melanie Durkheim are buried along side Gerson and Rosine Mauss, is remarkably well preserved. However, Durkheim's grave in the famous Montparnasse Cemetery in Paris is in sad disarray. The stone is crumbling, the chain had collapsed, and it does not look cared for. M. Halphen could not remember the last time he visited his grandfather's tomb. This state of neglect is in sharp contrast to the freshly cut flowers on Jean-Paul Sartre's grave and the graves of other famous persons in Montparnasse. I cannot avoid commenting here that the disregard for Durkheim's birth and death relative to other great thinkers seems analogous, in some ways, to sociology's state of dereliction relative to other intellectual disciplines and enterprises.

The Philosophy of Representationalism Applied to Durkheim's Life

Durkheim insisted that we can never know the world directly as a brute fact, but only as a representation. The world is always filtered through our ideas of it, but that fact in no way negates the "objectivity" of the world. Some of Durkheim's followers applied this theory to the lives of various heroes. Their approach is instructive in the sense that Durkheim, too, has become a misunderstood hero. They can suggest to us how Durkheim might have wanted to be approached, and how one should evaluate present day knowledge of him.

For example, Stefan Czarnowski ([1919] 1975) approaches the "cult" of St. Patrick as the national hero of Ireland. He immediately dismisses the possibility of ever knowing the real St. Patrick, because every hero is an incarnation of social values, a representation shaped by collective representations—a kind of totem. The hero represents the group. He exemplifies a social ideal and amplifies a public tradition. Czarnowski even believes that the true hero must be dead, because part of his function as a representation is to protect the group from dangers, real or imaginary. Similarly, in his study of the cult of Saint-Besse, Robert Hertz concludes that the collective imagination ignores dates, confounds names, alters events, and neglects historical truth. The life of a public figure is a product of the inventive spontaneity of the people and the reflective activity of writers (Hertz 1928, p. 189). All these statements apply to Durkheim as much as they do to any other hero. But is the representational approach doomed to a kind of intellectual nihilism because it denies the possibility of ever knowing objects directly?

Not at all. This is where the importance of Schopenhauer's claim that the will is the other side of the representation comes in. Consider Maurice Halbwachs's classic blend of Durkheimianism in *The Collective Memory*. Halbwachs ([1950] 1980, p. 69) accepts from the outset that memory is a social "reconstruction of the past achieved with data borrowed from the present." We recall events more easily that occurred within the context of a group and that are recalled within a group, even if we merely imagine the presence of the group: "Our most personal feelings and thoughts originate in definite social milieus and circumstances . . . a person remembers only by situating himself within the viewpoint of one or several groups and one or several currents of collective thought" (ibid., p. 33). It follows that "the succession of our remembrances, of even our most personal ones, is always explained by changes occurring in our relationships to various collective milieus—in short, by the transformations these milieus undergo separately and as a whole" (ibid., p. 49). For example, even if we could bring Durkheim back from the dead and interview him, it does not follow that he could tell us all that we want to know about his past. According to Halbwachs, Durkheim could increase his recall in the presence of his group of disciples, and would recall most easily events that had already been elaborated by some group.

It is doubtful that Halbwachs's statements would surprise an individual whose profession consists of tapping the memories of human subjects. Freud's psychoanalysis, for example, assumes that neuroses are antisocial structures (discussed in Meštrović 1982). How much of the neurotic's repression, for example, is due to the fact that the neurotic has chosen an isolated life-style? Repressed memories return when the analyst becomes a significant other in the patient's life and forces the neurotic to acknowledge the social presence of others and the consequences that presence entails.

In any event, Halbwachs (ibid., p. 51) writes, "a man must often appeal to others' remembrances to evoke his own past. He goes back to reference points determined by society, hence outside himself." And these social reference points are the product of the social will that is essentially continuous, which survives the death of individual agents and witnesses. We are back to Schopenhauer. As Halbwachs (ibid.) put it:

> History is neither the whole nor even all that remains of the past. In addition to written history, there is a living history that perpetuates and renews itself through time and permits the recovery of many old currents that have seemingly disappeared. [p. 64]

> Besides, death may end physiological life, but it does not abruptly halt the current of thoughts unfolding in the social circles of the person whose body has been buried. [p. 72]

> What remains are not ready-made images in some subterranean gallery of our thought. Rather, we can find in society all the necessary information for reconstructing certain parts of our past represented in an incomplete and indefinite manner, or even considered completely gone from memory. [p. 75]

Here is hope. The social will that gave rise to as well as crystallized the collective representations persists for a long time after the event in question has ceased to exist. The situation is roughly analogous to the trails of gas left by ionized particles even after the particles disintegrated. Present-day society can supply the necessary information for reconstructing aspects of Durkheim's past. And this reconstruction will not be inferior to the information we could have gathered had we lived in Durkheim's time, nor to the information we might gather were it possible to bring him back to life. For in all these cases, reality as well as memory are constructed, are representations. And as Halbwachs (ibid., p. 79) put it, "the need to write the history of a period, a society, or even a person is only aroused when the subject is already too distant in the past to allow for the testimony of those who preserve some remembrance of it. . . . The study of history in this sense is reserved only for a few specialists." The effect of this specialized history is too small to affect public opinion.

In the case of Durkheim, the public has not really had a chance to form an opinion. Freud's name is a household word, but Durkheim's name is unknown even to many social scientists. Paris and most French cities have named a street after Auguste Comte, but only Epinal, and there only a small back street, commemorates Durkheim's name. An official at city hall mentioned that choosing a street to commemorate Durkheim had caused quite a controversy, but would not elaborate. An amphitheater at the Sorbonne was finally named after Durkheim, but it is small and remote compared to the others. Statues of French scholars abound in the Latin Quarter of Paris, but Landowski's portrait of Durkheim is not included among them. (It sits in the home of Durkheim's grandson.) Even his descendants have practically no memories or representations of him. Durkheim is truly the unsung hero of sociology.

One is tempted to guess the reasons why Durkheim's memory has been allowed almost to die, in scholarly and in public circles. One could find fault with Durkheim's personality, accuse his followers of poor "public relations," or engage in other idle speculation. Yet scores of brilliant thinkers did not earn as much notice as Durkheim, and scores of mediocre personages have achieved greater fame. The point is that Durkheim stood for things that are difficult to grasp: the reconciliation of the object-subject debate, the science of morality, a new vision of society. He was truly ahead of his time. Collective representations have not had a chance to catch up with him, because the representations he was using in his teachings were hardly born in his lifetime.

The Effect of Religion on Durkheim's Objective Thought

Durkheim was descended from eight generations of rabbis, a distinguished dynasty. What influence did this fact have upon his sociology? Durkheim wrote that he discovered religion in 1895. What is the relationship of this alleged discovery to the fact that he did not become a rabbi? These questions have concerned only a literal hand-ful of scholars, among them Lacroix (1981), Filloux (1976, 1977), Besnard (1982, 1987) and Greenberg (1976), and have been almost completely ignored by the majority of Durkheimian scholars, partic-ularly in the English-speaking countries. They are important ques-tions that must be addressed because they have a bearing on the larger theme that concerns us: Was Durkheim's "will" essentially Jewish, or a self-conscious, cultivated form of austerity that exhibits affinities with Calvinism? Before we can understand how and why Durkheim sought to reconcile object and subject in sociology, we must understand how he reconciled them in his own life.

Bernard Lacroix (1981) offers a sensitive and intriguing interpre-tation of the relationship between Durkheim's interest in religion and the death of his father. Lacroix applies Freudian psychoanalysis to the impact of an important event in Durkheim's life. He speculates that Durkheim may have felt—albeit probably unconsciously—tre-mendous guilt on the occasion of his father's death, perhaps because Durkheim is sometimes alleged to have been destined to become a rabbi. The consequence of refusing this alleged destiny may have carried some psychical cost, and Lacroix may be correct to cite Durkheim's ensuing, self-diagnosed "neurasthenia" and various psy-chosomatic symptoms as part of that cost. Lacroix suggests that Durkheim's self-reported "discovery" of the importance of religion in 1895 was, in the psychoanalytic sense, an example of doing versus undoing. The religion that Durkheim had rejected in his personal life was now, supposedly, restored in a different form in his profes-sional life. Essential to Lacroix's argument is the claim that a hiatus in Durkheim's thought exists: before 1895 he was concerned primar-ily with political phenomena, and after 1895 he was concerned almost exclusively with religious phenomena.

Filloux (1976) is another Durkheimian scholar who places great emphasis on Durkheim's possible rabbinical training and its supposed consequences on his sociological thought. Filloux alleges that Durk-heim was steeped in the Talmud. The result, he claims, is that Durkheim's conception of religion in *Elementary Forms of the Religious Life* is essentially Talmudic. Like God, society—for Durkheim—is creation, life, paternity; the cradle of civilization, the source of man's ideas; it is "presence" (Filloux 1976, p. 261). Society causes man to experience a feeling of perpetual dependence (ibid., p. 262). Durk-heim supposedly substituted religious revelation for scientific revela-tion. Although he did not have disciples as a rabbi, he had disciples in his role as the head of the journal and school he established.

But did Durkheim attend a rabbinical school? Lukes (1985, p. 39) claims that he did: "Durkheim, however, was destined for the rabbinate and his early education was directed to that end: he studied for a time at a rabbinical school." In a footnote, Lukes attributes this claim to Durkheim's grandson, M. Etienne Halphen. But M. Halphen denied this claim in an interview with me. There is no historical evidence to suggest that any rabbinical school existed in Epinal. (A rabbinical school had existed in nearby Metz, but in 1858 it was moved to Paris.) Bauer's (1929) classic study of the French rabbinical school includes no mention of the Durkheim family. Of course, it could still be argued that Durkheim was exposed to the Talmud at the synagogue in Epinal; but again, there is no direct evidence to suggest that Durkheim was, in fact, exposed to the Talmud. Instead, M. Halphen suggests that there may have been very little pressure on Durkheim to follow in his father's footsteps. He adds that his own mother raised him and his two brothers completely without religion, they all married non-Jews, and his two brothers were even converted to Catholicism. Support for M. Halphen's representation of his grandfather can be found in Henri Durkheim's interview with Filloux, in Greenberg's (1976) analysis of Durkheim's background, and in the works of other scholars with regard to sons of rabbis in Durkheim's milieu, in general. Let us examine these in turn.

Filloux (1977) cites an interview with Henri Durkheim as evidence for his belief that Durkheim intended to become a rabbi prior to his radical break with his father's vocation. Philippe Besnard (1987), who has examined the text of this interview, disagrees with Filloux's conclusion. My own examination of this text leads me to side with Besnard. At best, Durkheim may have been expected—perhaps in a weak sense—to become a rabbi, but there is no evidence to suggest that he intended to become a rabbi.

Henri Durkheim was the son of Durkheim's brother Felix. One should wonder why, if so much pressure was allegedly put on Durkheim to become a rabbi, even more pressure was not exerted on his older brother, Felix. But Felix became a businessman, and Henri Durkheim mentions no conflict between Felix and Moïse Durkheim in that regard. The rabbi of Epinal and the Grand Rabbi of Metz have both indicated that in any case "pressure" is too strong a word. All of a rabbi's sons are expected to become rabbis, but that expectation is by no means coercive. Ultimately, they said, God decides what the child will become, and the rabbi indulges his son's decision.

According to the text of the interview in my possession, Henri Durkheim said about Durkheim and the rabbinate (in my translation): "I think that Cuvillier wrote in one of his first editions that Emile Durkheim was the son of a rabbi and that he was destined for the rabbinate. That is an error. . . . He never had this idea to become a rabbi. . . . He wanted to enter L'Ecole Normale, and like my grandfather, they were not rich." And in contradistinction to Lukes's (1985, p. 41) statement that "while at school [Durkheim] experienced a brief crisis of mysticism, under the influence of an old Catholic school-mistress, which he rapidly surmounted," Henri Durkheim said: "I have never heard Monsieur Durkheim say anything about a crisis of mysticism. I would never consider him as a mystic, so had he said anything about it, I would have been very surprised."

Filloux (1976) brought up the allegation by Georges Davy that at one point in his adult life, Durkheim allegedly said, "One should not forget that I am the son of a rabbi." Henri Durkheim responded: "It's possible. But, I never heard him say that, never. If it was a question of becoming a rabbi, it was because he was the natural son of a rabbi. But then my father [Felix Durkheim] did not pursue rabbinical studies either. My father wanted to go into business. . . . Finally, no, he [Emile Durkheim] did not want to become a rabbi. . . . It was never a question of him becoming a rabbi. If he said it, it was natural, but I do not know the context of the discussion in which he said it. I don't know."

Henri Durkheim indicated that, in general, Emile Durkheim "did not say he had religious beliefs—perhaps he had some, I don't know." When asked whether Durkheim had studied Hebrew and the Talmud, Henri Durkheim responded: "Well, it's probably true. But it is certain, certain that he renounced, completely, Judaism . . . and I never heard him say that he knew Hebrew." Rather than suggest that Durkheim's father influenced him with regard to the Jewish faith or the rabbinate, Henri Durkheim suggested that "his father influenced him psychologically, with rabbinical morality." And he made the interesting remark to Filloux that Durkheim's "religion was morality" and that "morality for [Durkheim] transcends society and community." M. Halphen read over the text of Henri Durkheim's interview and told me that he was in basic agreement with the spirit and facts of the interview, but that he did not know for certain what the facts were. And he added that he did not believe that his grandfather had studied to become a rabbi.

The image of Durkheim that emerges from Henri Durkheim's comments is remarkably similar to that of the young Freud in relation to his family (see Jones 1981). Like Freud, Durkheim was the intellectual in the family, who respected him for that reason. He directed the actions of the entire family not only after his father died, and not because his father had died but, in general, because he was the intellectual, according to Henri Durkheim. Durkheim worked constantly, from sun-up to sun-down, and was insatiable in his quest for knowledge. He was patriotic but not militant. According to Henri Durkheim, Marcel Mauss "was militant" and a "career socialist," but

"Durkheim certainly was not." Durkheim took a stand on the Dreyfus affair, but the stand was motivated by his loyalty to the Third Republic, not by Jewish sentiments, and it "did not leave a trace on his life."

Louis Greenberg offers an affectionate portrait of the relationship between Emile and his father, which is closer to the spirit of Henri Durkheim's remarks than the tone of conflict implied by Filloux (1976) and Lacroix (1981). Greenberg (1976, p. 625) writes: "[Moïse Durkheim's] family photograph presents a dignified figure of a man, but the absence of the beard, the modernity of his dress, and the very existence of the photograph contradict the stereotype of the orthodox, robed patriarch who traditionally shunned the camera." Moreover, Greenberg writes, Moïse Durkheim had a "decided taste" for the sciences and philosophy, a "scholar's interest" he could not cultivate through study because of his poverty. Greenberg suggests that Moïse may have encouraged his son to pursue science and philosophy precisely because Moïse himself could not bring those plans to fruition. Greenberg mentions a parallel situation in the relationship of Henri Bergson with his father. Why stop there? Sigmund Freud was another famous Jew whose father indulged his scientific interests (Jones 1981). In general, historical evidence exists to suggest that many Jews in Durkheim's time were encouraged by their fathers to assimilate into the larger culture (see Bauer 1929; Blumenkranz 1972; Charle 1984; Hertzberg 1968; Marrus 1971).

Greenberg suggests that Durkheim's childhood family life was warm and affectionate (consider Durkheim's subsequent passionate intellectual concerns with marriage and the family as the primary source of integration in a crumbling social world). He writes: "Emile Durkheim was not a cold fish by birth; while there was a propensity for literal-mindedness, his puritannical personality was really a cultivated disposition" (Greenberg 1976, p. 627). Rather than suggest that Durkheim opposed his father's will, as Filloux and Lacroix imply, Greenberg (p. 628) believes that Durkheim's

> debt to his Jewish heritage encouraged him to stress the evolutionary ties between modern man and his primitive forebears, rather than to place them in absolute opposition. He could, therefore, praise the rabbis whose subtle juridical skill had stretched the sacred law to its fullest in a futile endeavor to meet the demands of the new age. Nevertheless, Emile Durkheim became a convinced assimilator. "The Jews," he was to claim, "are leaving their ethnic character with extreme rapidity. In two generations it will be an accomplished fact." The needs of the modern world required that the rabbi shed his particularist and archaic robes to emerge as the universal scientist and teacher.

Durkheim's assimilation was consistent with the will of his times, a will accepted by most of the Jewish community in France following their legal emancipation as French citizens.

Greenberg (ibid., p. 629) is correct to cite Jules Bauer's (1929) observation that with few exceptions, rabbis in that milieu were not attracted to the prospect of making their children "ministers in Judaism." By all accounts, the Jews in Alsace-Lorraine were extremely poor. Rather, where the fathers had failed, the sons were encouraged to succeed: "It was not the father's values or personality that Emile rejected, but his career. Perhaps Emile's father understood this, the impoverished rabbi who had himself once displayed a marked taste for philosophy and the sciences and may have known the dreams of a student in Paris" (ibid., p. 630).

The Jewish Assimiliation Movement in France

Michael Marrus (1971) offers the best documented account of the status of Jews in Durkheim's time, which is supported by other accounts (Raphael and Weyl 1980; Schwarzfuchs 1982; Stauben 1860; Wistrich 1982). In 1900, there were only 86,000 Jews in all of France, by far the smallest Jewish population in any European country. The congregation that Moïse Durkheim led numbered only 390 in the year 1900 (Weymuller 1985, p. 282). Most French Jews had settled along the Rhine River in an effort to flee Germany. When Alsace-Lorraine was annexed to Germany in 1870, most of the Jewish population, already poor, moved west, leaving the poorest behind. Marrus and other authors emphasize that the Alsatian Jews were among the most backward and deprived in Europe. When they were granted citizenship following the French Revolution, most Jews had seized upon this fact as their opportunity for survival and advancement. In general, French Jews had "aligned themselves with the traditions of the French Republic, articulated a general political perspective which glorified their association with the Third Republic, and expected that they would be safe" (Marrus 1971, p. 85).

The goal of the Jews in France was total fusion and assimilation into French culture. Marrus delves into the life of a Jewish intellectual, one James Darmester, as an ideal-type of this assimilation. The externals of Darmester's life are remarkably similar to Durkheim's. Darmester's father was a rabbi, but the son studied science and abandoned the Jewish religion. His father died and he "discovered" religion. He became a proponent of Franco-Judaism, the ideology which held that the ideals of the French Republic were identical with those of the Jewish religion! It is interesting that one of these ideals was justice, a word used often in French literature as well as in the Talmud. The

Grand Rabbi of Metz made an interesting remark to me in this regard: "The Old Testament prophets were all socialists. They all criticized the rich and demanded justice." In any event, according to Marrus, Darmester typified the young French Jew at the turn of the century: "Always the theme was the same: Judaism contained within its doctrines, within its history, and even within its practices the seeds of good citizenship and devotion to the French fatherland" (Marrus 1971, p. 111).

The mingling of Jewish religion and the goals of modern France became the *official* doctrine of the Jewish community in France (ibid., p. 120). Jews in France did not associate themselves with extreme socialism, but steered a political middle course (which is also true for Durkheim's stand on socialism). They were unwilling to help fellow Jews who had immigrated from Russia in 1892 (ibid., p. 161), and they clung to their Frenchness in the face of all obstacles. Engagement in the Dreyfus affair was an issue of nationalism and rationalism, not Jewishness. To repeat: Henri Durkheim portrays Emile Durkheim's involvement in this nationalist tone.

The Grand Rabbi of Metz supported these observations in an interview with me. He said that being a good Jew in Durkheim's time meant hiding the fact of one's Jewishness. The Jews were expected by other Jews to adopt a French name (hence Emile David Durkheim), French manners, and French culture. Even if one kept to the tenets of orthodox Judaism, one was supposed to be "low-key." When the Dreyfus affair broke, the Jewish community was even more divided than the French population. Most Jews responded by reasserting their Frenchness or by keeping quiet (this point of view was confirmed for me by the rabbis I met in France), and most Jews felt that Dreyfus was guilty (ibid., p. 213). Even if Dreyfus was innocent, what upset the Jewish community most was that he had put—unwittingly or not—the fact of being a Jew into the forefront. What mattered most was one's commitment to France. Even Emile Durkheim's ([1898] 1975) published defense of Dreyfus took this patriotic approach and did not approach the problem from the point of view of anti-Semitism.

According to Marrus (1971, p. 99), Jewish writers in that period "with remarkable unanimity . . . agreed upon one point: anti-Semitism in France was a German import." They simply could not comprehend anti-Semitism as a French phenomenon. Emile Durkheim was no exception. Marrus (ibid., p. 99) writes:

> The sociologist Emile Durkheim, the son of an Alsatian rabbi, put this argument clearly to an interviewer in 1898. "Our anti-Semitism," he said, speaking of France, "is the consequence and the superficial symptom of a state of social malaise"; by contrast, the anti-Semitism which

one found in Germany or in Russia was "chronic" and "traditional." The conclusion to be drawn was that anti-Semitism was unpatriotic, anti-French, and pro German. Its triumph would mean the destruction of the French soul and her gifts to the world; the victory of anti-Semitism would be the victory of Germany.

In sum, the dominant collective representations of Durkheim's time urged assimilation. And this fact throws light on Durkheim's personal biography.

Durkheim's "Discovery" of Religion Reexamined

In the context of the preceding, the fact that Durkheim abandoned his father's religion and then "discovered" a more general "religion" of morality in adult life takes on a new meaning. Literally, it becomes a "social fact." Too many other Jews in his circumstances underwent a similar "crisis" for us to regard it as something peculiar to Durkheim. Let us approach Durkheim's personal crisis from the sociological perspective.

Philippe Besnard (1982, 1987) is critical of Lacroix's (1981) and Filloux's (1976) focus on Durkheim's alleged rabbinical crisis and its relationship to Durkheim's "discovery" of religion. Besnard (1982) notes the anomaly that Durkheim's father died in 1896 and that Durkheim's "discovery" of religion—if one dates it in relation to the famous letter he wrote that Lacroix (1981) cites—occurred in 1895. Clearly, one could, and Besnard does, argue that Durkheim discovered religion, at least sociologically, prior to his father's death. Lacroix retorted that Durkheim must have anticipated the death of his father, to which Besnard responded (1982) with the somewhat sarcastic observation that this must have been a long anticipation. And what of the death of Durkheim's mother in 1901? asks Besnard. Did it influence Durkheim's classic second preface to the *Division of Labor in Society,* published in 1902?

Despite the fact that he is critical of Lacroix and Filloux, Besnard (1982) offers his own version of how Durkheim's personal crises coincided with aspects of his sociological thought. In particular, Besnard offers a cautious, tentative suggestion to the effect that Durkheim's professional interest in anomie—which Besnard dates from 1896 to 1902—began with an intense but brief period of anomie in his personal life in the spring of 1896 that terminated in 1897. But one can apply Besnard's criticisms of Lacroix to Besnard's suggestion. It is not at all evident that Durkheim's interest in anomie was limited to the period 1896 to 1902, as Besnard (1987, pp. 135–39) insists (see my review in Meštrović 1988b). If anomie is understood to be a state of immoral *dérèglement*—which is how Durkheim ([1897] 1983, p. 281) referred to it (discussed in Meštrović and Brown 1985)—and its attendant vocabulary of agitation, sorrow, effervescence, and so on, one could argue that anomie dominated Durkheim's thought during his entire career.

The essential point here, a point usually overlooked because of the widespread mistranslation of *anomie* as the secular "normlessness," is that anomie is a concept tinged with religious and moral overtones. Both *anomia* and *dérèglement* imply immorality. This fact enables one to regard Durkheim's intellectual career as a unity. Durkheim was continually concerned with morality and its opposite, and there is no real break in his thought, regardless of the personal crises that he experienced.

Still, the suggestions regarding the impact of Durkheim's Jewish background upon his thought contain a grain of truth. It is possible to argue, as Lacroix (1981) likes to argue, that Durkheim's thought underwent a radical shift from political to religious concerns around the year 1895. In some ways, the society-as-a-symbol-of-God that Durkheim depicts *is* more like the Old Testament God of justice and fear than the New Testament God of love. Yet it does not necessarily follow that this aspect of Durkheim's thought betrays his Jewishness, at least not in the orthodox sense. John Calvin, and St. Augustine before him, tended to emphasize the Old Testament God in their theologies as well. (See also Reinhold Niebuhr's 1976 thesis in *Love and Justice* that the highest form of Christian charity is justice.) Greenberg (1976), too, has a point when he suggests that Durkheim's father may have been an atypical rabbi who might not have been distressed by his son's choice of a nonrabbinical career. Arguments can be made for and against the Jewish influence on Durkheim's thought, but no hard evidence has been unearthed to settle the matter. These are representations, not data. Perhaps what is required is that these representations be examined as Durkheim taught that representations should be studied.

First, Durkheim was more concerned with facts than with events. In philosophical usage extant in his time, events were temporary occurrences, while facts exhibited more of the quality of permanence. Events were demarcated in time and space, but facts were relatively independent of time and space. (I discuss this in relation to Durkheim and turn of the century thought in Meštrović 1985b.) Thus, the death of Durkheim's father was both an event (when one considers when and where it occured) and a representation, a fact (recall that Robert Hertz, [1907] 1960 treats death as a collective representation). Similarly, Durkheim ([1897] 1951) did not analyze suicide in relation to life's events, but in relation to social *facts*. His follower Célestin Bouglé expressed this point well: "What is of special interest to [the Durk-heimians] is not what passes away but what is repeated; institutions survive the flow of events" (Bouglé [1908] 1971, p. 6).

Similarly, Freud did *not* claim that one becomes neurotic due to life's events, but due to the accumulation and inadequate "wearing-away" of life's "traumas" (discussed in Meštrović 1982). Thus for Freud, a trauma is not just an event (Laplanche and Pontalis 1974). Rather, traumas presuppose the interaction of the human agent's reconstructed memories and the social milieu, an interaction that occurs in a relatively timeless unconscious. (It is interesting in this regard that in his *Collective Memory,* the Durkheimian disciple Maurice Halbwachs, [1950] 1980 combined the essence of Freud's conception of memory with Durkheim's social thought, and that both of these follow Schopenhauer's lead that memory is independent of the prin-ciples of sufficient reason.) This is an important point to consider given Lacroix's (1981) application of Freud's thought to Durkheim's life. Consider, for example, the fact that Freud was not deterred when he discovered that many of his patients had lied about their alleged seductions. Freud argued that the fantasies of seduction were as real, if not more real, in terms of their effects than the events of seduc-tion—which in any case were false. Similarly, Durkheim placed far more emphasis on collective representations considered as social *facts* than on personal events. Durkheim argued that one became neuras-thenic or succumbed to suicide not because of transient personal events, but because of the relatively more-permanent social facts.

It must be emphasized that Schopenhauer's philosophy explains both Freud's and Durkheim's treatments of memory, events, and facts in the sense that Schopenhauer ([1818] 1977) distinguished sharply between the "idea" which is subject to Kant's categories and the will which is completely independent of these rational categories. In the realm of the will, the categories of space, time and other principles of reason do not apply.

Let us apply these insights to the just-mentioned analyses of the relationships between Durkheim's personal biography—particularly in relation to his Jewish background and his father—and social thought. Precisely when certain events occurred in Durkheim's pro-fessional and personal biography is a somewhat irrelevant point. Of course, events are important, but events are refracted through collec-tive representations. Representations are prisms, not reflectors. An overreliance on events, at the expense of facts and the social milieu that gives them meaning, is a precarious undertaking. Such argu-ments lead to the kind of hair-splitting that we have just reviewed with regard to Lacroix (1981) and Besnard (1982). And what does it matter if one reduces the thought of an important thinker like

Durkheim to his coping with personal events? In that case, one implies that scientific objectivity—in any form—is completely impossible. Durkheim's social thought concerning religion is something more than a personal response to his father's death and the alleged guilt this may have caused.

Let us reexamine the same set of facts that concern Lacroix, Filloux, Besnard, and Greenberg from the Durkheimian perspective of totality (discussed in Meštrović 1987). Even though Durkheim rejected the role of the rabbi for himself, Durkheim—were he alive today—would probably have argued that he was shaped by certain collective representations of the Jewish religion, the Talmud, the history of Epinal, and the French Republic *as they were refracted* through Epinal, his family, and his personality. In other words, one should consider not only the effects of Durkheim's conscious rejection of Jewishness, but also the unconscious shaping of his personality by collective representations extant in his time. In this regard, Durkheim's theory is in line with Freud's, for Freud also believed that one's character is largely "set" in childhood, regardless of the conscious decisions one makes in later life. But our point is that given Durkheim's life-long insistence on the view that one's personality is largely shaped by collective representations, one should not focus primarily on Durkheim's conscious responses to certain events in his adult life.

From this more Durkheimian perspective applied to Durkheim's life, the relationship between Durkheim's personal and professional biographies takes on a more complex meaning than is apparently the case at present. For example, Durkheim's preoccupation with *anomie* may be understood not only relative to the adult reaction to his father's death. It may also have been the fulfillment of Durkheim's childhood wishes to become like his father because, after all, Durkheim consistently regarded *anomie* as the obverse of morality. What Durkheim and his father had in common was that they were both moralists. The fact that throughout his career, from the first to the last of his major writings, Durkheim was intent upon establishing a *science of morality* is often overlooked in Durkheimian scholarship. Traditionally, science and morality are considered to be poles apart. The fact that Durkheim sought to combine them may be due, in part, to his unconscious reconciliation of the representations that shaped him, representations that urged secularization and assimilation, and also representations that stressed a concern with morality.

Durkheim's concerns with religion should not be understood apart from his concerns with morality. His first classic work, *The Division of Labor in Society* ([1893] 1933), was an effort—in his own words—to illustrate how morality may be studied as a social fact, and he died in 1917 writing the introduction to *La Morale*, which he never completed.

Durkheim may have said, again as an adult, that he "discovered" religion in 1895, but he was always preoccupied with morality and immorality. His moralism may be understood independent of his father's death, as a refraction of the Durkheim family rabbinical tradition. It could be argued that although Durkheim consciously rejected the Jewish religion and the role of the rabbi, he was still a prophet of sorts.

One could claim—in a very Durkheimian fashion—that the collective representations that shaped Durkheim were never lost or destroyed, only transformed. That is the gist of Durkheim's argument concerning collective representations in general and religious representations in particular, found especially in his *Sociology and Philosophy* ([1924] 1974) as well as in *Elementary Forms of the Religious Life* ([1912)] 1965). While Durkheim did not become a rabbi, he may have transformed his father's philosophical and moral concerns into something new, his version of sociology.

This point requires special emphasis, as it is neglected in Durkheimian scholarship in general, and certainly with regard to the problem of his biography. Durkheim insisted throughout his career that collective representations are never wholly lost, neither "objectively" nor "subjectively." For Durkheim (as for Schopenhauer), the objective and the subjective are a unity. These representations undergo various metamorphoses. Moreover, like Freud, Durkheim claimed that these representations are unconscious, wholly or in part. Finally, collective representations are modified, retouched, shaped and, in Durkheim's words, "individualized" by human agents. Each of us comprehends collective representations in his own private and somewhat idiosyncratic way, but that fact in no way detracts from the objective quality of the collective representations. This is the gist of Durkheim's argument concerning representations, which we are applying to Durkheim's life.

Reconciliation With a Subjective Past

I believe that the representation of Durkheim in relation to his Jewish background that best accounts for his will—as manifested in his private and professional life—and the social will of his times is the following: He grew up in a poor but loving family that was not as orthodox in religious practice as it might have been, in times that stressed the assimilation of Jews. His elder brother experienced no conflict in moving away from the rabbinate and into business. Emile was marked as the intellectual in the family, a trait that gave him special honor and status within the family (reminiscent of Freud's family status). There was no question but that he would make his mark on the secular, not the religious, world. But in addition, his intellectualism bound him to his father. Father and son probably identified with each other in a way that made their relationship special. Morality, the bridge between the community of the past and the society of the future, was Durkheim's religion. It is not the same as religion, but it is religious. It is not secular and antireligious, nor is it ritualistic.

Consider the most-neglected aspect of Emile Durkheim's sociology, his quest for what he called the science of moral facts. He referred to it as such in his earliest lectures, published later as *Professional Ethics and Civic Morals* ([1950] 1983), to his last, albeit unfinished work, *La Morale* ([1920] 1976). And his major works were all concerned with this theme, not with positivism, realism, social order or the other representations that are typically proposed. For example, Lucien Levy-Bruhl—one of Durkheim's closest friends and followers—offers the following assessment of two of Durkheim's classics (1899, p. 464):

> M. Durkheim, in his *Division du Travail Social* and in his *Règles de la Méthode Sociologique*, endeavoured to treat the facts of moral life after the method used in the positive sciences—that is, not only to observe them carefully, to describe and classify them, but to find out in what way they are capable of becoming objects of scientific study, and to this end, to discover in them some objective element which will admit of exact determination, or if possible, of measurement. If the definition of the "social fact" were sufficiently exact, the greatest difficulty would be overcome, and social science could then progress rapidly.

But Durkheim's *Division of Labor in Society* is typically cited as a treatise on "social solidarity" and the problem of social order. His *Rules of Sociological Method* are usually understood as a bungled attempt to establish a methodology by which sociology could be scientific, positivistic, and value-free (see Douglas 1967; Lukes 1985).

And yet, consider Durkheim's openings in these works. In the first sentence of the first preface to *Division of Labor in Society* ([1893] 1933, p. 32), Durkheim wrrites: "This book is pre-eminently an attempt to treat the facts of the moral life according to the method of the positive sciences. . . . We do not wish to extract ethics from science, but to establish the science of ethics, which is quite different. Moral facts are phenomena like others; they consist of rules of action recognizable by certain distinctive characteristics. It must, then, be possible to observe them, describe them, classify them, and look for the laws explaining them. That is what we shall do for certain of them." And in the introduction to the *Rules of Sociological Method*, Durkheim claims that he is merely clarifying, proving, and illustrating the project he began in *Division of Labor in Society* (Durkheim [1895] 1982, p. 49).

Durkheim's quest for a science of moral facts is the reconciliation of all of the personal and professional dualisms and conflicts we have been discussing. It enabled him to be the moralist that his father was and the scientist his father had wanted to be. It allowed him to keep his Jewish heritage yet assimilate into the French republic. It wed fact and value, object and subject, science and morality, all of which have been understood traditionally as being poles apart. Science is supposed to be value-free, according to contemporary sociology's rhetoric, even though most natural scientists disagree. Durkheim's quest was so revolutionary in comparison with the collective representations that inform modern sociology that it was simply not recognized. For, as stated at the outset, the world is representation, and without the representation the world does not exist. Durkheim's and Schopenhauer's revolutionary moves in this regard were–and to some extent, still are–too far ahead of their times.

Durkheim's moralism, when it is mentioned in contemporary accounts, is usually depicted as an afterthought to his alleged concern with order, a footnote to his other concerns with solidarity and science or, finally, as an embarrassing bit of bias carried over from his nineteenth century upbringing, incompatible with "value-free science." But the fact is that *all* his major works were written in the spirit of trying to establish a science of moral facts, and the many topics other sociologists typically treat as primary were secondary for him in relation to this quest. And the notion of "value-free" science has been criticized so extensively, both within sociology and in science in general, that it is a wonder it is still cited. Of course the scientist must be impersonal and objective, but that does not rule out concerns with moral issues. Objectivity is a moral act, in Schopenhauer's ([1818] 1977) scheme of things, precisely because it puts the egoistic will in its place, at least temporarily.

Nor is there anything strange about Durkheim's quest for a science of moral facts in relation to his times. Many of his contemporaries were concerned with establishing morality on a scientific basis: Freud, Guyau, Nietzsche, Wundt, Levy-Bruhl, and so on—in fact, most of the same thinkers who took up Schopenhauer's problem of the will and representation. The intellectuals in Durkheim's time understood that the will had been unleashed in the world by the dissolution of the community and religion, which had previously absorbed it. This is the message of Tönnies's ([1887] 1963) *Community and Society*, which draws on Schopenhauer, and which Durkheim reviewed. What should be done about it? That is still the question, although it is rarely acknowledged in those terms. Durkheim's reply was not to retreat into the past nor to thrust into the future without continuity. It was to reform and renovate the best of the tradition of the past in order to deal effectively with the exigencies of the future.

CHAPTER 3

Renovated Rationalism

W HY RENOVATE RATIONALISM? This complicated question can be broken down into two component questions: Why renovate any epistemology? And, if something must be renovated, why rationalism, instead of realism or some other "ism" on the "objective" side of the dualism? My aim in this chapter is to show that Durkheim wanted to renovate previous epistemologies because they posit an irreconcilable hiatus between the object and subject. He felt that sociology could not progress as long as it was plagued by this dualism. And he wanted to renovate rationalism, not realism, because he believed—as do many contemporary philosophers—that at bottom we are all rationalists (see Flew 1985; Fodor 1981; Trigg 1985; Sylvan and Glassner 1985). We must be, because the world can only be known by us as representation. On this point, even Kant and Schopenhauer agree. It is impossible to be a true realist because realism, too, requires a subject and its representations. I shall illustrate the importance of these moves with reference to Durkheim's critique of pragmatism. Finally, I will focus upon his notion of the "totality" of knowledge, but first the notion of "representation" must be elaborated.

I shall emphasize the focus on representations in Durkheim's works as well as in the works of many of his colleagues in order to question Lukes's apparently uncritical depiction of Durkheim as a "social realist." It is curious how Lukes (1985, p. 79) arrives at this label: "This is what was postulated by Durkheim's doctrine of 'social realism' (as it came to be called by its opponents)." Moreover, in citing evidence for the label given to Durkheim by his opponents, Lukes footnotes Deploige (1912), who engaged Durkheim in a bitter polemic. Similarly, Lukes (1985, p. 67) quotes a historian to the effect that in 1884 France, "one attitude of mind, one doctrine dominated and excited French intellectual life: scientific positivism, issuing from

Auguste Comte," and that "this attitude of mind was certainly shared by Durkheim." Scores of scholars have uncritically adopted these starting points when reading Durkheim's works. Yet evidence abounds that at the turn of the century, Comte's influence was waning and Schopenhauer's influence in France was at its height (Baillot 1927; Ellenberger 1970; Simmel [1907] 1986). My strategy will be not to rely on Durkheim's opponents, but to examine the interests of his colleagues in the wake of Kant's devastating critique of realism.

Representations and Their Relation to Renovated Rationalism

The French word *représentation* cannot be translated accurately into English. Literally, it means "idea." Durkheim made frequent and problematic use of this concept, as when he claimed in *Rules of Sociological Method* that he "had expressly stated and reiterated in every way possible that social life was made up entirely of representations" ([1895] 1982, p. 34). In *Elementary Forms of the Religious Life* he claimed that "social life, in all its aspects and in every period of its history, is made possible only by a vast symbolism" that includes all kinds of "representations" ([1912] 1965, p. 264). When Durkheim praised Saint-Simon as the rightful founder of sociology, it was on the grounds that Saint-Simon was the first to claim that the social system is nothing but a system of ideas (Durkheim [1928] 1958, p. 128). In *Suicide* he claimed that "essentially social life is made up of representations" (Durkheim [1897] 1951, p. 312). In *Moral Education*, too, Durkheim asserted that society "is a complex of ideas and sentiments, of ways of seeing and of feeling, a certain intellectual and moral framework distinctive of the entire group" ([1925] 1961, p. 277). Durkheim's *Evolution of Educational Thought* ([1938] 1977) traces the development of reason in relation to social structure since the fall of the Roman Empire in the context of how persons represent reality in different epochs. Bouglé felt that this aspect of Durkheimian thought needed special emphasis, claiming in the preface to *Sociology and Philosophy* that "Durkheim was one of those who insisted most upon the fact that 'society is above all a composition of ideas' " (Bouglé [1924] 1974, p. xxxvii). Indeed, anyone who reads the works of Durkheim's followers will find that they referred constantly to "representations" in their analyses, and that, in general, they seem to have been under the sway of their master's powerful claim that "without doubt, collective life is only made of representations" (Durkheim [1900] 1973, p. 16).

This emphasis on representations by Durkheim and his followers led them far from the tenets of positivism and realism into a mysterious domain they eventually came to call "renovated rationalism." In the first preface to *Rules of Sociological Method,* Durkheim denied outright that he was a positivist and said that he preferred the label "rationalist," but made it clear that this was no ordinary rationalism ([1895] 1982, p. 33). In the second preface, he became more heated: "Whereas we had repeatedly declared that consciousness, both individual and social, did not signify for us anything substantial, but merely a collection of phenomena *sui generis,* more or less systematized, we were accused of realism and ontological thinking. While we had expressly stated and reiterated in every way possible that social life was made up entirely of representations, we were accused of eliminating from sociology the element of mind" (ibid., p. 34).

Durkheim is *still* accused of realism and of eliminating the concept of mind from his sociology. Durkheim explained the way in which representations may be considered simultaneously as objects and subjects in his essay "Individual and Collective Representations" in 1898, an argument which parallels the gist of Schopenhauer's *World as Will and Idea* closely. His best illustration of the manner in which representations are objects despite their being ideas is to be found in his earliest treatment of religion, his 1897 essay on the incest taboo. It was published as the first article in the first issue of the famous journal he founded, *L'Année sociologique.* Durkheim ([1897] 1963, p. 114) wrote: "One cannot repeat too often that everything which is social consists of representations, and therefore is a result of representations. However, this act of becoming a collective image, which is the very essence of sociology, does not consist of a progressive realization of certain fundamental ideas. These fundamental ideas, at first obscured and veiled by adventitious beliefs, gradually liberate themselves and become more and more completely independent." It is as if these representations possessed a metaphysical "will" of their own. Durkheim's ponderous moves regarding representationalism cannot be reduced to any current "ism." He was definitely reaching for something new.

Much of *Moral Education* is devoted to an explication of the rationalism Durkheim claimed is "in the blood" of the French, such that "in general, a Frenchman is to some degree a conscious or unconscious Cartesian" (Durkheim [1925] 1961, p. 253). Despite the limitations of Cartesianism, he insisted that "we must remain impenitent rationalists, but our rationalism must be rid of its simplicism" (ibid., p. 265). Similar wording occurs in the conclusion of *Evolution of Educational Thought:* "Still today, we must remain Cartesians in the sense that we must fashion rationalists, that is to say men who are concerned with clarity of thought; but they must be rationalists of a new kind who know that things, whether human or physical, are irreducibly complex and who are yet able to look unfalteringly into the face of this complexity" ([1938] 1977, p. 348). "Simple rationalism" is a system of ideas that is sufficient unto itself, but that does not take account of external "reality." It is dogmatic. Still, "reality" cannot be known except through some form of rationalism. Hence, one must remain a rationalist, but one's rationalism must take account of empiricism—it must be renovated, not abandoned.

A similar move is the foundation for Durkheim's argument in *Pragmatism and Sociology,* wherein he writes that pragmatism exposes the "weaknesses of the old rationalism, which needs to be reformed if it is to meet the demands of modern thought and take into account certain new points of view introduced by modern sciences. The problem is to find a formula which will preserve what is essential in rationalism and answer the valid criticism that pragmatism makes of it" (Durkheim [1955] 1983, p. 2).

The Elementary Forms of the Religious Life is actually a sophisticated inquiry into the social origins of the *rationalist* distinction between sacred and profane representations, although it is almost never read from this perspective. Sociologists have failed to account for his thought-provoking assertion that "The rationalism which is imminent in the sociological theory of knowledge is thus midway between the classical empiricism and apriorism" (Durkheim [1912] 1965, p. 31). Compare Durkheim's claim with Schopenhauer's ([1818] 1977, vol. 1, p. 32) that "it must be observed that we did not start either from the object or the subject, but from the idea, which contains and presupposes them both." This intriguing epistemological position is the basis of Durkheim's renovation of rationalism ([1912] 1965, p. 32):

Thus renovated, the theory of knowledge seems destined to unite the opposing advantages of the two rival theories, without incurring their inconveniences. It keeps all the essential principles of the apriorists; but at the same time it is inspired by the positive spirit which the empiricists have striven to satisfy. It leaves the reason its specific power, but it accounts for it and does so without leaving the world of observable phenomena. It affirms the duality of our intellectual life, but it explains it, and with natural causes. The categories are no longer considered as primary and unanalyzable facts, yet they keep a complexity which falsifies any analysis as ready as that with which the empiricists content themselves. They no longer appear as very simple notions which the first comer can very easily arrange from his own personal observations and which the popular imagination has unluckily complicated, but rather they appear as priceless instruments of thought which the human groups have laboriously forged through the centuries and where they have accumulated the best of their intellectual capital. A complete section of the history of humanity is resumed therein.

This non-Kantian, nonpositivist, non-Cartesian, very complicated epistemological stance is also the focus of his sequel to *Elementary Forms of the Religious Life*, Durkheim's essay on *homo duplex*, "The Dualism of Human Nature and Its Social Conditions" ([1914] 1973), and of his lectures (delivered in 1914 and 1915) entitled "Pragmatism and Sociology" ([1955] 1983).

Georges Davy ([1950] 1983, p. xviii) also presents a complicated view of Durkheim's epistemology as something that is neither materialism nor idealism:

> We must avoid ambiguity in the word "thing." It is not a matter of seeing only a material datum in the social phenomenon. Durkheim always disclaimed any such materialism—but he was only against regarding it as a given fact—*given*, that is, like any thing we encounter just as it is and not imagined or fabricated according to what one believes it might be or desires it to be. That said, the fact being given as a thing in no way presumes that it should be only a material *thing*, and in no way excludes it also, or at the same time, being an *idea*, a belief, a sentiment, a habit or behavior, which are, no less than matter, realities, existing and having effect and therefore capable of being observed.

What Durkheim was philosophically is quite difficult to fathom. It is clear that he and his followers sought to reject naive positivism, naive empiricism, and naive rationalism. Anyone who has read *L'Année sociologique* from its first issue and is familiar with the works of his followers will agree that the sociological method of these sophisticated thinkers—most of whom held degrees in philosophy—has very little in common with what passes for sociological methodology today, or with what passed for sociological methodology in Durkheim's time. Durkheim and his followers were neither realist nor subjectivist, neither positivist nor Cartesian, nor were they just dodging the issue. Above all, they did not compartmentalize reality into any dominant "ism." They sought to reconcile and synthesize the epistemological "isms" that continue to dominate contemporary social thought. In this regard, they were following the path that Schopenhauer ([1818] 1977) had already opened with his attempt at reconciling the dualisms that Kant had exposed, and that many of their contemporaries were pursuing (Ellenberger 1970).

Lukes (1982, pp. 1–27) regards Durkheim's focus on the representational character of sociology's domain as limiting, "strange," and leading to a "sterile prescription for the social sciences." This is because Lukes regards Durkheim as a social realist scientifically (Lukes 1985, pp. 79–85, 316–18; idem 1982, p. 11). From this epistemological stance–which is *not* Durkheimian, and which Durkheim rejected explicitly–the claim that society is a system of ideas has to seem bizarre. How can ideas exist independent of agents? As Lukes (1982, p. 9) put the matter, "If, as [Durkheim] came to think, in social life 'everything consists of representations, ideas and sentiments,' are they not conceptions, albeit collective, of participants and witnesses?" This is meant to be a rhetorical question, but for Durkheim, the answer is a flat "no." Lukes alternates between reducing Durkheim's epistemology to subjectivism or realism. He misses the point that for Durkheim, as for Schopenhauer, the representation bridges object and subject.

The other great influence on Durkheimian scholarship, the work of Parsons, is just as problematic. For example, in *The Structure of Social Action*, Parsons (1937, p. 349) claimed that because of his alleged positivism, Durkheim was biased in favor of the use of "facts of the objective verifiability of which there can be no question such as division of labor, suicide rates, legal codes, etc., while he is suspicious of such 'subjective' entities as 'ideas' and 'sentiments.'" In fact, Durkheim (1908) doubted the possibility of "objective verifiability" and relied more on the one "well-designed experiment" than anything like modern replication. The very opposite of what Parsons claimed is true: Durkheim's sociology rests on the premise that society is a system of *ideas,* and he was suspicious of "facts" that cannot be questioned. Nor was Parsons correct to claim that Durkheim derived his category of *choses* (things) from the methodology of the "hard sciences" (Parsons 1937, p. 352). Durkheim was explicit in expressing his debt to the philosophers on this point, and in any case, sought to reconcile our present-day, neat distinction between the humanities and science, especially in his *Evolution of Educational Thought* ([1938] 1977). But Parsons (1937, p. 359) was completely off the mark when he wrote that "Durkheim's famous category of representations is undoubtedly simply a name for the scientist's subjective experience of the phenomena of the external world [and] collective representations . . . are his 'ideas' concerning the 'social environment.'" Durkheim's thought has been reduced, again, to subjectivism. How many times had Durkheim ([1895] 1982; [1924] 1974) warned that collective representations elude the consciousness of agents, witnesses, and society itself? Parsons concluded that Durkheim "ended where he began, at the conception of a common subjective element" (Parsons 1937, p. 360). Parsons set the tone for misreading Durkheim that persists into the present.

Contrary to some of these contemporary misunderstandings of Durkheim's epistemology, his focus on representations was commonplace in his time, in France as well as western Europe in general. Parsons was totally inaccurate in his depiction of Durkheim's alleged subjectivism and alleged antipathy toward ideas. And Lukes overstates the influence of Comte's positivism at the same time that he completely ignores Schopenhauer. Durkheim's renovated rationalism was a fresh attempt to reconstruct the social sciences from the remnants of age-old epistemological problems. It is of more than historical interest, although its historical context should not be ignored. It speaks to the modern epistemological crises in sociology.

Representationalism in Historical and Cultural Context

There was nothing strange about Durkheim's thoughts on representations. In fact, the term *représentation* and its German equivalent *Vorstellung* were standard terms not only among Durkheim's disciples but also for the Freudian school, the phenomenologists, and other important intellectual movements in Europe at the time (Ellenberger 1970; Lalande [1926] 1980; Laplanche and Pontalis 1974; Simmel [1907] 1986). Representations had been discussed in the drawing rooms of Vienna and Paris for at least a century before Durkheim appeared on the scene (Janik and Toulmin 1973). This concern with representationalism was nurtured by several currents that can ultimately be traced back to Plato. As a result of Kant's ([1788] 1956) devastating critique of pure empiricism, some philosophers turned to the task of analyzing the basic data of experience as the structured phenomena "representations." Schopenhauer was one such thinker and devoted almost all of volume 2 of his *World as Will and Idea* ([1818] 1977) to the theme that Kant was on the right track, but did not develop his insight sufficiently. As Schopenhauer (ibid., p. 6) put it, "Kant's greatest merit is the distinction of the phenomenon from the thing in itself." This move barred any retreat to crude empiricism and realism, the very doctrines Lukes (1985) ascribes to Durkheim. As stated previously, Schopenhauer's influence upon turn-of-the-century thought was immense, and Durkheim was among those who apparently subscribed to Schopenhauer's philosophy. Ellenberger (1970, p. 208) summarizes Schopenhauer's achievement as follows: "Kant distinguished the world of phenomena and the world of the thing in itself, which is inaccessible to our knowledge. Schopenhauer called the phenomena representations, and the thing in itself will, equating the will with the unconscious as conceived by some of the Romantics; Schopenhauer's will had the dynamic character of blind, driving forces, which not only reigned over the universe, but also conducted man. Thus man is an irrational being guided by internal forces, which are unknown to him and of which he is scarcely aware."

In his *Vocabulaire technique et critique de la philosophie*, André Lalande ([1926] 1980, pp. 920–22) offers an analysis of the history of the term *représentation*. According to him, the concept of "representation" rests on two fundamental but opposing ideas, that of something actually present and able to be sensed versus its "replacement" as an image in the mind of the observer. Descartes pushed this opposition to its extreme in his *Meditations*. The term can be traced back even further to the Christian idea that various symbols can represent the body and blood of Christ and of course, to Plato's "Ideas.". Kant, Schopenhauer, Freud, even Durkheim, all take up Plato on this point (see Meštrović 1982). Durkheim ([1912] 1965) dared to trace representationalism even beyond Plato, to primitive totemism, in which totems represent the group.

Historians and philosophers of the social sciences have not yet explained why representationalism gained momentum in the late nineteenth century. Its progress was slow after Descartes, through the writings of Malebranche, Leibniz, Hegel, Kant, and Schopenhauer. Then it suddenly gained crucial importance in the thought of leading philosophers and precursors of the social sciences: Ribot, Renouvier, Espinas, Herbart, Freud, Jung, Meillet, Wundt, Hamelin, Taine, Fechner, Bergson, Kraepelin, and Guyau—although this list is not exhaustive. Fields of inquiry that have come to be known as psychology, sociology, linguistics, and psychiatry owe their inception to the concept of representationalism. Nineteenth century continental thinkers took it for granted that "mind" and "body" were mysteriously interrelated, but that mental ideas and representations were something quite other than epiphenomena of the body.

Durkheim's followers were philosophers, for the most part, and seem to have been keenly aware of the intellectual interconnections in this milieu concerning this terminology. Levy-Bruhl's (1899) analysis has already been mentioned. Bouglé (1938, p. 19), too, makes an interesting link between Durkheim and Hegel: "In Bordeaux, Durkheim started where Espinas left off . . . social facts being, according to him, above all the collective representations which reveal themselves to men. . . . This is sometimes considered as imitating Germany. For is not collective consciousness the distant descendant of *Volksgeist,* if not of the 'objective spirit' of Hegel?" (see also Knapp 1985).

In some significant ways, Hegelianism and Cartesianism intermingled, so it would be difficult to unravel their respective spheres of influence. But many strands actually that led to representationalism. Schopenhauer, alone, harps on Malebranche, Plato, Kant, and Hegel—and Durkheim was aware of the contribution of all these thinkers. According to Pierre Halbwachs, Maurice Halbwachs wrote his doctoral dissertation on Leibniz and was a disciple of Bergson for a time; both of these thinkers were engaged with the concept of representation. Durkheim was on the best of terms with Hamelin (1921, 1927, 1952) and wrote the preface to his work on representations (1921). Durkheim's admiration for Espinas has already been mentioned. Another of Durkheim's teachers, Charles Renouvier (1892), was one of the first French philosophers to take up Schopenhauer's philosophy in relation to Kant's representationalism. Renouvier (1892) has nothing but praise to offer for Schopenhauer's philosophy (yet Lukes 1985, p. 55, refers vaguely to Renouvier's "neo-Kantianism" without mentioning Schopenhauer). This list of multiple, and some mutual, influences can be extended to a great length. It is impossible to state precisely who influenced whom, but it is possible to conclude that no self-respecting philosopher could have ignored Schopenhauer's philosophy or the topic of representationalism at the turn of the century.

Marcel Mauss extends this list of interconnections to include George Herbert Mead, Freud and the Freudians, Jung, Piaget, and the "alienists" concerned with what has come to be known as "mental illness." Mauss ([1950] 1979a, p. 12) sees no fundamental opposition between sociology and psychology due to this fact, only a difference in focus: "But already, since I have spoken of collective representations and practices, i.e., of habitual actions and ideas, I have necessarily spoken in psychological language. . . . That is why Durkheim, the pupil of Wundt and Ribot, Espinas, Ribot's friend, and the rest of us, the followers of these teachers, have always been ready to accept the advances of psychology." But Mauss is scornful of thinkers who ignored representations, referring to Herbert Spencer's ideas, for example, as "brutal over-simplifications" (ibid., p. 3).

In no way is this analysis meant to exhaust the importance of representationalism to the origins of the social sciences. Nor is our focus on Schopenhauer meant to be dogmatic or to imply that Durkheim's thought should not be compared and contrasted with other representationalists. It ought to be. Schopenhauer is a convenient choice because Lalande (1960) points him out as one of Durkheim's favorite philosophers, and because Durkheim ([1887] 1976a; [1887] 1976b) addresses the works of many of his contemporaries in the context of Schopenhauer's philosophy. But Schopenhauer was representative of his times and influenced many who influenced Durkheim. The more important point is that the sharp divisions, compartmentalization, and "turf" barriers that characterize contemporary social sciences were apparently not intended by their precursors. They were willing to study representations in a myriad of forms.

Freud reproduced much of Durkheim's conceptual system with his use of the notion of *Vorstellung*, the German translation of *représentation* (Laplanche and Pontalis 1974, pp. 200–5, 373–74, 447–49; Meštrović 1982). Freud, too, was influenced by Wundt and Schopenhauer (Ellenberger 1970; Jones 1981) and possibly even directly by

Durkheim. Freud's (1913) *Totem and Taboo* is replete with references to the Durkheimians, and Freud kept up with the Durkheimian journal, *L'Année sociologique*. Both Freud and Durkheim developed the idea that representations can take on a life of their own—somewhat independent of the human agent—so that these representations evolve, combine and regroup to form new representations (Meštrović 1982). In other words, representations exhibit their own "will" to some extent. Both thinkers were concerned with this kind of "free association" and its consequences for understanding religion, irrationality, and pathology.

Despite this enormous effervescence of thought, the works of Durkheim's and Freud's followers remain buried in obscurity. Wundt, Espinas, Herbart, Ribot, and Renouvier have been almost completely omitted from introductory social science textbooks. Freud's and Durkheim's thought has been incorporated into the social sciences along the lines of positivistic methodology: portions that are allegedly "empirically verifiable" are kept, and the rest are discarded. Mauss ([1950] 1979a, p. 2) may have spoken too soon when he claimed that "the heroic age—forgive me the phrase—of Weber and Fechner, of Wundt and Ribot is long over. . . . no one disputes the advances of our two sciences [psychology and sociology] any longer." On the contrary, these alleged advances are disputed now more than ever, even by social scientists. How and why the nineteenth century focus on representationalism was recast into a positivistic, pragmatist scenario is a mystery worth pursuing, although I will note here simply that it is inaccurate. For example, Durkheim is typically aligned with Comte's positivism. But the fact remains that Durkheim and his followers were highly critical of Comte. Comte was a naive rationalist in their view of things (Bouglé 1938; Levy-Bruhl 1899). They were careful to claim that their approach was "positive in spirit" but not positivist.

At present, representationalism is still discussed in philosophy and art and is beginning to be re-introduced into the discourse of the social sciences. Thus Skinner's behaviorism has been criticized on the basis of representational arguments, although often unwittingly, and certainly not by invoking psychology's pioneers. Symbolic interactionism, according to Mauss ([1950] 1979a), holds many affinities with representationalism, but contemporary interactionism is diffuse and beset with its own internal crises of understanding (Joas 1985). Positivistic methodologies are currently under attack by philosophers of social science, who regard them as a dead issue philosophically (Flew 1985; Trigg 1985). Nevertheless, these dead doctrines continue to dominate the social sciences, which are typically described as being in a state of crisis.

My intent here is not to venture further into sociology's epistemological crises. Rather, it is to suggest that Durkheim's representationalism and renovated rationalism are fresh, solid alternatives with contemporary relevance that need to be unearthed. Durkheim claimed that society is essentially a system of representations. His renovated rationalism is a tool for understanding these phenomena. Unlike traditional rationalism, renovated rationalism affirms that reason is a collective and impersonal product of historical development. Reason is not an a priori faculty for Durkheim, but is a social faculty; it varies in relation to social structure. In this regard, Durkheim was most non-Kantian. This point is so obvious that attempts by La Capra (1972) and Lukes (1985) to align Durkheim with Kantianism seem incomprehensible. Renovated rationalism recasts epistemological problems that continue to plague the social sciences, among them fact versus value, subject versus object. It is a new attempt to recover the social sciences from these problems and is worth taking seriously.

Critique of Pragmatism

Without a doubt, Durkheim's most virulent and passionate critique of any "ism" is to be found in his *Pragmatism and Sociology* ([1955] 1983). Durkheim appears to have abhorred pragmatism. It is not that he was against practicality; on the contrary, he stressed continually that sociology must be practical and must offer practical solutions to social problems. Rather, he feared the epistemology of pragmatism, which he regarded as a denial of representationalism. Pragmatism seeks to apprehend reality directly, and it opens up infinite possibilities for the will. Thus Durkheim must have regarded it with the same scorn that he felt toward the Renaissance, as an invitation to intellectual and moral anomie. Pragmatism denies that the world is representation and unleashes the will.

In his introduction to Durkheim's *Pragmatism and Sociology* (in Durkheim [1955] 1983, p. xxxvii), Allcock observes: "what [Durkheim] finds in pragmatism is no less than *intellectual anomie,* in that there is insufficient regulation of that which passes for truth in society. This point is the fulcrum of his entire discussion of pragmatism and incidentally it points the way to a reappraisal of the general drift of Durkheim's sociology." I agree. In *Elementary Forms of the Religious Life,* written before *Pragmatism and Sociology,* Durkheim ([1912] 1965, p. 29) claims that: "This duality of our nature has as its consequence in the practical order the irreducibility of a moral ideal to a utilitarian motive and in the order of thought, the irreducibility of reason to individual experience."

In that statement Durkheim summarizes the two forms of anomie that most concerned him. He found "the economic life" in Western societies the most obvious example of the reduction of a moral ideal to a utilitarian motive, which thereby unleashed the will and subjected it to the infinity of desires. And he found pragmatism an example of the reduction of reason to individual experience, which also unleashed the will. In pragmatism, anything is possible. Pragmatism is an optimistic philosophy, and Durkheim seemed to share Schopenhauer's severe sentiment that optimism is by nature monstrous. Consider Durkheim's attack on pragmatism's optimism in the context of the following remark by Schopenhauer ([1818] 1977, vol. 1, p. 420): "Optimism, when it is not merely the thoughtless talk of such as harbour nothing but words under their low foreheads, appears not merely as an absurd, but also as a really wicked way of thinking, as a bitter mockery of the unspeakable suffering of humanity."

Thus, in *Pragmatism and Sociology,* Durkheim makes it clear that he regards pragmatism as a public "danger" ([1955] 1983, p. 1), which is how he referred to economic anomie in *Professional Ethics and Civic Morals* ([1950] 1983). On the opening page, Durkheim ([1955] 1983, p. 1) describes pragmatism as *"an attack on reason* which is truly militant and determined," as an "irrationalism" that is "a total negation of rationalism," and as a reversal of "the entire philosophical tradition." Pragmatism seeks to destroy "the cult of truth" much as sophism did in the time of Socrates (ibid., p. 2).

Pragmatism never poses the problem of truth (ibid., p. 6) and, because it emphasizes action based on the appearance of truth, it is nothing but a "logical utilitarianism" (ibid.) that denies the sacrosanct quality of truth, profaning it and degrading it (ibid., pp. 66–67). Its criteria for "truth" are subjectivist (ibid., p. 48); pragmatism denies the need for rules (p. 57); and it supports moral subjectivism (p. 74). It is therefore antiscientific: "The essence of the scientific mind is that the scientist takes up a point of view which is sharply opposed to that of the pragmatist" (ibid., p. 78).

It is possible to demarcate Durkheim's critique of pragmatism along the lines of representationalism and the will. He thought that pragmatism denies the very notion of representationalism. There is "no reason to look beneath appearances" for the pragmatist, he wrote, adding that in pragmatism, "We must deal only with the world as it appears to us, without worrying about knowing whether there is anything else" (ibid., p.4). He refers to William James's "radical empiricism" as a move beyond traditional empiricism, a move in the wrong direction, because "Empiricism and rationalism are basically only two different ways of affirming reason. Each in its own way insists on something which pragmatism tends to destroy, the cult of truth" (ibid., p. 2). For pragmatism, Durkheim (ibid., p. 35) believes, "the whole of reality and the whole of thought are on the same plane and are part of the same process." Durkheim cannot accept this position as being philosophically plausible because, as we have seen, the concept of representation assumes that reality and knowledge are separate.

On the level of will, Durkheim apparently believes that "pragmatism is above all an attempt to liberate the will" (ibid., p. 64). There are no constraints in pragmatism. The only caveat he adds is that this liberation refers more to thought than to action. In other words, Durkheim does not believe that pragmatism is actually as "practical" as it is sometimes purported to be; rather, it seeks to "soften" truth, to make it more "plastic" and malleable. Ultimately, pragmatism cannot distinguish between truth and falsehood, and for this reason Durkheim rejects its scientific value.

Durkheim's *Pragmatism and Sociology* does *not* play a preponderant role in contemporary analyses of his thought. It has given rise to some book reviews, however, and in some of these, the reviewers argue that pragmatism is more complicated than Durkheim makes it out to be. (It may also be true that pragmatism had been vulgarized even in Durkheim's time, as suggested by Rochberg-Halton 1986.) Without entering into a polemic, the following points are worth noting in order to appreciate the value of Durkheim's critique. First, he is aware that James, Peirce, Dewey, even the Chicago School—which he mentions by name—have their own interpretations of pragmatism and, out of these, he seems to feel some affinity with Dewey. Second, he is not interested in pragmatism *per se* but in its relationship to renovated rationalism and representationalism. To lose sight of this fact is to miss his motive in delivering these lectures. Third, although his comments may be offensive to many because pragmatism has taken firm root in American social science, it should be noted that despite Durkheim's passion, his reasoning is commensurate with André Lalande's ([1926] 1980, pp. 803–7) much cooler treatment of pragmatism in his *Vocabulaire technique et critique de la philosophie*. Finally, anyone who reads William James's *Essays in Pragmatism* will probably agree that Durkheim does not misrepresent James's position. James ([1879–1907] 1948, p. 161) *did* write that "truth happens to an idea." James (ibid., p. 163) *did* attack rationalism, and he *did* claim that "truth lives, in fact, for the most part on a credit system" by "passing" as long as nothing and nobody challenges it.

In fact, once one gets beyond Durkheim's passion, he appears to have taken a very intellectual, "high-brow" approach to pragmatism. He attacked it on the level of truth and science, not practicality, because he believed that James was discounting these notions. James did write that pragmatism has affinities with nominalism, utilitarianism, and positivism—the very doctrines Durkheim continually attacked—and that it was essentially "anti-intellectualist" (ibid., pp. 145–46). I would like to suggest that Durkheim took offense at this pragmatist stance on grounds similar to Schopenhauer's. Schopenhauer ([1818] 1977, vol. 1, p. 45) wrote:

> It has often been said that we ought to follow truth even though no utility can be seen in it, because it may have indirect utility which may appear when it is least expected; and I would add to this, that we ought to be just as anxious to discover and to root out all error even when no harm is anticipated from it, because its mischief may be very indirect, and may suddenly appear when we do not expect it, for all error has poison at its heart. . . . This is the power of truth; its conquest is slow and laborious, but if once the victory be gained it can never be wrested back again.

Similarly, Durkheim referred to "the cult of truth" in overtones of sacredness. He could never accept James's seemingly nonchalant attitude that truth is whatever happens to an idea or is accepted. It is no wonder that Durkheim, the moralist who worshipped science, attacked James as he did.

CHAPTER 4

Anomie, the Unleashing of the Will

IT IS CURIOUS that a large portion of the edifice of contemporary sociology has been constructed on what Parsons (1937) called "human action," the belief that persons are rational agents capable of choosing goals and means voluntarily and of pursuing them. For Parsons, anomie is some kind of confusion in the relationship of the human agent to these goals and means. This contemporary edifice is contradictory and at odds with the philosophical foundation of Durkheimian sociology, as well as with the sociologies of other important thinkers at the turn of the century. The notion of "will," not "human action," informed nineteenth-century philosophical and social thought. André Lalande ([1926] 1980, p. 1221) notes in his treatment of "will" that this term designates a fact different from deliberate action; that it implies passion and desire and does not necessarily imply effort. Rather, the "will" refers to the tyranny of passions imposed on us by nature. Diderot and Rousseau referred to the "General Will." Kant distinguished between good and evil "will." William James referred to a "Will to Believe" and Nietzsche to a "Will to Power." Fouillée designated a fact he called "Will to Consciousness." But of these, perhaps the most important influence on Durkheim was Schopenhauer's "Will to Life."

Schopenhauer's notion of "will" influenced other important precursors of modern sociology in the nineteenth century in various and important ways. It is well known that Freud built a large part of his psychoanalysis on the principle that we are all "lived" at the same time that we live our lives. Freud's understanding of the "id" and the politics of desire are a direct offshoot of Schopenhauer's concept of the "will" (Ellenberger 1970; Jones 1981; Magee 1983). I dare say that even Freud's insistence that all dreams are reflections of a wish (will)—a claim that alienated him from Jung, in particular—is essentially a refraction of a similar comment Schopenhauer made on dreams and wishes. Georg Simmel's ([1907] 1986) notion of "life" as a force that creates its own path regardless of human agency is also indebted to Schopenhauer. Wilhelm Wundt (1907), an important thinker who influenced both Freud and Durkheim, posited an "individual will" in opposition to a "social will," clearly an echo and extension of Schopenhauer. In several reports Durkheim wrote on German social thought following his visit to Germany, he refers to Schopenhauer's influence on leading thinkers, as well as to the "innumerable" conferences held on Schopenhauer in Germany at that time (Durkheim [1889] 1976c, p. 480). Schopenhauer seems to have been a "hot topic" in Durkheim's milieu.

Consider the influence of Schopenhauer's notion of will, and its attendant pessimism, on Durkheim's sociology. Contrary to Spencer, Durkheim ([1893] 1933) did not envision the division of labor as the outcome of human agency nor of any other utilitarian calculation. What was unique about Durkheim's evolutionary scheme is that he believed that the division of labor was a natural, spontaneous force that creates itself regardless of what individuals desire or think they desire; in other words, a product of social, not individual, will. Durkheim's understanding of anomie as the "bottomless pit" of human desires is almost exactly like Schopenhauer's understanding of the infinite will and is strikingly similar to Freud's "id." Even the details of Durkheim's definition and treatment of suicide are like Schopenhauer's! The term "pessimism" definitely characterizes Durkheim's sociology for, like Schopenhauer, Durkheim believed that suffering was an inevitable given of the human condition that could perhaps be controlled but could never be eliminated. Schopenhauer's notion of will and his philosophy of pessimism explain more about Durkheim's sociology than any theory of "human action."

But it is a mistake to conclude that for this reason, Durkheim was a determinist who abandoned the notion of human freedom, agency, and individualism. To drive this point home, one of his followers, Paul Fauconnet ([1922] 1958, p. 32), refers to Durkheim's sociology as "individualism." Fauconnet is correct. Durkheim defended individualism and referred to it both as a collective representation—a social force that compels us to respect individual rights and dignity—and an individual phenomenon, egoism, will, something like Freud's narcissism. (We shall take up this problem in a subsequent chapter.) It is important to note that Schopenhauer posed a problem that Durkheim and other thinkers in his time had to resolve, namely, how can one embrace the individualism that will be the religion of the future without succumbing to egoism?

Suicide is special to Schopenhauer's philosophy. If man is doomed to an infinity of desires, if the achievement of any desire merely brings on new desires and hence new insatiability, why *not* commit suicide? Albert Camus (1955) begins a famous essay with precisely that question, referring to it as *the* problem of philosophy. We would suggest that Durkheim may have regarded the problem of the meaning of life as *the* question for sociology. This is because for Durkheim, it is society that restrains the will and thereby makes life bearable. Contrary to Parsons and Merton, for Durkheim the will is irrational, and it *is* based on biological needs in conflict with society, on "the body." Durkheim's sociology is a long reply to Schopenhauer.

Schopenhauer on the Relationship of the Will to Suicide

Schopenhauer ([1818] 1977, vol. 1, p. 253) writes the following about the will and its relationship to suffering:

> All willing arises from want, therefore from deficiency, and therefore from suffering. The satisfaction of a wish ends it; yet for one wish that is satisfied there remain at least ten which are denied. Further, the desire lasts long, the demands are infinite; the satisfaction is short and scantily measured out. But even the final satisfaction is itself only apparent; every satisfied wish at once makes room for a new one; both are illusions; the one is known to be so, the other not yet. No attained object of desire can give lasting satisfaction, but merely a fleeting gratification; it is like the alms thrown to the beggar, that keeps him alive to-day that his misery may be prolonged till the morrow.

Because the infinity of desires is a given of human nature, according to Schopenhauer (ibid., p. 410), "suffering is essential to life" and is "inevitable." "So far as the life of the individual is concerned," Schopenhauer (ibid., p. 418) writes, "every biography is the history of suffering." And it cannot be otherwise because "the will, of which human life, like every phenomenon, is the objectification, is a striving without aim or end. We find the stamp of this endlessness imprinted upon all the parts of its whole manifestation" (p. 414).

It is no surprise that Schopenhauer (p. 420) cannot tolerate optimism, but the depth of his feeling is somewhat disconcerting: "Let no one think that Christianity is favorable to optimism; for, on the contrary, in the Gospels world and evil are used as almost synonymous." Durkheim, too, regarded the modern Christian religions as more pessimistic than the "primitive" religions (see his [1897] 1951,

p. 313; [1912] 1965, p. 354). But Durkheim felt drawn to Christianity, and the pessimistic representations that constitute it may have been part of the attraction for him.

For Schopenhauer, the opposition of the will to the idea corresponds roughly to the distinction between the heart and mind, respectively. The will encompasses dreams, impulses, affection, passions, sentiments, and all that is obscure, unconscious, and emotional. Like Durkheim, Schopenhauer associates the will with "the body." The mind stands for reflection, thought, abstraction, control, and conceptualization. For Durkheim, society is almost pure "mind." But the heart is stronger than the mind! Schopenhauer denounces abstract thinking in favor of intuition. He insists that reflective thought stops when we sleep, but the will never stops operating. In sum, we have in Schopenhauer's thought an extreme version of *homo duplex*, of the dualism of human nature.

Observe the far-reaching influence of Schopenhauer's version of *homo duplex* upon Durkheim's thought, readily apparent in his essay "The Dualism of Human Nature and Its Social Conditions" ([1914] 1973). For example, in *Professional Ethics and Civic Morals*, Durkheim ([1950] 1983, pp. 91-109 passim) opposes the State as an organ of thought and reflection to the "will of the people" depicted as a mass of unbridled passions. Like Schopenhauer, Durkheim argues that the "will" of the people is stronger than the State. He denies that democracy is rule of the will of the people, because any such rule would be too unstable (discussed in Meštrović 1988a). Rather, democracy is effective communication between the State as "the organ of thought" and the will of the people. Similarly, he sets collective representations in opposition to egoistic desires; society and morality (which consist of mental images, representations) opposite "the body"; religion as a system of representations opposite individual sensations, and so on. For Durkheim, as for Schopenhauer, life reduces itself, to a large extent, to an opposition between will and idea, heart versus mind.

Schopenhauer rages against egoism as the very source of immorality. For when the individual sees no interests but those of his own will, he is likely to trespass on the will of others. Such is the source of all wickedness, whether it takes the form of homicide—the most obvious form of violating someone else's will to live—deceit, breach of contract, despotism, or numerous other violations. Schopenhauer does not believe that the egoist is happy; on the contrary, the egoist is miserable, and his misery is stamped on his countenance. This is because he is never satisfied. The more he achieves, the more he wants, and his wants are infinite because he does not respect the will of others.

Schopenhauer ([1818] 1977, vol. 1, p. 404) saw the obvious, that "the suffering and misery of life may easily increase to such an extent that death itself, in the flight from which the whole of life consists, becomes desirable." This seemingly obvious connection between suffering and suicide—although it is present in Durkheim's thought—is actually absent in most post-Durkheimian studies of suicide. Contemporary researchers have operationalized the lack of integration and correlated it with suicide without touching upon the issue of suffering. Alvarez has a point when in *The Savage God* (1970) he suggests that despite all that has been written on suicide from a sociological point of view, we understand less, not more, than was known about it in Durkheim's time. This is because contemporary sociology has been guided by the "human action" perspective in which human suffering does not play a preponderant role. Consider the influential treatment of the relationship between anomie and suicide in Parsons's writing, for example. Parsons (1937) alleges that anomie is primarily a state of social chaos and confusion between goals and means that may, in extreme cases, lead to suicide. But why would confusion and "meaninglessness" in society lead the individual to suicide? In comparison, Schopenhauer's linkage between the suffering caused by the infinity of desires and suicide is actually quite intricate.

First, Schopenhauer ([1818] 1977, vol. 1, p. 511) asserts that "the more intense the will is, the more glaring is the conflict of its manifestation, and thus the greater is the suffering." This may be the reason why Durkheim suspected that poverty protects against suicide and wealth contributes to it. Poverty restrains the will whereas wealth and success feed it; the more intensely it is fed, the more suffering it causes (Durkheim [1897] 1951, p. 254). "How is this possible? How can something considered generally to improve existence serve to detach men from it?" Durkheim asks (ibid., p. 246). Only after he delivers his famous discourse on anomie as the "bottomless abyss" of passions does Durkheim give an answer, an answer that again echoes Schopenahuer: "When there is no other aim but to outstrip constantly the point arrived at, how painful to be thrown back! . . . Since imagination is hungry for novelty, and ungoverned, it gropes at random. . . . At least the horizon of the lower classes is limited by those above them, and for this same reason their desires are more modest. Those who have only empty space above them are almost inevitably lost in it, if no force restrains them" (ibid., p. 257).

Second, Schopenhauer does *not* define suicide as either the abandonment of the will to live or as the will to die. Rather, Schopenhauer ([1818] 1977, vol. 1, p. 515) offers this complicated definition:

Suicide, the actual doing away with the individual manifestation of will, differs most widely from the denial of the will to live, which is the single outstanding act of free-will in the manifestation. . . . Far from being denial of the will, suicide is a phenomenon of strong assertion of will; for the essence of negation lies in this, that the joys of life are shunned, not its sorrows. The suicide wills life, and is only dissatisfied with the conditions under which it has presented itself to him. He therefore by no means surrenders the will to live, but only life, in that he destroys the individual manifestation. He wills life—wills the unrestricted existence and assertion of the body; but the complication of circumstances does not allow this, and there results for him great suffering. The very will to live finds itself so much hampered in this particular manifestation that it cannot put forth its energies.

To put it mildly, this is an extremely ponderous assessment. Let us seek out affinities with Durkheim's thought.

Durkheim remarks in *Moral Education* ([1925] 1961, p. 212) that even a person who decides to commit suicide by drowning will struggle to live:

In general, the prototype of selfish drives is what we call, improperly enough, the instinct of preservation—in other words, the tendency of every living creature to keep alive. That tendency makes its action felt without our thinking of the pleasures that life might have for us. It is felt even when life has only pain in store for us, and when we know it. Thus, a suicide who jumps into the water makes every effort to save himself; although the fact of his immersion has not changed his situation nor the way in which he evaluated it. The fact is that he clung to life more than he knew himself. . . . Since the love of life is deeply rooted, one must have endured much suffering to end it.

Schopenhauer's influence is evident in this intriguing passage.

Consider Durkheim's controversial definition of suicide in which the agent "knows"—but does not intend—that his acts will produce death: "The term suicide is applied to all cases of death resulting directly or indirectly from a positive or negative act of the victim himself, which he knows will produce this result" ([1897] 1951, p. 44). Jack Douglas (1967) alleged that Durkheim defined suicide as an intentional act, but "failed" to check whether any of the cases in his book actually intended death. Strictly speaking, Durkheim never defined suicide in terms of intentions. In a follow-up to *Suicide*, Maurice Halbwachs ([1930] 1978, p. 291) reaffirmed many years later that Durkheim never meant to define suicide in terms of willing death or consciously rejecting the will to life: "Durkheim did not say, 'the act accomplished by the victim with the intention or prospect of putting himself to death.'" Halbwachs (ibid., p. 294) added that "when Durkheim defines suicide as an act which the victim knows must produce death, he does not say that this act is voluntary." Rather, suicide is a weakening of the will to live due to great suffering, what Marcel Mauss ([1950] 1979a, p. 24) called loss of "morale" that is dependent on social causes. Compare Schopenhauer's passage above with Durkheim's summary of the exhausting effects of suffering upon the agent afflicted with anomie: "Effort grows, just when it becomes less productive. How could the desire to live not be weakened under such conditions?" (Durkheim [1897] 1951, p. 253).

It is interesting in this context that Durkheim does not regard altruistic suicide—which *does* involve the intentions—as "true suicide." But Schopenhauer had already claimed that suicide is widely different from acts of will-lessness. The "true suicide, the sad suicide" (Durkheim [1893] 1933, p. 247) is a victim of a diseased will but does *not* abandon the will. Abandoning or even controlling the will would have precluded the suffering that excessive willing caused in the first place. Thus, suicide is a disease of the will caused by intemperate willing. It is a vicious cycle.

Finally, Schopenhauer ([1818] 1977, vol. 1, p. 516) claims that "just because the suicide cannot give up willing, he gives up living." Philosophers agree that Schopenhauer was a strong advocate of abandoning the will as far as possible through conscious, voluntary asceticism, contemplation, and discipline. Durkheim certainly stood for these things as well, but there is an important difference between Schopenhauer and Durkheim in this regard. Durkheim apparently did not believe that contemporary individuals could practice self-initiated asceticism on a large scale. There are simply too many objects to desire that have been thrust on the horizon. Schopenhauer did not believe many persons could achieve "will-less-ness" either, but he aimed his philosophy at a select group of geniuses, and resigned himself to a life of suffering in any case. Durkheim conceived of society as the constraint that would check man's inherently insatiable will. But for society to accomplish this task, it would have to be healed of anomie. An anomic society can only breed anomie in its members.

Anomie Reexamined in Relation to the Will and Suffering

The contemporary understanding of Durkheim's concept of *anomie* as "normlessness" was begun by Parsons (1937) and Merton (1957). But it is important to emphasize that although both Parsons and Merton attribute this incorrect understanding of anomie to Durkheim, Durkheim never used the term "normlessness." Lukes never challenges Parsons and Merton on this issue, and goes on to criticize Durkheim on the basis of an alleged use of a concept that Durkheim never used: "[Durkheim] failed to realize that anomie can itself be seen as a norm, culturally prescribed and accepted, rather than a state of normlessness" (Lukes 1985, p. 218). Moreover, Durkheim never adopted the theory of "human action" that Parsons and Merton wrongly attribute to him. In fact, Durkheim was an advocate of a version of the very position that Merton sought to discredit in the opening lines of his famous "Social Structure and Anomie." Merton (1957, p. 185) writes:

> Until recently, and all the more so before then, one could speak of a marked tendency in psychological and sociological theory to attribute the faulty operation of social structures to failures of social control over man's imperious biological drives. . . . In the beginning, there are man's biological impulses which seek full expression. And then, there is the social order, essentially an apparatus for the management of impulses, for the social processing of tensions, for the "renunciation of instinctual gratifications," in the words of Freud. . . . With the more recent advancement of social science, this set of conceptions has undergone basic modification.

While the position that Merton seeks to discredit is not an exact rendition of Durkheim's position, it is close enough. Both Freud and Durkheim adopted Schopenhauer's understanding of the tyrannical will. But this is the position Merton wishes to sever from Durkheim's thought, and consequently from social theory.

Our aim, on the contrary, is to refine and restore it. Merton's position is too well established for it to be replaced or even challenged effectively. We will show that Merton is incorrect to attribute his understanding of anomie as "normlessness" to Durkheim, and that the consequences of Merton's understanding are vastly different from Durkheim's. "Normlessness" apparently causes no suffering; Durkheim's anomie does. "Normlessness" apparently does not cause a weakening of the will to live but only deviance, whereas Durkheim's understanding of what now passes for "deviance" is more complex. "Normlessness" assumes a rational agent capable of accepting society's goals and means, whereas Durkheim's anomie assumes that man's will is by nature dangerous to himself and to society. "Normlessness" is difficult, if not impossible, to imagine, for there will always be some norms in any situation. But Durkheim's understanding of anomie as immorality can be conceptualized.

More important, "normlessness" simply cannot explain the origins of anomie. If anomie is social and is not related to the tyranny of man's biological body (his will), then it must be caused by society itself. But if that is the case, where do the desires originate in Merton's overly rationalist scheme of things? If the id-like, desiring, "lower" pole of the dualism of human nature has been eliminated, then the source of anomie must be society, not the individual. But why would society produce its own sickness? If society is the rational organ that Merton makes it out to be, how can it produce irrationality? And even if it did, how would it transmit anomie to its members? In other words, because Merton does not assume a dualism of human nature, as Schopenhauer and Durkheim do, his version of anomie is subject to contradictions. It is a position that negates itself.

In the following section, we will demonstrate the link between anomie, suffering, and the tyrannical will in Durkheim's thought as a refraction of Schopenhauer's thought. The importance of these connections is that it shows that Durkheim attempted for sociology what Freud achieved for psychoanalysis: both thinkers introduced the irrational will into rational theory. Endless litanies of praise have been sung to Freud's memory for this move, but sociologists have yet to acknowledge Durkheim in this regard. In addition, we wish to offer an alternative to Besnard's (1987) argument that Durkheim was not really a sociologist of anomie, and to Orru's (1987) claim that anomie has many divergent meanings but no one meaning. Our aim, instead, is to disengage Durkheim's version of anomie from Merton's, and to point to the concept of immorality that seems to underlie anomie's many surface meanings.

Anomie as *Dérèglement*

The one and only explicit synonym for anomie that Durkheim ever used is *dérèglement*. This fact is noted by Andre Lalande ([1926] 1980, p. 61), quoting from Durkheim, *Le Suicide*, p. 281: "Anomie. . . . Absence d'organisation, de coordination. 'L'état de dérèglement ou *d'anomie.*'" "Normlessness" and "deregulation" are poor translations of *dérèglement,* for several reasons. First, they did not enter into common English usage until the 1960s and certainly did not exist in Durkheim's time. *Dérèglement* is difficult to render in English. It carries with it in French the connotations of immorality and suffering, but it is perhaps best translated as derangement. The French poet Rimbaud used *dérèglement* to refer to a general kind of disordering. Anomie as *dérèglement* implies a condition of madness or a state akin to sin. This coincides with the observation that more than twenty words denoting sin were translated as *anomia* when the Bible was translated by St. Jerome and others (Meštrović 1985a), as well as with the fact that Durkheim was a scientific moralist. Anomie is a scientific term for immorality. If, as Henri Durkheim suggested, morality was Durkheim's religion, anomie was considered by him to be a secular version of sin.

The origin and spelling of anomie are typically attributed to Durkheim's *Division of Labor in Society* (1893). In fact, however, Guyau used the term *anomie* as early as 1885 in his *Esquisse d'une morale sans obligation ni sanction:* "C'est l'absence de loi fixe, qu'on peut désigner sous le terme *d'anomie*, pour l'opposer à l'autonomie des Kantiens" (Guyau [1885] 1907, p. 165). Guyau used the term again in 1887 in his *Non-religion of the Future* to describe moral anomie, the emancipation of the individual will from religious dogmatism. Durkheim reviewed Guyau's book, specifically noted the influence of Schopenhauer on Guyau (Durkheim [1887] 1976b, p. 157), and noted that the problem of modern living is that the individual will has been unleashed. But Durkheim felt that anomie could never be moral: "Nous croyons au contraire [to Guyau] que *l'anomie* est la négation de toute morale" (Durkheim [1893] 1976, p. 282).

According to the Littré *Dictionnaire de la langue française* ([1863] 1963, vol. 2, p. 1672)—the rough equivalent of the Oxford English Dictionary, whose author was a disciple of Comte—the principal meaning of *dérèglement* is derangement: *"Dérèglement, dérangement* are words expressing two nuances of moral disorder: What is *dérangé* is disarranged *[hors de son rang]* or is without place. What is *déréglé* is out of rule *[hors de la règle]*. The state of *dérèglement* is more serious than that of derangement."

If we examine just one of Littré's sources, we can gain understanding of the connotative meanings of *dérèglement* from the context of its use. Consider Bossuet's ([1731] 1836, pp. 43–79 passim) treatise on concupiscence. Bossuet describes the state of *dérèglement* in terms of affliction, *mal, égarement*, corruption, *péché*, agitation, *tourments*, agitations, *infini de misères*, troubles, *tourmenter, maladie, désordre, dangereux, souffrir, impiété, intempérance, dessèchement, misérable captivité*. Both Bossuet and Durkheim focus on the themes of evil, impatience and, above all, suffering in their discussions of *dérèglement*. Durkheim's thought is a refraction of Schopenhauer's philosophy, much as Schopenhauer's pessimism is a refraction of Christian emphases on evil, sin, and suffering.

Anomie and *Suicide*

In *Suicide*, Durkheim ([1897] 1951, p. 247) echoes Schopenhauer when he writes: "Unlimited desires are insatiable by definition and insatiability is rightly considered a sign of morbidity. Being unlimited, they constantly and infinitely surpass the means at their command; they cannot be quenched. Inextinguishable thirst is constantly renewed torture." Moreover, in modern times, "appetites, not being controlled by a public opinion become disoriented. . . . with increased prosperity desires increase" (ibid., p. 253). Thus, "the state of derangement *[dérèglement]* or anomy is . . . further heightened by passions being less disciplined, precisely when they need more disciplining" (ibid.; in French, [1897] 1983, p. 281). In short, the will, the id, desire, have been set loose in modern societies. But most people do not realize what has happened!

In fact, according to Durkheim, the business and economic sector of society has enshrined this state of undisciplined desires as one of the cornerstones of modern economic theory. Durkheim ([1897] 1983, p. 287) claims that anomie is most prevalent in the business world because business has made *dérèglement* into a *règle:* "La passion de l'infini est journellement présentée comme une marque de distinction morale, alors qu'elle ne peut se produire qu'au sein de consciences *déréglées* et qui erigent en *règle* le *dérèglement* dont elles souffrent. . . . Et comme c'est dans le monde économique que ce desarroi est à son apogée, c'est la aussi qu'il fait le plus de victimes" (emphasis added).

Spaulding and Simpson's translation (in *Suicide* [1897] 1951, p. 257) of the phrase that includes the word *dérèglement* as "a rule that is a lack of rule" is awkward, although it is far better than the translation "normlessness." By contrast, the notion of establishing a *règle* that is *dérèglement* may be found in the *Littré* and in theological analyses of sin. Because this is an important passage, we venture to offer our translation based on the preceding analysis: "The passion for infinity is commonly presented as a mark of moral distinction, even though it cannot appear except in deranged consciences which establish as a rule the derangement from which they suffer. . . . Since this disorder is at its apex in the economic world, it has most victims there." Durkheim goes on to argue that government is to blame for this state of affairs because it "has become its tool and servant" instead of being the *régulateur* of economic life ([1897] 1983, p. 283). Durkheim's accusation rests on the assumption that a government's failure to moderate the profane desires of infinite economic acquisition is something like sin. More than that, he is saying that failure to discipline the will is unhealthy, and the institutionalization of this unhealthy move is something like madness.

Another important passage that has been given a consistently misleading translation concerns the alleged "non-regulation" of egoists (Durkheim [1897] 1951, p. 288; and in French, [1897] 1983, p. 325):

> Two factors of suicide, especially, have a peculiar affinity for one another: namely, egoism and anomy. . . . It is indeed, almost inevitable that the egoist should have some tendency to non-regulation; for, since he is detached from society, it has not sufficient hold upon him to

regulate him. . . . Inversely, an unregulated temperament does not lack a spark of egoism; for if one were highly socialized one would not rebel at every social restraint.

[In French]: "Il est notamment deux facteurs du suicide qui ont l'un pour l'autre une affinité spéciale, c'est l'égoïsme et l'anomie. . . . Il est même presque inévitable que l'égoïste ait quelque aptitude au *dérègle-ment;* car, comme il est détaché de la société, elle n'a pas assez de prise sur lui pour le *régler.* . . . Inversement, le *dérèglement* ne va pas sans un germe d'égoïsme; car on ne serait pas rebelle à tout frein social" [emphasis added]. In this passage, Durkheim is saying that egoism and *dérèglement* exhibit an affinity for one another, not that egoists and anomics are "unregulated." Spaulding and Simpson's phrase "for if one were highly socialized" was apparently added gratuitously to the text. In addition, we repeat that the notions of non- or de-regulation did not exist until very recently, even in English.

The fact that egoism, anomie, and derangement are a kind of unity is important. This trilogy is a refraction of Schopenhauer's philosophy in the sense that he, like Durkheim, equates the boundless will with egoism, and claims that its end result is wickedness, madness, strife, and many kinds of folly. But this connection is important also for highlighting the way in which Durkheim's understanding of anomie differs from the Parsonian-Mertonian version. Parsons's "socialization" and "regulation" do not imply an egoistic will that strives to tear them down. As stated previously, they merely provide for consistency in society, and this consistency is supposed to trickle down to its individual members. But for Durkheim, egoism is the "lower" side of *homo duplex* and is dangerous. Durkheim defines egoism as a state "in which the individual ego asserts itself to excess in the face of the social ego and at its expense" ([1897] 1951, p. 209). One does not "socialize" and "regulate" such rebellion, because it is impossible to do so. Rather, for Durkheim, one establishes a social arrangement such that the "lower" side of *homo duplex* is continually ruled by the "higher," which is society. Similarly, Durkheim attacks major Western social institutions for establishing *disarrangements* such that the "lower," desiring pole of *homo duplex* is unrestrained. Parsonian-Mertonian theory cannot account for this phenomenon, because it denies the existence of an id-like component to human nature. The religious flavor of Durkheim's conceptualization is unmistakable. Disobedience, willfullness, rebellion—these traits characterize man's original sin in Paradise. But these traits also characterize anomie. For Durkheim, the offense is against society, but for him, society is definitely on a symbolic plane with God.

In *Suicide,* in addition to economic anomie, Durkheim treats several varieties of anomie, among them conjugal, marital, religious, political, and intellectual. In all these cases, man's imperious will has been unleashed, a societal institution fails to contain it, and the result is suffering. For example, Durkheim felt that marriage was supposed to "close the horizon" on man's passion for a love object and make him content. But in modern societies, with increasing divorce rates and lowered respect for the institution of marriage, the effect is disillusionment, despair, and eventually, increased suicide rates for society as a whole. In general, the other French words Durkheim uses to describe this state of anomie as *dérèglement* ([1897] 1983, pp. 271–326 passim) constitute a vocabulary that was used by seventeenth century theologians when they wrote about sin and madness. I do not think this is a coincidence.

Durkheim described Western society as being in effervescence, pain, and in feverish, futile frenzy: "We must not be dazzled by the brilliant development of sciences, the arts and industry of which we are the witnesses; this development is altogether certainly taking place in the midst of a morbid effervescence, the grievous repercussions of which each one of us feels" ([1897] 1951, p. 368). Moreover, this morbid restlessness, a symptom of derangement, has been made into a rule, and is regarded as normal: "Yet these dispositions [toward anomie] are so inbred that society has grown to accept them and is accustomed to think them normal. It is everlastingly repeated that it is man's nature to be eternally dissatisfied, constantly to advance, without relief or rest, toward an indefinite goal" (ibid., p. 257). But we have seen that for Schopenhauer, as for Durkheim, these infinite, indefinite longings are the signs of the will, which, if it has its way, wills itself to destruction.

Anomie in Politics and the Modern Division of Labor

Leçons de sociologie: physique des moeurs et du droit, published in English as *Professional Ethics and Civic Morals,* is a compilation of lectures Durkheim gave at Bordeaux from 1890 to 1900 and repeated at the Sorbonne in 1904 and 1912. The French subtitle makes it clear that this book is about a science of moral facts, which is how Durkheim referred to these lectures shortly before he died (Durkheim [1920] 1976, p. 330). Indeed, Durkheim begins the book with the claim that: "The science of morals *[la physique des moeurs]* and rights should be based on the study of moral and juridical *facts.* These facts consist of rules of conduct that have received sanction" ([1950] 1983, p. 1; in French, 1950, p. 5; emphasis added).

Studying this book, one can trace the continuities in Durkheim's thought. It resembles the introduction to *Division of Labor in Society*

(1893), whose theme is the problem of how one can recognize moral facts, and similar concerns with morality that preoccupied Durkheim up to his last, albeit unfinished, manuscript, *La Morale* (begun in 1917). In *Leçons*, Durkheim attacks classical economic theory, the lack of ethics in the business profession, and problems in democracy; in short, it is a book about anomie. He criticizes these Western institutions primarily on the grounds that they have failed to contain man's imperious will. But he does not want to dismantle them as the Marxists do. Rather, he wants to reform these cancerous Western institutions. Anomie is the explicit focus of this work, as Durkheim declared in summing up his discussion of the above-mentioned social problems: "Elle [la vie publique] tient à un état *anomique* qu'il faut, non pas subir, mais travailler à faire cesser" (Durkheim 1950, p. 130, emphasis added). Durkheim's explicit use of *anomique* in this book was translated into English as "lawless," thus obscuring the continuities in his thought, especially the relationship between his concerns for anomie and a science of moral facts.

Durkheim perceived classical economic theory, which emphasizes self-interest as opposed to the cosmopolitan religion of humanity, to be a fertile source of anomie. This is because man's economic appetites will not be satisfied on their own accord. Something must restrain them. Similarly, referring to business as "les fonctions économiques, aussi bien l'industrie que le commerce," Durkheim (1950, p. 14) writes that all the professions except business have their code of ethics. These ethics are outside the realm of the "common conscience," and their function is to contain egoism. He maintains (ibid., p. 15) that in commerce, there are no professional ethics: "C'est que dans toute cette région [le commerce] de la vie sociale, il n'existe pas de morale professionnelle." He asks whether this state is normal and answers that, according to classical economic theory, it is. Yet this is only because both capitalism and socialism "do no more than raise a *de facto* state of affairs which is unhealthy, to the level of a *de jure* state of affairs" (Durkheim [1950] 1983, p. 10). All the major social functions have been made secondary to unrestrained economic functions (Durkheim 1950, p. 16). The only *règle* in economics is that of self-interest, which is insufficient for morality (ibid., p. 18). In short, *anomie* as it is exhibited in business is an amoral condition that amounts to a public danger: "Ce caractere amoral de la vie économique constitue un danger public" (ibid.).

Durkheim castigates the utilitarians for deluding themselves (*s'abuser*) by thinking that the desires of the masses will be calmed through laissez-faire capitalism when, on the contrary, it only rouses their impatience for gain (ibid., p. 22). Durkheim then links his discussion of economic anomie to political anomie ([1950] 1983, p. 96), arguing that democracy understood as government ruled by the will of the people leads to anomie (ibid., p. 108). This is because the individual's desires in the political arena are as subject to the "mal de l'infini" as they are in the economic arena, so that "the primary duty is to work out something that can relieve us by degrees of a role for which the individual is not cast" (ibid.).

In the now-classic second preface to *Division of Labor*, Durkheim writes ([1902] 1933, p. 1): "We repeatedly insist in the course of this book upon the state of juridical and moral anomy in which economic life actually is found." Apparently, Durkheim viewed *anomie* as the major theme of *Division of Labor*. He continues (p. 2): "It is this anomic state that is the cause, as we shall show, of the incessantly recurrent conflicts, and the multifarious disorders of which the economic world exhibits so *sad* a spectacle" (emphasis added). Durkheim calls anomie "anarchy" (p. 3) and an "evil" (p. 5). He explains: "Si *l'anomie* est un *mal*, c'est avant tout parce que la société en *souffre*, ne pouvant se passer, pour vivre, de cohésion et de régularité" ([1902] 1967, p. vi, emphasis added). Durkheim considers anomie evil because it causes suffering, which is a very Schopenhauerian reason.

Durkheim devotes a chapter to the question whether the progress of the division of labor is linked to increased happiness, and answers in the negative. This is because the transition from mechanical to organic solidarity engenders suffering, so that with the advance of the division of labor, "the general happiness of society is decreasing" ([1893] 1933, p. 249). He illustrates this point with reference to suicide. Altruistic suicide in primitive societies was not the result of unhappiness. But "the true suicide, the sad suicide, is in the endemic state with civilized peoples" (ibid., p. 247). *Anomie* is linked to suffering and pain *(douleur, souffrance, tourment)*. It follows that the abnormal, anomic suicide will be sad—not blandly "normless."

The Division of Labor in Society is a profoundly pessimistic book, a veritable echo of Schopenhaeur. Durkheim refers to the "uneasiness" that was felt in his own time (ibid., p. 219). He denies the theory that human desire to increase happiness is the origin of the division of labor (ibid., p. 233). He grants that modern man enjoys more pleasures than the primitive man, but adds, "if we are open to more pleasures, we are also open to more pain" (p. 242). And he foreshadows a move he would make explicit many years later in *Elementary Forms of the Religious Life:* "Is it not very remarkable that the fundamental cult of the most civilized religions is that of human suffering?" (p. 243). To be sure, he denies that there is any necessary relation between the advance of the division of labor *per se* and human unhappiness (p. 250), but he also denies that it is related to increased happiness. In other words, if the problem of man's newly freed will could be resolved, the division of labor could lead at least to contentment. The problem is with the emancipated will, not with the division of labor.

Anomie and Socialism

Le Socialisme was completed in 1896, although it was not published in its entirety until 1928. It is important to note that Durkheim criticized capitalism *and* socialism; his thought is neither conservative nor liberal, but something new. In this neglected work, Durkheim writes of the necessity for setting "a limit on the state of disarrangement, excitement, frenzied agitation, which do not spring from social activity and which even make it suffer" ([1928] 1958, p.204). Durkheim lays the blame for this state of *dérèglement* on classical economic theory: "la faute en est à la science économique" ([1928] 1978, p. 41). Along with the classical economists, Saint-Simon and his followers are all accused of promoting *dérèglement:* "What caused the failure of Saint-Simonianism is that Saint-Simon and his disciples wanted to get the most from the least, the superior from the inferior, moral rule from economic matter *[la règle morale de la matière économique]*" (Durkheim [1928] 1958, p. 240; in French, [1928] 1978, p. 253). According to Durkheim, such aspirations are "impossible." The economic structure emphasizes egoism and materialism and therefore cannot be a source of morality, only of the will.

Anomie is presented in terms very similar to its depiction in *Suicide, The Division of Labor in Society,* and *Professional Ethics and Civic Morals.* Durkheim begins with the claim that, however skillfully ordered, economic functions cannot cooperate harmoniously nor be maintained in a state of equilibrium unless subjected to moral forces that surpass and contain them (Durkheim [1928] 1958, p. 197). This is because it is a general *law* of all living things that needs and appetites are normal only when contained: "Et, en effet, c'est une *loi* générale chez tous les vivants que les besoins et les appétits ne sont normaux qu'à condition d'être bornés. Un besoin *illimité* se contredit" ([1928] 1978, p. 211, emphasis added). Durkheim continues ([1928] 1958, p. 199): "As there is nothing within an individual which constrains these appetites, they must surely be contained by some force exterior to him, or else they would become insatiable—that is, morbid. . . . This is what seems to have escaped Saint-Simon. To him it appears that the way to realize social peace is to free *economic appetites* of all restraint *[frein]* on the one hand, and on the other to satisfy them by fulfilling them. But such an undertaking is contradictory" (emphasis added; in French, [1928] 1978, p.213). The result of enfranchising the "appétits économiques" is that "les appétits se *dérèglent* et l'ordre économique se désorganise" (ibid., p. 215, emphasis added). In Schopenhauer's terms, socialism allows the will to reign unchecked, which is an invitation to unhappiness and social malaise.

The similarity between this section of *Le Socialisme* and the famous discourse on anomie in *Suicide* is unmistakable. Again, Durkheim's argument rests on the now familiar claim that insatiability is a sign of disease ("l'insatiabilite est un signe de morbidité" ibid., p. 212). His solution, therefore, "is to know, under the present conditions of social life, what moderating functions are necessary and what forces are capable of executing them" ([1928] 1958, p. 199). This solution is repeated on the last page of the manuscript in a more complete form, which is worth citing in French: "Le problème doit donc se poser ainsi: chercher par la *science* quels sont les freins *moraux* qui peuvent réglementer la vie économique, et, par cette réglementation, contenir les égoïsmes, et par conséquent permettre de satisfaire les besoins" (Durkheim [1928] 1978, p. 253, emphasis added). When discussing *dérèglement* in *Le Socialisme*, he uses the now-familiar vocabulary of *anomie*, tinged with pathos and references to suffering ([1928] 1978, pp. 27–39, 217–47 passim). Durkheim refers to Marx and the socialists as giving the world a "shriek of pain" that can be traced to the collective malaise that interests Durkheim. Socialism, in general, is "un cri de *douleur* poussé par les hommes qui sentent le plus vivement notre *malaise collectif*" (ibid., p. 27, emphasis added). But socialism and Marxism, for Durkheim, are not scientific. They are merely representations of the modern problem of an unleashed will (Durkheim [1897] 1986).

Moral Education and Anomie

Moral Education, the translation of lectures Durkheim gave between 1902 and 1907, includes a long discussion on rules and morality. Note that he thought educational institutions could be used to teach secular morality. The "impuissance à se contenir" ([1925] 1963, p. 33) that is characteristic of anomie is a sign of disease *(morbidité)*: "If such sentiments [impatience] develop to the detriment of other feelings it is a sign of derangement *[dérèglement]*, the pathological character of which is well known to clinicians" ([1925] 1961, p. 38). He gives an example of anomie that is similar to *Suicide*: "Should the rules of conjugal morality lose their authority, should husband-wife obligations be less respected, should passions and appetites ruled by this sector of morality unleash themselves, being even exacerbated by this same release *[se dérègleront, s'exaspéreront par ce dérèglement même]*. . . such passions would entail a disillusionment which translates itself graphically into statistics of suicide" (ibid., p. 33; in French, [1925]

1963, p. 37). Essentially, Durkheim is applying Schopenhauer's thought to the sociology of the family.

In economic life, too, ambitions for gain become overexcited *[sur-exciteront]* and inflamed *[s'enfièvreront]* and result in a rise in the annual quota of suicides. These are all examples of the "mal de l'infini qui travaille notre temps" (ibid., p. 37). The summary of this discussion in *Moral Education* is reminiscent of *Rules of Sociological Method* ([1895] 1982, p. 95) in suggesting how one shall recognize the abnormal. Thus Durkheim writes in *Moral Education:* "The notion of the infinite, then, appears only at those times when moral discipline has lost its ascendancy over man's *will*. It is the sign of attrition that emerges during periods when the moral system, prevailing for several centuries, is shaken, failing to respond to new conditions of human life, and without any new system yet contrived to replace that which has disappeared" ([1925] 1961, p. 43, emphasis added). Schopenhauer could have written these lines.

Another passage in *Moral Education* brings home the theme of unhappiness in relation to suicide: "Whenever moral rules lack the necessary authority to exert, to a desirable degree, a regulatory influence *[leur action régulatrice]* on our behavior, we see society gripped by a dejection *[tristesse]* and pessimism *[désenchantement]* reflected in the curve of suicides" (ibid., p. 68). For Durkheim, as for Schopenhauer, the unrestrained will is the cause of pessimism. According to Durkheim (ibid., p. 42), this is because

> The totality of moral regulations really forms about each person an imaginary wall, at the foot of which a multitude of human passions simply die without being able to go further. For the same reason—that they are contained—it becomes possible to satisfy them. But if at any point this barrier weakens, human forces—until now restrained—pour tumultuously through the open breach; once loosed, they find no limits where they can or must stop. Unfortunately, they can only devote themselves to the pursuit of an end that always eludes them.

We have already seen that Durkheim regarded the present era and the Renaissance as two epochs in which anomie has played a major role. He makes an interesting allusion to the rise of Buddhism in this regard: "During periods when society is disorganized *[désintegrée]* and, as a result of its decadence has less power to exact the commitment of individual wills, and when, consequently, egoism has freer reign—these are calamitous times. The cult of the self and the notion of the infinite go together. Buddhism is the best illustration of this relationship" (ibid., p. 72; in French, [1925] 1963, p. 61).

In his critique of Kant, which echoes Schopenhauer's ([1813] 1899) closely, Durkheim points out that rationality and autonomy are not sufficient for establishing a system of morality. According to Durkheim ([1925] 1961, p. 112), "it is because in fact we are not purely rational beings; we are also emotional creatures [such that our desires] incline us toward individual, egoistic, irrational, and immoral ends." This is a "real antagonism" and man is "divided against himself" (p. 113)—phrases that Schopenhauer also liked to use.

Again, Durkheim's vocabulary in *Moral Education* is the same language of pain and agitation used in other discussions of anomie (Durkheim [1925] 1963, pp. 6–61 passim). In a transcript of a course that Durkheim gave in 1909, reproduced in Karady's *Textes*, one finds a terse but interesting summary of the themes we have been discussing. Durkheim ([1909] 1976, p. 309) writes: "L'impuissance, pour une énergie organique, à se contenir est signe de morbidité. . . . Où sera la limite? Corrélation de tristesse et du sentiment de l'infini. . . . La réglementation matrimoniale a pour but de mettre des bornes aux sentiments et appétits que le mariage met en jeu. Quand cette réglementation n'est plus respectée, quand les divorces augmentent, les suicides augmentent aussi. Les désirs n'arrivant plus à se satisfaire, le suicide est la conclusion naturelle. . . . La maîtrise de la volonté suppose avant tout la limitation des besoins."

The Evolution of Educational Thought, a translation of lectures Durkheim gave in 1904 and 1905, takes anomie as its basic theme. According to Durkheim, "from their origins the schools carried within themselves the germ of that *great struggle between the sacred and the profane,* the secular and the religious, whose history we shall have to retrace" ([1938] 1977, p. 26, in French, 1938, p. 34, emphasis added). The secularization of education—literally a form of sacrilege, given the religious origin of schools—became most intense in the "moral crisis" of the Renaissance ([1938] 1977, p. 225), a period Durkheim describes by using the vocabulary of anomie. As stated previously, Durkheim describes the Renaissance as a period in which aspirations tended toward "l'infini," as marked by intemperance and immorality, and "un fléchissement général du sentiment moral" (1938, pp. 218–43 passim). Durkheim characterizes the Renaissance as follows: "Le XVIe siècle est donc une époque de crise pédagogique et morale" (ibid., p. 260). The humanism of the Renaissance is understood by Durkheim in the context of "our whole present-day moral system [which] is dominated by the cult of the individual person" ([1938] 1977, p. 325). But the problem posed by the Renaissance has not yet been solved; namely, how should one pursue humanism in education without succumbing to egoism (ibid., p. 228)? This problem persists today.

The Cult of Sorrow and Suffering

Durkheim's pessimism emerges most forcefully in *The Elementary Forms of the Religious Life* and its sequel, "The Dualism of Human Nature and Its Social Conditions." In *Elementary Forms*, he writes: "If there is any one belief which is believed to be peculiar to the most recent and idealistic religions, it is the one attributing a sanctifying power to sorrow [*douleur*]" ([1912] 1965, p. 354; in French, [1912] 1979, p. 450). Similarly, "society itself is possible only at this price" ([1912] 1965, p. 356). Durkheim continues: "Though exalting the strength of man, [society] is frequently rude to individuals; it necessarily demands perpetual sacrifices from them; it is constantly doing violence to our natural appetites, just because it raises us above ourselves. If we are going to fulfil our duties towards it, then we must be prepared to do violence to our instincts . . . it is . . . inherent in all social life" (ibid., p.356; in French, [1912] 1979, p. 452).

Fearful that he was misunderstood in *Elementary Forms*, Durkheim repeated the idea that society is possible only at the price of *douleur* in his gloomy, Freudian-like sequel "The Dualism of Human Nature and Its Social Conditions" (1914). Because Durkheim's thesis of *homo duplex* continues to be misunderstood, we shall emphasize its context. It is important to note that like Schopenhauer (and also like Freud, Plato, St. Augustine, Calvin, and a host of classical thinkers), Durkheim definitely links the "lower," desiring part of *homo duplex* with "the body" ([1914] 1973, p. 162):

It is not without reason, therefore, that man feels himself to be double: he actually is double. . . . In brief, this duality corresponds to the double existence that we lead concurrently; the one purely individual and rooted in our organisms, the other social and nothing but an extension of society. . . . The conflicts of which we have given examples are between the sensations and the sensory appetites, on the one hand, and the intellectual and moral life, on the other; and it is evident that passions and egoistic tendencies derive from our individual constitutions, while our rational activity—whether theoretical or practical— is dependent on social causes.

The "lower" half of *homo duplex* is the organismic, individual, bodily will that does its work apart from and contrary to consciousness. The "higher" half is composed of the social phenomenona of consciousness and reason. Recall that for Durkheim, society is a system of representations. Durkheim's position is highly dramatic and extreme. He is not saying that human nature results in tension at times. Like Schopenhauer, he is saying that man is essentially, unalterably, inescapably subject to pain, sorrow, and tension because of the conflict between the will and idea.

Moreover, the pain and sorrow that stem from this dualism can never be abolished, but only maintained within tolerable limits—which is also Schopenhauer's contention. And the tension will get worse as society progresses, because the individual will is becoming increasingly liberated:

> The painful *[douloureux]* character of the dualism of human nature is explained by this hypothesis. There is no doubt that if society were only the natural and spontaneous development of the individual, these two parts of ourselves would harmonize. . . . In fact, however, society has its own nature. . . . Therefore, society cannot be formed or maintained without our being required to make perpetual and costly sacrifices. Because society surpasses us, it obliges us to surpass ourselves; and to surpass itself, a being must, to some degree, depart from its nature—a departure that does not take place without causing more or less painful tensions. . . . We must, in a word, do violence to certain of our strongest inclinations. Therefore, since the role of the social being in our single selves will grow ever more important as history moves ahead, it is wholly improbable that there will ever be an era in which man is required to resist himself to a lesser degree, an era in which he can live a life that is easier and less full of tension. To the contrary, all evidence compels us to expect our effort in the struggle between the two beings within us to increase with the growth of civilization. [ibid., p. 163]

Shortly after writing this, Durkheim begin writing *La Morale* and died.

Freud has been given all the credit for his version of Durkheim's thoughts, above, which Freud published in 1930 in *Civilization and Its Discontents*. Durkheim had said it more eloquently in 1912, repeated it more forcefully in 1914—and he is *still* accused of being the extreme sociologue who denigrated or ignored man's psychological nature. No one can read his essay on *homo duplex*, nor the works which lead up to it, with any degree of sensitivity and agree with contemporary assessments of his thought as "oversocialized." Durkheim was keenly aware that the individual is the enemy of civilization at all times. And in positing this extreme version of man's propensity for egoism and wickedness, he was merely echoing a long and distinguished line of religious and philosophical moralists, including John Calvin. It is no wonder that he posed for Landowski's statue of Calvin.

Conclusions

Merton (1957, p. 161) writes that "as initially developed by Durkheim, the concept of anomie referred to a condition of relative normlessness in a society or group." This understanding of anomie is not supported by Durkheim's writings. Durkheim never used the word normlessness. There is no etymological, historical, or contextual support for reading *anomie* as normlessness. More important, Merton's "normlessness" does *not* assume a dualism of human nature. Durkheim's concept of *anomie*, in sharp contrast, does. And Durkheim's *homo duplex* is but a refraction of Schopenhauer's will versus the idea, and Plato's desires versus Ideas long before that, with many representations of this dualism in between (Meštrović 1982).

Durkheim's concept of *anomie* is far removed from Merton's bland, secular, and painless concept of "normlessness." Durkheim was a moralist—albeit a scientific moralist—who was sensitive to the pain and sorrow caused by immorality. He did not think of *anomie* as simple confusion, but as evil. And he thought of it as evil because it unleashes the unrestrained will. He launched his career in sociology by inquiring, in his introduction to *Division of Labor*, into the method for studying "moral facts" scientifically ([1893] 1933, p. 424). He was attempting to move beyond the fact-value distinction that has plagued philosophers and social scientists since the writings of Kant. *Elementary Forms* ends his career-long discussion of morality on the note that sociology is "destined to open a new way to the science of man" ([1912] 1965, p. 495), precisely because it has the potential to overcome the dualisms posed by Kant. Durkheim died writing the introduction to his next book, *La Morale*. In this introduction he claims that "moral facts" can be studied as "natural things" and that the expression he had used in teaching this new science was "Physics or Science of Mores [*moeurs*] and of Law" (Durkheim [1920] 1976, p. 330). This expression is obviously a reference to *Leçons de sociologie: physique des moeurs et du droit*, the longest-running series of lectures in Durkheim's career. Because the title had apparently raised some controversy, Durkheim proposed that "We shall therefore call it 'Science of Morality' or 'Science of Moral Facts,' understanding thereby that it deals with moral phenomena or moral reality as it can be observed either in the present or in the past, just as physics or physiology deal with the facts they study" ([1920] 1978, p. 202). Durkheim obviously felt that these "moral facts" were as impersonal as "social facts," enabling the sociologist to move beyond the impasse of pure speculation reached by theologians and philosophers concerned with ethics.

Durkheim's concern with anomie and *dérèglement* bespeaks his concern with a science of morality. And these concerns were part of his quest to reform sociology. Any sociology that ignores or, indeed, fosters anomie—however unwittingly—was suspect to him. And any sociology that ignores the will is likely to fall into these errors.

CHAPTER 5

Intellectual Anomie and the "Cult of Truth"

OF ALL THE VARIETIES of anomie, intellectual anomie has been the most neglected by sociologists. As early as 1893, Durkheim discussed anomie in relation to science and truth, what we shall call intellectual anomie, within the context of general anomie in his *Division of Labor*. He glides back and forth easily from economic anomie to intellectual anomie. The gist of his argument is that like the other varieties of anomie, intellectual anomie does not result directly from the division of labor within science—the proliferation of many sciences and specializations—but from compartmentalization. Using Marcel Mauss's ([1950] 1979a) vocabulary, one could say that Durkheim objects to the fact that the "totality" of science and truth has been lost in modern times. Using Schopenhauer's ([1818] 1977) vocabulary, one could say that even intellectual "will" has to be restrained, for it, too, is inherently insatiable. Let us examine this argument closely. According to Durkheim ([1893] 1984, p. 293), "Up to very recent times, science, not being very much divided, could be studied almost in its entirety by one and the same person. Thus there was a very strong feeling of unity about it." But in modern times, specialization has resulted in the emergence of many particular sciences and particular problems. "Science, carved up into a host of detached studies that have no link with one another, no longer forms a solid whole," Durkheim laments (ibid., p. 294). The totality of human knowledge is lost.

Durkheim (ibid., p. 296) makes an interesting connection with political anomie: "What the government is to society in its entirety philosophy must be to the sciences. Since the diversity of the sciences tends to break up the unity of science, a new science must be entrusted with the task of reconstituting it." Durkheim's philosophical temperament emerges fully in this comment. He makes it clear in *Professional Ethics and Civic Morals* (and elsewhere) that the government must take on the "higher" role of superintending the will of the people. A similar kind of "governor" is required in science! Alas, Durkheim observes, contemporary philosophy is as subject to compartmentalization as the other disciplines, so that modern philosophy cannot fulfill this regulatory role (a sentiment echoed more recently by Bloom 1987). "The cult of truth" must take philosophy's place. This "cult" is a kind of religion, the counterpart of the "cult" of individualism. Like any other kind of religion, it transcends egoism.

The essence of this "cult" of truth is that the scientist, regardless of his specialization, must remember that he is linked to other scientists by the fact that he values truth. For Durkheim, the quest for truth is not "value-free," as it is purported to be in positivistic sociology. Rather, truth itself is a value. He distinguishes between the "letter" versus the "spirit" of science (ibid., p. 299). This obviously religious allusion is commensurate with the religious connotations of anomie as a kind of sin. In fact, Montgomery (1984) has demonstrated that scientific bias was typically understood as a kind of sin in Durkheim's time. Durkheim believes that science "is not wholly contained in the few propositions that it has definitively demonstrated" ([1893] 1984, p. 299). By contrast, positivistic sociology focuses almost exclusively on what is provable. Durkheim (ibid.) continues:

> Beside this present-day science, consisting of what has already been acquired, there is another, which is concrete and living, which is in part still unaware of itself and still seeking its way: beside the results that have been obtained, there are the hopes, habits, instincts, needs, and presentiments that are so vague that they cannot be expressed in words, yet so powerful that occasionally they dominate the whole life of the scientist. All this is still science: it *is even the best and major part of it*, because the truths discovered are very few in number beside those that remain to be discovered, and, moreover, to master the whole meaning of the discovered truths and to understand all that is summarized in them, one must have looked closely at scientific life whilst it is still in a free state, that is, before it has been crystallized in the form of definite propositions. . . . Each science has, so to speak, a soul that lives in the consciousness of scientists. Only a part of that soul takes on substance and palpable forms. The formulas that express it, being general, are easily transmissible. But the same is not true for that other part of science that no symbol translates externally. Here everything is personal, having to be acquired by personal experience. [emphasis added]

In this incredible passage, Durkheim is essentially applying the concept of *homo duplex* to science. The personal, subjective, private—

one might say intuitive—aspects of the scientific process are as important as the external, public, and objective aspects. Science, like anything else, is a "total" phenomenon. In Schopenhauer's terms, science, too, is will *and* idea. Science should not be compartmentalized, Durkheim believed, such that only the external, objective aspects (the letter of science, science as idea) are valued. Nevertheless, this compartmentalization is the essence of contemporary training in sociology. Training to become a contemporary sociologist, one is far more likely to be exposed to Max Weber's troublesome dictum that science is value-free than to Durkheim's claim that it must be a total phenomenon.

Addressing a problem in his day that still plagues the modern sciences in general and the social sciences in particular, Durkheim (ibid., pp. 303–4) writes:

> There are hardly any disciplines that harmonize the efforts of the different sciences toward a common goal. This is especially true of the moral and social sciences, for the the mathematical, physical, chemical and even biological sciences do not seem to such an extent foreign to one another. But the jurist, the psychologist, the anthropologist, the economist, the statistician, the linguist, the historian—all these go about their investigations as if the various orders of facts that they are studying formed so many independent worlds. Yet in reality these facts interlock with one another at every point. . . . They afford the spectacle of an aggregate of disconnected parts that fail to co-operate with one another. If they therefore form a whole lacking in unity, it is not because there is no adequate view of their similarities, it is because they are not organized. . . . It is because they are in a state of *anomie*.

In the context of Durkheim's assessment above, one can understand why the studies of the Durkheimians were so cross-disciplinary. They sought to overcome intellectual anomie. It cannot be emphasized enough that contemporary sciences are still in "insufficient contact" with one another, that they remain "too distant from one another to be aware of the bonds that unite them" (ibid., p. 306). Modern university departments are easily characterized as empires that avoid contact with other empires.

With his characteristic pathos, Durkheim depicts the psychological and physiological consequences of this alienation on the part of scientists: fatigue, anxiety, restlessness, disillusionment, and the other vocabulary of anomie. Just as in the economic order the worker is separated from his family and the person who employs him, the anomic scientist is separated from other scientists and the "cult of truth" that ought to rule him. The scientist can lose sight of the sacredness and importance of his task. Mountains of facts are piled up within an area of specialization and testify to the unrestrained, disconnected will; but disconnected from other sciences, these facts often remain obscure and relatively useless to society.

But Durkheim's critique runs deeper than this. Intellectual anomie permeates the lives of the general population in the form of pragmatism, which he attacked bitterly in his *Pragmatism and Sociology*. We must remember that Durkheim continually expressed the belief that sociology must be practical. He was not against pragmatism on the grounds of relevance and practicality. Pragmatism, according to Durkheim ([1955] 1983), abandons the "cult of truth" entirely. This move exacerbates intellectual anomie, because it makes it even more difficult to grasp the connectedness among facts and truths. It leads to trial-and-error techniques that eventually lead to disillusionment with science in general, because the will to truth is never satisfied. If Durkheim is correct that anomie in general and intellectual anomie in particular are unhealthy and produce suffering, one would expect that pragmatism may be a direct contributor to human unhappiness. And if that is true, Durkheim has proposed an important caveat to the ancient philosophical understandings of truth as one source of health and contentment (see especially Plato's dialogues). The consequences of this Durkheimian move for the sociology of knowledge and for sociology in general are enormous. Simply put, individuals in societies that recognize the totality of truth should be healthier, mentally and physically, than individuals in "intellectually anomic" societies. Pragmatism should be related to increasing suicide rates and other forms of deviance, because it increases the chances for human suffering and unhappiness. This fascinating insight that flows out of Durkheim's sociology has not been examined up to now. Before it can be understood fully, we need to examine the "cult of truth" more closely.

The Cult of Truth

In his neglected *Evolution of Educational Thought*, especially, Durkheim ([1938] 1977) traces the evolution of rationality in relation to social structure. The "cult of truth" was as unimportant in primitive societies as the "cult of the individual." Both "cults" evolved laboriously, and in parallel, as societies progressed from mechanical or organic solidarity. But the evolution was uneven in the West. The ancient Greek worship of reason, best illustrated by the writings of Plato and Aristotle, was subjected to the anomie of sophism. The scholastic progress made by Christian monks was toppled by the Renaissance, a period that Durkheim depicts as a long period of anomie. Then came the Enlightenment, in which reason again flowered only to be toppled again, this time by excessive empiricism. The opposition between the humanistic study of man versus the objective study of the external world is part of *homo duplex* (Durkheim makes this especially clear in his 1914 essay on the dualism of human nature). In non-anomic societies, these two polarized ways of approaching knowledge should be regarded as a totality, a unity. Durkheim ends *Evolution of Educational Thought* by calling for a curriculum that will emphasize humanistic and strictly scientific studies equally. This is the promise of sociology as apprehended by him: it is the queen of the sciences because it restores the unity of knowledge and flows from it.

According to Durkheim (ibid.), the Protestant Reformation began the restoration of the balance of *homo duplex* that had been toppled by the Renaissance. Protestantism was concerned with the secular, and this concern led naturally to science. And the science of the Enlightenment was a "total science," not an excess in any direction. Durkheim also considers the Jesuit Counter-Reformation movement in this context. Both the Reformation and the Jesuits restored the balance of *homo duplex,* even though they appear to work in contrary directions. If early Catholicism resulted in the anomie of the Renaissance because it took man too seriously, Protestantism leads to the modern anomie of pragmatism because it takes the world too seriously. In both cases, the will must be restrained.

Thus, Durkheim would say, we are currently in the midst of yet another period of intellectual anomie that is related to the general anomie of post-industrial societies in the West.

Apart from *Evolution of Educational Thought*, all of Durkheim's comments on science emphasize that it should be studied as a totality. In *Moral Education* he regards the development of moral individualism and rationalism as a unity. In the conclusion of *Elementary Forms* he claimed that the concept of "totality" itself has been the most neglected of philosophical categories: "And yet there is perhaps no other category of greater importance; for as the role of the categories is to envelop all the other concepts, the category *par excellence* would seem to be this very concept of *totality.* The theorists of knowledge ordinarily postulate it as if it came of itself" ([1912] 1965, p. 489). Durkheim adds that "the concept of totality is only the abstract form of the concept of society" and in a footnote (p. 490), "At bottom, the concept of totality, that of society and that of divinity are very probably only different aspects of the same notion."

It is no wonder that in the remainder of the conclusion, Durkheim argues against what has come to be known as the fact-value distinction and denies any fundamental opposition between science and morality. "Sociology appears destined to open a new way to the science of man" (ibid., p. 495) because it affirms the totality of knowledge in the very fact that it affirms society. To apprehend society is to apprehend the category called "totality." Humankind had to struggle for centuries to understand society as something more than the sum of its parts, something that should not be reduced to its substratum–and that substratum is the mass of individual wills. Society is simultaneously an object and subject to its members, an object composed of human subjects that acts upon them but that is also fashioned by them. Likewise, the experience of conceptualizing objects of knowledge as "totality" is new to humankind. It is so new that mankind is torn between the awareness of the totality of knowledge and pragmatism.

Durkheim corners pragmatism into a series of well-conducted arguments that have been repeated by modern philosophers of science, albeit without citing Durkheim, (see Flew 1985; Trigg 1985). They run as follows: if the criteria for truth shall be how useful truth is, then anything can be said to be useful from some point of view. But if everything is useful, then one may as well abandon the notion of truth, for then anything can be made to be true—which is to say, useful—in some way. Or consider the extreme position of cultural relativism, the claim that there are no absolute truths, only truths relative to specific contexts (a view attacked with great force by Bloom 1987). If that is true, then it is not true, since it can be denied relative to certain contexts; it negates itself. It implies that science and sociology are nothing but complex activities. As Trigg (1985, p. 33) put it, "Why should sociologists find it plausible to suggest that science is not the discovery of truth but merely one rule-governed social activity among others?" Trigg (p. 41) continues: "The idea that all standards are embedded in particular social practices and that 'objective' claims have validity against a particular social background is self-defeating. It destroys itself, since it can no longer claim the kind of truth it needs if others are to take notice of it." This is because even the cultural relativism position can be accepted or rejected based on subjective opinion. And subjective opinion is based on will, which is inherently unstable and insatiable.

Actually, both Durkheim and Trigg, as well as some other contemporary philosophers who criticize pragmatism and its derivatives in this fashion, are still using rationalism as a tool to make their criticisms. Contradictions are a sin as long as one adheres to some version of rationalism (some cult of truth) not to versions of pragmatism. Durkheim was aware that the real dangers of intellectual anomie stem from this very fact. In positing that truth is created and based on utilitarianism, pragmatism denies constraint. Logic itself, the logic that enables one to expose the contradiction in a principle, is an affirmation of rationalism and constraints imposed upon our think-ing. Without constraint, the passion for truth is as subject to the malady of infiniteness as other deranged passions that constitute anomie. In other words, in intellectual anomie anything can be true; no hard and fast criteria oblige or enable one to distinguish truth from falsehood. Williams James ([1879–1907] 1948) took pride in this "softness" of truth, its malleability, plasticity, and amorphousness. But for Durkheim, as stated previously, such amorphousness is a characteristic of primitive mentality.

As in other forms of anomie, this freedom from the constraints of truth appears to be a deceptively attractive trait, at least at first. But ultimately, it leads to the disillusionment and despair that are the hallmark of other kinds of anomie. If nothing is true because the appearance of truth is sufficient, then one will never be satisfied nor content with truth. If the capture of truth is nothing but a ritual, a game dependent upon a number of others who also play the game; if it is a conquest that has to be re-conquered over and over again, what is the point of valuing truth? Other truths will always seem more attractive than the one conquered. Ultimately, one will become disil-lusioned with the very possibility of truth. Such societies will fall prey to propaganda, "disinformation campaigns," unscrupulous advertis-ing, and other forms of deceit. Durkheim rightly alludes to the sophists in Plato's time in this regard, because sophistry, like contem-porary pragmatism, places a premium on the appearance of truth as opposed to truth (witness the debate between Socrates and Thrasy-machus in *The Republic*).

Durkheim ([1955] 1983, p. 1) remarks that sociology and pragma-tism are "children of the same period." The popularity of pragmatism "must be based on something in the human consciousness" as it has evolved (p. 2). That something is the realization that truth is a human product and a product of history, an insight shared by sociology and pragmatism. In other words, truth involves object *and* subject. But for Durkheim, although truth is a human product, it is also a *collective* product. For pragmatism, truth is ultimately personal, subjective, and the product of the individual. Pragmatism denies a large portion of the *homo duplex* within the *homo duplex* that is an essential part of Durkheim's sociology.

This is a mistake, Durkheim wrote. Reality is constantly changing and evolving, but truth can and must change with it. Collective representations are simultaneously flexible *and* rigid in that society's standards change, but society always draws the line beyond which the passions must not go. The "copy" (representation) evolves with the model, but there *is* an affinity between our concepts, emphasized by rationalism, and things as they exist in "reality," emphasized by pragmatism and its derivatives. This affinity is part of the "totality" of truth; it is also the very point that William James attacks. The reconciliation of object and subject, truth and reality, is the basis of Durkheim's ([1955] 1983) claim that rationalism must be *renovated*, not abandoned, before sociology can fulfill its mission. Rationalism's value is that it presupposes an active subject acting upon an objective world. Nevertheless, it must be renovated, because traditional rationalism can degenerate into a self-sufficient, dogmatic game of concepts that is overly divorced from "reality." According to Durkheim, the whole of "the philosophic tradition is rationalistic" (see also Durkheim ([1925] 1961, p. 4). In the preface to the *Rules of Sociological Method*, indeed, he claimed that with regard to sociology, the "main objective is to extend the scope of scientific rationalism to cover human behavior" ([1895] 1982, p. 33). This is an extremely ponderous claim when one considers how vehemently rationalism had traditionally opposed various empiricisms (see Lalande [1926] 1980, pp. 889–90). And it is important to set this claim in the context of contemporary attempts to "empiricize" and pragmatize the socal sciences. Durkheim sought to link the behavioral sciences with versions of rationalism, *not* of empiricism.

Contemporary philosophers writing on representations, like Jerry Fodor (1981), affirm Durkheim's argument, albeit unwittingly. For example, Fodor demonstrates that empiricism *cannot* really claim that what is in the mind must first be present in the senses. It cannot assume that the mind is a blank slate acted upon by an objective world. The world can be perceived only through representations, and mental representations are actually mental "objects." In the long run, at bottom, everyone is a rationalist, even the empiricists and pragmatists. One must be a rationalist to apprehend the world, because the world can be apprehended only through representationalism—again, this is how Schopenhauer begins his *World as Will and Idea*. There is no way to escape this conclusion without succumbing to naive empiricism and realism, the belief that the world is obvious and immediately apparent to all. But there can be no doubt that the majority of contemporary philosophers and social scientists have failed to take their European founding fathers seriously on this point and have opted instead for various versions of naive pragmatism and its derivatives (for discussions, see Rochberg-Halton 1986; Turner 1986).

Durkheim was a philosopher, to be sure, but he brought to philosophy an awareness that dominant modes of thought are also shaped by social forces. Pragmatism is more than a philosophical error. For Durkheim, it is a form of sacrilege, an attack on the "cult of truth." It is a *reversal* of the philosophical respect for reason and truth, a genuine *dérèglement*.

Affinities to Critical Theory

Durkheim's thought borders on what has come to be known as critical theory. We make the allusion cautiously, because critical theory, like other theories in sociology, is amorphous and subject to internal controversies. It is not entirely clear to what extent critical theory is indebted to Marx, Freud or the rest of the *fin de siècle* spirit outlined by Ellenberger (1970) and Bloom (1987). (We have already mentioned Bouglé's 1918 attempt to find *some* philosophical affinities between Marx and Durkheim). Nevertheless, Durkheim is in essential agreement with Max Horkheimer (1947), Walter Benjamin (1968), Erich Fromm (1955, 1962), and other members of the so-called Frankfurt School who applied Marx's concept of alienation to reason itself. Only Durkheim goes a step further, implying that intellectual anomie causes pain and suffering to the entire social body, not just to the working classes, and that it can lead to pathogenic effects like suicide! Let us elaborate on this connection.

In *The Eclipse of Reason* Max Horkheimer (1947) argues that the present crisis of reason consists in the fact that conceiving of objectivity at all is negated or regarded as a delusion. Subjectivism, which was regarded by some ancient philosophers as only a part of total reason, is now understood to be all there is to reason. For Aristotle and Plato, the Good was absolute, independent of the observer. Today, to be "reasonable" means to be able to take adequate steps in relation to a subjectively perceived goal. Formerly, rationality was an instrument for determining which goals one should choose. Formerly, objective reason implied an all-embracing structure. Today, everything is subjective. Pragmatism is the outcome of this subjectivization of reason. Truth is supposed to be tested in action, experimentation of all kinds that produces concrete answers to concrete questions as posed by the interests and will of individuals. Pragmatism in general reflects the spirit of the prevailing business culture: one who reasons correctly is one who can achieve desired aims. Formerly, an intelligent person was not one who could merely reason in relation to goals, but one whose mind was open to perceiving objective truths.

Horkheimer makes the observation that the original democratic principles of ancient Greece and colonial America were based on the principle that the rights of man resided in an objective principle, not in majority opinion. Today, deprived of its rational foundation, "the democratic principle becomes exclusively dependent upon the so-called interests of the people, and these . . . do not offer any guarantee against tyranny" (Horkheimer 1947, p. 28). Durkheim had made a similar argument in his *Professional Ethics:* democracy understood as the will of the people is an invitation to anomie as long as this will is understood primarily as subjective opinion. Subjectivism is too unstable to serve such an important function.

Horkheimer (ibid., p. 75) believes that in modern times, truth itself has been split: "The physical sciences are endowed with so called objectivity, but emptied of human content; the humanities preserve the human content, but only as ideology, at the expense of truth." I would add that the social sciences have themselves been split between these extremes. In addition, hadn't Durkheim ([1938] 1977) warned against such compartmentalization? "Thought today is only too often compelled to justify itself by its usefulness to some established group rather than by its truth" Horkheimer (p. 86) writes. Similarly, Durkheim ([1955] 1983) raged against utilitarianism because it degrades truth. Horkheimer (p. 101) writes: "Pamphlets on how to improve one's speech, how to understand music, how to be saved are written in the same style as those extolling the advantages of laxatives. . . . Every word or sentence that hints of relations other than pragmatic is suspect; when a man is asked to admire a thing, to respect a feeling or attitude, to love a person for his own sake, he smells sentimentality and suspects that someone is pulling his leg or trying to sell him something." To read Horkheimer's account of how reason has been eclipsed is an experience similar to reading Durkheim's statements on intellectual anomie. Yet the link between Durkheimianism and critical theory has never been made in sociological theory.

Even Horkheimer's proposed solution is similar to Durkheim's. Essentially, both thinkers call for a reconciliation of objective and subjective reason—for totality, not taking sides. The latest symptoms of taking sides are positivism, pragmatism, the tyranny of advertising, and the degradation of art. Reason must reject the alienated modern *and* ancient versions of reason, critique it, and restore reason to its true nature. Or as Durkheim ([1955] 1983, p. 2) put it, rationalism must be renovated and reformed.

Or consider the work of another important member of the Frankfurt School, Walter Benjamin (1968), particularly his essay "The Work of Art in an Age of Mechanical Reproduction." Benjamin argues that mechanical reproduction is completely new. For the ancient Greeks, with minor exceptions (the making of bronzes and coins), art was always unique. Today, we have printing, lithography, photography, and film, among other kinds of reproduction. But "even the most perfect reproduction of a work of art is lacking in one element: its presence in time and space, its unique existence at the place where it happens to be" (ibid., p. 222). When Benjamin claims that reproduction kills the "aura" of a work of art, he is unknowingly echoing Durkheim's sentiments on "totality." And when Benjamin makes the bold leap that modern man in general has lost the sense of aura, that can be translated into Durkheimian terminology as the claim that modern man's thinking has been compartmentalized. (These moves by Benjamin and Durkheim also reverberate, in part, with Schopenhauer's theory of the sublime in *The World as Will and Idea*.) Humankind has grown so used to this state of alienation and anomie that "it can experience its own destruction as an aesthetic pleasure of the first order" (ibid., p. 244). War is enjoyed. In Durkheimian terms, society's members have become so accustomed to pain and suffering that they no longer recognize them as symptoms of distress.

Durkheim's Notion of *Contrainte* in Relation to the Will

Durkheim's *Rules of Sociological Method*, first published in 1895, might best be summarized as a book about social constraint *[contrainte]*. He regarded *Rules* as a sequel to *Division of Labor*, which, as we have seen, was concerned primarily with establishing a science of moral facts. The notion of constraint is ubiquitous to Durkheim's thought from the first to his last major works. The interesting thing about the notion of *contrainte* is that it is a response to Schopenhauer's problem of the will. Just what is constrained in Durkheim's conceptualization of science? The answer is that it is the *will*. So long as the egotistical will reigns freely, objective science is impossible.

In a preface to *Rules*, Durkheim explains that social facts are "distinguishable through their special characteristic of being capable of exercising a coercive influence on the consciousness of individuals" ([1895] 1982, p. 43). Thus, social facts are described in terms of their "coercive influence," "coercive power," and "coercion" in general. This is the social dimension. On the psychological level, Durkheim refers to their "compelling," "constraining," and "obligatory" power. Essentially, social facts are experienced psychologically as habits. On the physiological level, social facts are experienced as force, pressure, and a sense of ineluctable necessity. Social facts also convey a sense of "heaviness" and "weight." Social facts are not fleeting, temporary events. Rather, they are found in "habit" and "tendency" and imply a sense of permanence. In addition, one must "submit" to the social fact. Durkheim also distinguishes between normal and abnormal constraint, and indeed, devotes a controversial chapter in *Rules* to the distinction between the normal and the pathological. He further distinguishes his theory of social constraint from the theories of Hobbes and Machiavelli. Why does Durkheim focus on *contrainte* and its synonyms rather than on some more traditional and better known characteristic of scientific objectivity? The answer is probably because he felt that previous understandings of science were overly subjective and backward.

Given Durkheim's tremendous sensitivity to etymology and the collective meanings of words, it is no surprise that his use of *contrainte* is orthodox, literally "by the book." *Contrainte* and *contraindre* are derived from the Latin verb *constringere,* which means to constrict or draw tightly. The synonyms for *contrainte* that emerge in dictionaries turn out to be among Durkheim's most favorite, or at least most frequently used, words: *coercition, force, pression, violence, discipline, loi, règle* (see Lalande [1926] 1980, p. 184; Littré [1863] 1963). To constrain, in English or French, is to force, compel, coerce, necessitate and violate *(Oxford English Dictionary* 1972). These are emotionally charged concepts. They imply that the individual's will has reached an obstacle it cannot dominate. Durkheim frequently refers to the violence that society perpetrates upon the individual. In most of his works, Durkheim was searching for moral rules that would exert a benign kind of constraint on the individual. He was always aware that *contrainte* connotes violence and pain, and he never took this price lightly.

In the preface to *Rules* Durkheim ([1895] 1982, p. 43) explains that his *preliminary* definition of a social fact was *not* meant to be "a sort of philosophy of the social fact." He was *not* "explaining social phenomena in terms of constraint," but wanted "merely to indicate how, by outward signs, it is possible to identify the facts." And he adds, "Thus we readily admit the charge that this definition does not express all aspects of the social fact and consequently that it is not the sole possible one . . . there is no reason why [the social fact] should possess only the one distinctive property." Durkheim ([1912] 1965, p. 243) repeated this defense many years later in *Elementary Forms,* arguing that *contrainte* is not the only *sign* of social facts, but it is an easily identifiable one.

The understanding of *contrainte* as a sign for identifying social facts forces one to reappraise the way "social facts" have been depicted in sociological literature. *Contrainte* is a sign in the sense explained in the *Littré* ([1863] 1963, vol. 2, p. 1152), that *it opposes the will:* "Contraindre exprime simplement un obstacle opposé à ma volonté, quelque chose qui me serre, qui me lie." This is the key to understanding why Durkheim harps on constraint as a feature of the social fact, but it has been completely missed by students of Durkheim. Consistent with this meaning, Durkheim is constant in his claims that society is not the product of individual wills; it is, rather, a phenomenon sui generis that opposes the individual will. Thus, "a social fact is identifiable through the power of external coercion which it exerts or is capable of exerting upon individuals" (Durkheim [1895] 1982, p. 56). This is also why he claimed that social facts are "external" to the individual—he apparently meant simply that they do not originate with the individual will. And social facts are like "things" because in philosophical usage, "things" are forces not of our choosing or creation (Lalande [1926] 1980, p. 139). This is also why Durkheim ([1895] 1982, p. 128) refuses to equate the more psychological concept of inhibition with social constraint: "Inhibition is, if one likes, the means by which social constraint produces its *psychical* effects, but is not itself that constraint" (emphasis added).

For Durkheim, then, one will be able to find, recognize, and identify social facts by searching for ways in which they constrain individual will. The constraint is a sign, one of several possible signs. One runs into a social fact like one runs into a table or a wall—it is a "thing" that opposes the individual. It hurts to run into a table or a wall, and it hurts to run into a social fact. There is no inherent moral or social philosophy of constraint *per se* implied in Durkheim's thought; that is, he is not claiming that all constraint is moral or just. Once these social facts are identified—and they must be distinguished as being normal or pathological, as he takes pains to emphasize in *Rules*—then they must be evaluated. But the scientific elaboration and practical consequence stem from the application of rationalistic principles to what has been discovered, not from accepting or rejecting out-of-hand the constraints found.

Facts Versus Events

Thus far we have explored only one aspect of the totality of social facts, the context of *contrainte*. But social facts are, after all, *facts*. Durkheim's notion of a "social fact" has been pragmatized to such a great extent that the full import of it being a fact, as opposed to an event, has not been appreciated. Facts are capable of exercising *contrainte;* it is rare to refer to events as constraining. Philosophers distinguish sharply between facts and events (see Angeles 1981, p. 52; Archie 1977; Brand 1982; Foulquie 1978, pp. 267–69), and so does Durkheim. This is no doubt the reason why Durkheim discounts event-explanations, as in this comment in *Suicide* ([1897] 1951, p. 298): "The most varied and even the most contradictory *events* of life may equally serve as pretexts for suicide. This suggests that none of them is the specific cause" (emphasis added). Schopenhauer ([1813] 1899), too, discounted events as explanations for suicide or as causal explanations in general (discussed in Magee 1983). And this is also why Durkheim maintained that only social facts can cause other social facts. Durkheim's *Suicide,* especially, has been subjected to intense criticisms from the positivistic perspective on the explanation of causes (Douglas 1967), but these criticisms have not paid attention to Durkheim's philosophical distinction between facts and events.

As background for this segment of the discussion, consider the etymology of the word "event," the Latin *eventus,* which means result, effect, or issue. In philosophical usage, it is a temporary appearance distinguished from a fact (Lalande [1926] 1980, p. 310). The etymology of "fact" means permanent or fixed (ibid., pp. 337–39). By contrast, an event involves a process, a change in the properties of something. In *Truth,* Alan R. White (1970, p. 80) elaborates on this philosophical distinction:

> Facts, unlike events, situations, states of affairs, or objects, have no date or location. Facts, unlike objects, cannot be created or destroyed, pointed to or avoided. . . . Facts, unlike states of affairs, do not begin, last or end. . . . A distinction can be drawn between the occurrence of an event or the existence of an event or the existence of a state of affairs and the fact that such an event occurred or that such a state of affairs exists. Contrariwise, facts, but not events, situations, or states of affairs, can be disputed, challenged, assumed, or proved. Facts can be stated, whereas events and situations are described. . . . *fact* is a notion which applies neither to items in the world, such as features, events, situations etc., nor to what is said about the world, like (true) statements, but to *what* the world is like, to *how* things, necessarily or contingently, are.

Translated into Durkheimian terminology, White is saying that facts are representations capable of exercising constraint, and that events are not. Facts are not things in this world, but representations of them. But representations necessarily imply a relationship between subject and object. And facts carry a weight of necessity that events, in their essence, cannot.

In recent years there has been a veritable explosion of philosophical literature on the fact-event distinction (for a review, see Brand 1982). It is amazing that Durkheim foreshadowed this contemporary debate so many years ago. Yet, one finds the scaffolding for Durkheim's moves even in Claude Bernard's ([1865] 1957) *Introduction to the Study of Experimental Medicine,* which was the rage in Durkheim's time. Bernard's book is still used as a text in physiology, and Bernard has been spared the attacks that have been made on Durkheim. Like Bernard, Durkheim was attempting to move away from positivistic methodology and to find the equivalent of the one well-designed or crucial experiment that would yield facts (Hirst 1975). *Rules* concludes that the comparative method could serve the place of Bernard's experiment, a claim that is credible only if one appreciates that by "experiment," Bernard did *not* put an emphasis on "empirical verification," which is the staple of contemporary experiments in social science: "The experimental method is nothing but *reasoning* by whose help we methodically submit our ideas to experience—the experience of facts" (Bernard [1865] 1957, p. 2, emphasis added). This ponderous definition is an important component of understanding what Durkheim meant by a fact.

Schopenhauer ([1813] 1899), too, saw no point in repeating observations. For him, the essence of the scientific experiment was correct, heightened observation of phenomena—what he termed genius, *not* what we call empirical verification. Schopenhauer's thought on experimentation influenced many thinkers other than Durkheim.

For example, let us review the broad outlines of the similarities between Bernard's *Introduction to the Study of Experimental Medicine* and Durkheim's *Rules of Sociological Method*. Durkheim cites Bernard explicitly in claiming that sociology must emulate the experimental method in which the scientist does not "produce" facts but "operates" on phenomena (Durkheim [1888] 1976, p. 13). Indeed, Bernard claimed that "pile up facts or observations as we may, we shall be none the wiser" ([1865] 1957, p. 16). In other words, facts are not just observable objects independent of the subject. Rather, the scientist acts on objects, brings about the appearance of phenomena: he invents, produces, and induces facts. The scientist interacts with the object; mere observation is not enough. In the wake of Kant, the "observation" of "material objects" was called into question. How, then, does one "observe" non-objects like social phenomena? The scientist must render judgment on the facts. Durkheim ([1893] 1933, p. 36) echoed Bernard: "To subject an order of facts to science, it is not sufficient to observe them carefully, to describe and classify them."

Durkheim makes his position on this matter most explicit in his neglected debate with historians at a meeting of the French Philosophical Society in 1908 (published as "L'inconnu et l'inconscient en histoire"). Durkheim complained that historians were overly concerned with specific *events,* a concern which could never yield scientific laws. Sociology should not be concerned with events, but with facts. He explained that when one considers facts A and B, the matter of how frequently the relationship of A-B is established is not the important point to consider. If it is a law, it is enough that there is a potential for the relation to be repeated. After all, the logician accepts that a law is established if an experiment is conducted well. After the law is established, it is of no importance whether the *facts* repeat themselves. Certain phenomena, he went on, like the "teratological" (those concerned with monstrous or rare phenomena, like suicide), are instructional precisely because they are unique, exceptional, and at times, extreme. Durkheim asserted: "If I know A is the cause of B, I know A will always be the cause of B. The link that joins them exists as a positive reality beyond time and space" (1908, p. 233). (I place great emphasis on Durkheim's remark concerning the independence from the Kantian categories of time and space as this is also one of Schopenhauer's major arguments in his *Fourfold Root of Reason* [1813] 1899.)

Durkheim continued with an illustration: "It is popularly stated that Marat died from being stabbed with a knife, unless it is found that the overheated bath caused his death before the stabbing did. At any rate, it is not because stabbing *precedes* death that it is the cause. A stabbing causes death because it touches an essential organ, thus by virtue of a general law." Durkheim had made a similar argument in the *Rules* ([1895] 1966, p. 79) many years earlier, that science cannot review all facts but must rely on the critical experiment: "Even one well-made observation will be enough in many cases, just as one well-constructed experiment often suffices for the establishment of a law."

Facts do not need to repeat themselves, and *cannot* repeat themselves. Facts are representations, and representations will vary depending upon the specific circumstances and the specific questions a particular scientist is producing in relation to phenomena. This is another way of asserting that facts are total phenomena. They presuppose the interaction of subject and object. Nevertheless, facts are unlike events because facts are constant. This is a seeming paradox in the thought of Bernard and Durkheim. Bernard ([1865] 1957, p. 10) insists that "effects vary with the conditions which bring them to pass, but laws do not vary." Like Durkheim, Bernard ([1865] 1957) declared that:

> If an hypothesis is not verified and disappears, the facts which it has enabled us to find are none the less acquired as indestrucrible materials for science. [p. 24]

> If we find disconcerting or even contradictory results in performing an experiment, we must never acknowledge exceptions or contradictions as real. That would be unscientific. We must simply and necessarily decide that conditions in the phenomena are different, whether or not we can explain them at the time. [p.70]

> An experimenter who has made an experiment . . . may happen not to get the same results in a new series of investigations as in his first observation. . . . What is to be done? Should we acknowledge that the facts are indeterminable? Certainly not, since that cannot be. We must simply acknowledge that experimental conditions, which we believed to be known, are not known. . . . Facts never exclude one another, they are simply explained by differences in the conditions in which they are born. So an experimenter can never deny a fact that he has seen and observed, merely because he cannot rediscover it. [p. 71]

In much of contemporary social science, if a hypothesis is not verified, it and the theory upon which it is based are said to be "falsified," and are "thrown out" of the canons of science.

Although at odds with much of what passes for sociological methodology today, Durkheim's position is consistent with what he called "renovated rationalism," with contemporary philosophical thinking on the nature of facts, and of course, with Schopenhauer's argument in *Fourfold Root of the Principle of Sufficient Reason* ([1813] 1899). Foulquié (1978, p. 269) notes that facts exist only in relation to a theory, citing Le Roy's dictum that "facts cannot exist in science, at least starting from a certain level of precision, unless they are a function of a theory or of a group of theories that alone are capable of giving them meanings." Bertrand Russell and a host of other illustrious philosophers are cited by Foulquié (1978) to the effect that facts are significant only in relation to an ensemble of theory or representations. There are no pure, brute facts in science that can speak for themselves. A brute fact is defined as a datum that is experienced immediately in an observation. A scientific fact consists of the same data made more precise by interpretation and integration either into a general representation or a theory.

What are called "empirical findings" in sociology are also representations—symbols, replacements of "reality"—not positivistic "hard facts" that are supposed to be obvious to everyone. In this sense, facts can never repeat themselves, because each time they are approached, the object, human subject doing the analysis, and witnesses "observing" the interaction between object and subject have changed. Each fact is relative to the configuration of object, subject, and witnesses. Human will interacts with objective reality, because the scientist's will dictates which questions will be asked of nature and how they will be asked. This is the consequence of approaching facts as "total" phenomena. Because representations are always unconscious in part, the full import of facts can never be fully apprehended by consciousness. This is what Claude Bernard ([1865] 1957, p. 53) claimed to be the essence of the experimental method: "Experimental truths . . . are unconscious and relative, because the real conditions on which they exist are unconscious and can be known by us only in relation to the present state of our science."

Intellectual breakthroughs occur when collective representations have changed to the extent that facts come to be appreciated. "Objects" *become* facts through social interaction. This explains why Durkheim thought that geniuses are not original in the sense that they discover new facts. Rather, they "discover" what everyone else already "knows," albeit unconsciously and imperfectly. Geniuses are merely more perfect instruments for refracting these facts back to society.

Again, Durkheim seems to have been echoing both Schopenhauer and Bernard. Claude Bernard (ibid., p. 34) wrote that: "Facts also exist which mean nothing to most minds, while they are full of light for others. It even happens that a fact or an observation stays a very long time under the eyes of a man of science without in any way inspiring him, then suddenly there comes a ray of light, and the mind interprets the fact quite differently and finds for it wholly new relations."

Undoubtedly, Durkheim's views on science are threatening to contemporary social science. They deny the essential need for vast sums of research money, equipment, and other aspects of the contemporary research process that have restricted it to a privileged elite. They even deny the need for statistical correlations (discussed by Turner 1988). The essential thing in research is correct reasoning applied to the "real" world. No study, no experiment is inherently inferior or a failure; all such experiments have something to teach as long as one applied rationalism to them. One might be tempted to object that Bernard's and Durkheim's "one well-designed experiment" cannot possibly yield scientific truths. But in the first place, many such one-time experiments in the physical sciences—from Galileo's to Einstein's—have yielded important facts. Even more important, science and scientific truths for Bernard, Durkheim, and perhaps for many physical scientists as well, are *not* one-time things-in-themselves dependent upon correlations. Science is simply consciousness and as such is always growing, always a matter of degree.

Science and the Unconscious

Schopenhauer is widely recognized as one of the forerunners of the concept of the unconscious (Ellenberger 1970; Magee 1983). In the context of his philosophy, the will does not require consciousness. Plants have will, but no consciousness. Moreover, even in creatures with consciousness, the will operates even when the consciousness is not operative, as in sleep. The will never rests, and it is always opposing consciousness. Like Schopenhauer, Freud, and others in his time who accounted for the unconscious, Durkheim held an elaborate theory of consciousness and its relation to the unconscious. In fact, he regarded science primarily as heightened consciousness, as "more" consciousness.

Durkheim ([1924] 1974) felt that representations escape and are unknown to the consciousness of witnesses, agents, even the "collective conscience" (for a discussion see Lalande [1926] 1980, pp. 173–76). Consciousness is not inherent in the idea of a representation—this is another important dimension in Durkheim's sociology. Again, it is commensurate with nineteenth century interest in the unconscious across several disciplines (Ellenberger 1970). Yet Durkheim's concept of the unconscious has been distorted, ignored, and even obscured, while Freud's theory of the unconscious is widely known. Moreover, Durkheim's concept of the unconscious has not been incorporated into sociological theory. This is because positivistic methodology assumes that everything it purports to study can be consciously "observed," and that incorporation of the unconscious into research is supposedly "unscientific" because the unconscious cannot be "observed."

It is difficult to write about the unconscious relative to science because of this widely held belief. A moment's reflection illustrates how incorrect it is. Positivistic methodology assumes what is frequently called "naive empiricism," that reality is readily observable and that "facts speak for themselves." No respectable contemporary philosopher would endorse naive empiricism. Facts require theory in order to "exist," which implies that prior to theory they are unconscious. And the "will" is always lurking in the unconscious, ready to contaminate our attempts at disinterested observation of "reality."

The concept of the unconscious challenges both objectivism and subjectivism. The world can never be known objectively in the fullest sense of the term, because a large part of it always escapes consciousness. But even with regard to his own subjective point of view, the human agent is not always aware of everything that is his point of view, because a large part of it is hidden even from himself.

Durkheim regards introspection as an invalid technique of human inquiry. Thus in *Sociology and Philosophy* ([1898] 1974, p. 20) he writes: "In fact, within each one of us a multitude of psychic phenomena occur without our apprehending them." In *Suicide* ([1897] 1951, p. 43) he asks: "How discover the agent's motive and whether he desired death itself when he formed his resolve, or had some other purpose? Intent is too intimate a thing to be more than approximately interpreted by another. It even escapes self-observation. How often we mistake the true reasons for our acts!"

In *Professional Ethics* ([1950] 1983, p. 80) he writes: "Within every one of us then, there is at all times a host of ideas, tendencies and habits that act upon us without our knowing exactly why or wherefore. To us they are hardly perceptible and we are unable to make out their differences properly. They lie in the subconscious." In an essay on Marxism, Durkheim claimed ([1897] 1982, p. 167): "For men never do perceive the true motives which cause them to act. . . . This is therefore even more true when we act under the influence of social causes which we fail to perceive even more because they are more remote and more complex." This is one of the rare points of agreement between Durkheim and Marx: both acknowledge that conscious-ness is inferior in relation to the will, which is the true guide of human action (another echo of Schopenhauer). Thus "social life must be explained not by the conception of it formed by those who participate in it, but by the profound causes which escape their consciousness" (ibid., p. 171).

In the neglected debate "The Unknown and the Unconscious in History" (1908, p. 230) Durkheim claimed that both witnesses *[té-moins]* and agents of events can be mistaken about what they think they observed, and adds, "if that is true about individual psychic facts it is even more true when it is about social events because the causes escape the consciousness of the individual." If one accepts that introspection is invalid, then, Durkheim asked, "What in the world could the individual consciousness know about the cause of facts which are considerably more complex?" (p. 231).

Durkheim's belief that speculation concerning collective represen-tations is as invalid as introspection implies that the sociologist must take the same attitude toward social institutions that the psychologist must take toward the individual's self-reports. In both cases, apparent causes must be distinguished from other, more primary causes. Thus, the sociologist must distinguish between society as it "really" is and as it "appears to itself": "The society that morality bids us desire is not the society as it appears to itself, but the society as it is or is really becoming. The consciousness which society may have of itself which is expressed in general opinion may be an inadequate view of the underlying reality. . . . It is also possible that . . . certain principles . . . . may for a time be relegated to the unconscious and so appear not to exist" (Durkheim [1898] 1974, p. 38). He made this point most clearly in 1908: "Suppose that there is a collective conscience, then conscious facts must be included and explained as well as unconscious facts" (p. 238). Social consensus, agreement about norms, and all other exclu-sive reliance on public opinion are scorned by Durkheim. The "will" works despite this conscious camouflage.

According to Durkheim, the method to be followed in investigating conscious social facts is exactly the same as the method used to understand unconscious social facts. This is because "In fact, what is conscious is also full of obscurity . . . what is conscious and what is unconscious are equally obscure and in both cases the method whereby one can know the causes is identical" (p. 235). According to Durkheim (p. 244), "The unconscious is often nothing more than less consciousness. In short, there is no problem about knowing the unconscious. In reality, you are only partially setting up the problem of sociology, which is the problem of the collective conscience." For Durkheim, science is not a set of rules nor a body of knowledge based upon a paradigm acceptable to the opinion of scholars. Rather, as Durkheim put it in *Division of Labor*, "science is nothing else than consciousness carried to its highest point of clarity" ([1893] 1933, p. 52). In other words, for Durkheim science lies on the continuum of conscious—unconscious. It is the process of wrenching knowledge from the unknown and the unconscious, wherein the will is always working.

CHAPTER 6

Morality as Religion

DURKHEIM'S *Elementary Forms of the Religious Life* ([1912] 1965) has fascinated sociologists, for diverse reasons. Park and Burgess (1921) cited it as a pioneer effort in delineating society as a source of social control. Parsons (1937) understood it as a sign of Durkheim's disenchantment with positivism and return to idealism. More contemporary commentators like Pickering (1984), Lukes (1985), and Jones (1986) comment on its "empirical" import as a kind of ethnography of sorts about Australian aborigines, and in that regard find it lacking. Indeed, it is difficult to pick out "the" major theme of *Elementary Forms*. In it, Durkheim seems to have something to say about almost everything: the aborigines, magic, religion, Kant and his famous categories, the future of sociology, and so on. Nevertheless, it is possible to state clearly what it is *not* about. Contrary to Park and Burgess, Durkheim never uses the word *côntrole* in this book—he uses *contrainte*. Contrary to Parsons, Durkheim states that his epistemological position is "renovated rationalism," which borrows from idealism *and* realism. And of course, from the point of view of this renovated rationalism, the fact that *some* anthropologists have entered the Australian bush and been unable to confirm Durkheim's observations is of little consequence. Facts do not speak for themselves in any kind of rationalism, renovated or the old-fashioned varieties. Facts require theory. Facts "exist" only as refractions of theory.

Once the false leads are set aside and Durkheim's radical epistemological move is highlighted, the continuities with Durkheim's previous work become apparent. In the *Elementary Forms*, written in Durkheim's twilight years, he combines the seemingly disparate themes of his "renovated rationalism" and a Freudian-like, Schopenhauer-like gloom that persists in all his writings. His 1897 essay on incest foreshadows *Elementary Forms* intimately; both works begin with the startling claim that society is essentially a system of representations that take on a life or "will" of their own. These representations exert "constraint" on individuals. Society is possible only at the cost of pain caused to the individual by the collective representations. Both Durkheim and Freud posited violent antagonisms that result from the dualism of human nature, and both were obsessed with compulsions and constraints. One is tempted to say that Durkheim's assertions, above, are like echoes of Freud's trilogy on society and religion: *Totem and Taboo* (1913), *Civilization and Its Discontents* (1930), and *The Future of an Illusion* (1927). But one is tempted in this direction only because Freud's melancholy pronouncements on culture are better known and more freely admitted than Durkheim's. Durkheim's Freudian-like ideas concerning religion appeared before Freud's works. Durkheim's neglected essay "Incest: The Nature and Origin of the Taboo" (1897), was widely regarded as a kind of first draft for his *Elementary Forms* (1912). Both were cited by Freud in *Totem and Taboo*, as well as other articles by Durkheim and his followers on related topics such as magic and sacrifice. Durkheim died in 1917, and Freud's other two famous works on society and religion appeared in 1927 and 1930. Freud's enigmatic pronouncements on human culture could well be regarded as refractions of Durkheim's thought. Yet Freud and Durkheim were both writing in the tradition that Schopenhauer had established. This is freely admitted for Freud, and needs to be acknowledged with regard to Durkheim's conception of religion.

Bringing Freud into this discussion, and especially comparing *Totem and Taboo* with *Elementary Forms* and its 1897 precursor, serves to highlight Schopenhauer's influence on Durkheim's thought. Freud's psychoanalysis is difficult to wed to any existing modern social science, because it breaks through the categorical barriers these professions have erected. Freud intended that psychoanalyis comment on most studies of culture. In his autobiographical study, he referred to himself primarily as a student of culture. But Durkheim had made a similar claim for sociology as he understood it in 1897, many years before Freud, in his first preface to *L'Année sociologique*. Freud cited this and subsequent issues of *L'Année sociologique*, the only sociological journal at the time. Freud thought of himself as a scientist, but continues to be attacked for being nonscientific primarily because most of his assertions are alleged not to be "empirically verifiable" (Fisher and Greenberg 1977). The same charge continues to be made about Durkheim. But this only reinforces the point that Freud's and Durkheim's epistemologies, which are both indebted to Schopenhauer's reconciliation of objectivism and subjectivism, are radically different from the epistemologies that inform contemporary social sciences and contribute to their crises.

Both Freud and Durkheim continue to be misunderstood and attacked with regard to their pronouncements on religion. Freud's authoritative biographer, Ernest Jones (1981), notes that Freud considered *Totem and Taboo* to be his greatest work, superior even to his cherished *Interpretation of Dreams,* and that he was bitterly disappointed at its poor reception. Similarly, Durkheim regarded *Elementary Forms* as his crowning achievement, but it was and continues to be his most criticized work. Both works are misunderstood because they are usually read from the vantage point of one or the other pole of the object-subject debate, which both thinkers tried to transcend. We shall begin with the radically new epistemology that is the basis of both classics, and reread them in relation to that epistemology. We shall lead to the point that, as Henri Durkheim put it, morality was Durkheim's religion. For Durkheim, one is left with religion as soon as the sacred is distinguished from the profane. Totemism, Christianity, "the cult of the individual," as well as many other phenomena not usually considered to be religion by contemporary sociologists, are considered by Durkheim to be religious phenomena. To put it another way, *Elementary Forms* is really a sequel to Schopenhauer's *World as Will and Idea,* because both works focus on the origin, nature, and consequences of various phenomena that are derived from the will, among them, the ideas of force, cause, God, and society.

Epistemological Parallels Between Freud and Durkheim

Consider the broad outlines of Freud's *Totem and Taboo* in relation to Durkheim's comments on the same phenomena. In the prefatory remarks, Freud cites the influence upon his thinking of Wilhelm Wundt's *Volkerpsychologie* and of Jung. Durkheim ([1912] 1969) reviewed *Volkerpsychologie* and studied under Wundt from 1885 to 1886. Lucien Levy-Bruhl, an intimate friend of both Durkheim and Jung (according to Levy-Bruhl's granddaughter), may have cross-fertilized several schools in Europe at the time. The influence of Levy-Bruhl may explain the coincidence that Jung was fond of using the Durkheimian concept of "collective conscience," while Durkheim used the Jungian concept of the "collective unconscious." Wundt was among the first to break away from the Kantian object-subject distinction with his focus on the objective study of "ideas"—hence, the Durkheimian focus on representations and the Freudian equivalent of Vorstellung. Wundt (1907) was among the first to cite the need to establish morality on a scientific basis; this no doubt was one influence among many on Durkheim's "science of moral facts" as well as on

Freud's excursions into morality. (It would be interesting to pursue Wundt's other influences on Freud and Durkheim.) The point is that Wundt was the father of what have emerged as the disciplines of contemporary psychology and sociology, that he influenced both Freud and Durkheim, and that his epistemology focused on the scientific study of "ideas," not material objects or subjective experiences. And Wundt, too, was influenced by Schopenhauer (Ellenberger 1970).

The Jungian dimensions of Freud's work also reverberate in Durkheim's thought. The seemingly Jungian idea that representations are plastic, malleable, and subject to "free association" had been made by Durkheim in his 1897 essay on incest. Durkheim had argued that the representation of "sacredness" could attach itself synthetically to *any* idea or object. For example, he traces back the horror of blood to the idea that blood stands for the life-force (will) of the ancestor of the tribe. Blood is sacred and taboo, and anything that comes in contact with it is made taboo. The other idea typically attributed to Jung, that many primitive representations persist in modern times, is also Durkheimian. Durkheim had argued on several occasions early in his career that representations are never totally obliterated. Rather, they combine and associate with other representations to form new myths, legends, and folklore. Freud, Jung, and Durkheim took the extreme position that nothing from the past, collective or individual, is ever lost, even though it is reconstructed in the process of retrieval.

This Schopenhauerian understanding of representations—commonplace in Freud's and Durkheim's time—is the key to understanding what was unique in Freud's and Durkheim's treatment of religion, and why they continue to be misunderstood. Society is a system of collective representations that are fundamentally different from the ideas of its individual members. But these representations become partially autonomous realities with their own will. Thus, they become divorced from the subjective experiences of individuals *and* from the social structure. We have here an epistemological move radically different from the idealism and subjectivism typified in Max Weber's writings and in the social determinism of Marx, for example. Like Durkheim, Freud treats the human agent's *and* society's ideas as if they had a life of their own, as if they were agents within the agent, and, independent of the agent, capable of attracting, repelling, and affecting each other. Thus Durkheim ([1924] 1974, p. 31) writes in *Sociology and Philosophy:*

[Collective representations] have the power to attract and repel each other and to form amongst themselves various syntheses, which are determined by their natural affinities and not by the condition of their matrix. . . . They are immediately caused by other collective representations and not by this or that characteristic of the social structure. The evolution of religion provides us with the most striking examples of this phenomenon . . . the luxuriant growth of myths and legends, theogonic and cosmological systems, etc., which grow out of religious thought, is not directly related to the particular features of the social morphology. Thus it is that the social nature of religion has been so often misunderstood.

Undoubtedly, Durkheim's conceptualization bears a striking resemblance to the psychoanalytic notion of the "free" association of ideas. More important, both Durkheim and Freud applied this conceptualization of "free" association to societies as well as to individuals. Thus, both attempted to correct what they perceived to be the misunderstanding of religion as either the outcome of some sort of individual agency (the need for meaning or the result of other needs and motives) *or* the determined outcome of social structure. Consistent with Durkheim's epistemological position of renovated rationalism, they treat the ideas of religion as the fantastic, independent outcome of a basic number of representations created in the past. Neither the individual's motives nor the social structure is essential to the symbolism that religion creates. In a sense, religion creates itself; it has a will of its own. This is the new philosophical idea Durkheim and Freud tried to introduce into the social scentific study of religion. It has yet to be acknowledged in this form.

For the purposes of this analysis, the reader should focus on representations Freud and Durkheim thought were basic to religion, the gulf between the sacred and the profane, and follow the synthetic attachment of these ideas to other ideas. The fundamental philosophical idea that binds the analyses of Freud and Durkheim is exemplified by a crucial explanatory passage from Durkheim's essay on incest ([1897] 1963, p. 114): "One cannot repeat too often that everything which is social consists of representations, and therefore is a result of representations. However, this act of becoming a collective image, which is the very essence of sociology, does not consist of a progressive realization of certain fundamental ideas. These fundamental ideas, at first obscured and veiled by adventitious beliefs, *gradually liberate themselves and become more and more completely independent"* (emphasis added). Durkheim repeated this Schopenhauerian idea years later in the opening pages of *Elementary Forms* ([1912] 1965, p. 231), claiming that "social life, in all its aspects and in every period of its history, is made possible only by a vast symbolism" that includes all kinds of "representations." To ignore these powerful claims is to miss the entire point of Durkheim's sociology of religion and how it influenced

Freud. Our purpose here is to expose the ways in which Durkheim and Freud elaborated upon this crucial, enigmatic, and philosophically novel move.

It follows that these liberated, independent, social representations exert constraint upon and compel the agent to think and behave in seemingly bizarre and irrational ways. Neither individual agency nor the social structure has any relation to any compulsion. The ideas have created themselves, but they carry a coercive power. In the preface to *Totem and Taboo*, Freud likens the idea of taboos to Kant's categorical imperative, but adds that unlike Kant's imperative, social compulsions can be wholly or partially unconscious. Similarly, Durkheim's introduction to *Division of Labor* (1893) begins with a critique and elaboration of Kant's categorical imperative relative to social constraints. The important point here is that Freud's concept of "compulsion" bears an uncanny resemblance to Durkheim's concept of *contrainte*. For both thinkers, these compulsions and constraints are unconscious; they disregard the human agent's wishes, and they are independent of the social structure. Indeed, all of Freud's major moves in *Totem and Taboo* seem to have been anticipated by Durkheim.

Durkheim's Essay on Incest Reexamined

Durkheim's essay "Incest: The Nature and Origin of the Taboo" was the first essay published in the first issue of the celebrated journal he founded in 1897, *L'Année sociologique*. Pickering (1984) suggested that it foreshadowed Durkheim's *Elementary Forms,* but Pickering does not address Durkheim's epistemology. We shall analyze the ways in which Durkheim's epistemology in his 1897 essay foreshadowed *Elementary Forms* and *Totem and Taboo*, even, indeed, many of the key ideas of psychoanalysis. The chief similarity lies in the analysis of the origin and behavior of representations essential to religion. This linkage, in turn, forces one to reevaluate the contemporary appraisal of Durkheim's sociology of religion.

Let us put ourselves in Freud's place when he read Durkheim's 1897 essay on incest. What would have struck the future father of psychoanalysis—who was also familiar with Schopenhauer's works—with the most intensity? The kernel of Durkheim's argument is this: society may be conceptualized as a system of ideas that exists primarily in the minds of its members who institutionalize them, albeit unconsciously. These institutions, in turn, force and compel society's members into behavior *and* other ideas, the motives for which they are unable to give a rational and intentional account. The essay that Freud read is an analysis of the origins of the very ideas of force, compulsion, constraint, and their attendant vocabulary—in a word, of the will. Some of these compulsions and constraints are irrational, disgusting, and otherwise destructive or disturbing—collectively neurotic, Freud might have said—but they persist nevertheless. Their persistence is so strong that many modern irrationalities and neuroses may be traced to primitive irrationalities and neuroses. These ideas and connections are not obvious, but are "obscured and veiled." The sociologist, like the psychoanalyst, must tear away the veils. Freud was also probably struck by Durkheim's focus on the themes of blood, sexuality, and religion, and the way he combined these themes. These turned out to be central themes of *Totem and Taboo* as well, albeit in a somewhat refracted version of Durkheim's argument.

Durkheim argues that the totem is perceived as the original ancestor of the group. Since its life force resides in blood, "all blood is terrible and all sorts of taboos are instituted to prevent contact with it" ([1897] 1963, p. 83). In other words, blood is sacred, and one reacts to it by separating it from the vulgar, pedestrian and, in a word, the profane. Thus, "the taboo is none other than this abstention, organized and elevated to the height of an institution" (p. 96). Durkheim does not delve into the origins of the reasons why the ancestor's blood had been spilled in the first place—Freud did that, with his emphasis on the killing of the primal father—but he leaves no doubt that the collective representation of blood is "charged," so to speak, with some sort of mysterious energy.

According to Durkheim, "the blood is taboo in a general way, and it taboos all that enters into contact with it. . . . Thus the woman, in a rather chronic manner, is the theater of these bloody demonstrations" (p. 85). Women are associated with blood during the burst of puberty, menstruation, the sexual act, and childbirth. Thus, during these phases in a female's life, women are taboo, and they are removed from contact with social life, often cruelly and irrationally. The abstention associated with women and blood is an extension of the general taboo associated with blood as the life-force of the group (p. 90): "The religious respect that blood inspires proscribes any idea of contact, and, since the woman, so to speak, passes a part of her life in blood, this same feeling involves her, marks her with its imprint, and isolates her."

In other words, these collective representations associated with blood are subject to "contagion," "diffusion," and "dispersion"; they "permeate" and "associate" themselves synthetically with other representations. Human agents do not diffuse these ideas, nor are these ideas the result of any sort of political, geographical, or social structure. Rather, the ideas beget other ideas. It must have been easy for Freud to characterize this phenomenon as a kind of collective free association of ideas, ideas that "bind" themselves to other ideas. This is the way Durkheim explains the war between the sexes, the "mystery" that women hold for men, the separate languages that men and women speak even though the masculine language typically dominates. The separation of the sexes is not only intermittent but becomes chronic: "Each part of the population lives separated from the other" (p. 77).

Durkheim (p. 113) is explicit in linking this separation of the sexes to the representation of blood:

> In all probability, one must say that, if in our schools, in our daily meetings, a sort of barrier exists between the two sexes; if each of them has a determined form of clothing imposed by habit or even by law; if the male has functions which are forbidden to the female, even though she might be well suited to fulfill them, and if the reciprocal is true; if, in our daily relationships with women, the men have adopted a special language, special mannerisms, etc., this is in part due to the fact that, some thousands of years ago, our fathers structured the reality of blood in general, and menstrual blood in particular, in the manner that we have suggested.

The sexual act itself, because it often involves blood, becomes dangerous, and requires institutional transformations to render it harmless. This is the origin of the institution of marriage, which Durkheim claims still bears the imprint of its religious, sacred character. The sexual act profanes the sacred, which the institution of marriage makes sacred again. In general, the psychological distinction between the sexes is something like religion: "The two sexes must avoid each other with the same care as the profane flees from the sacred, and the sacred from the profane; and any infraction of this rule invokes a feeling of horror which does not differ in its nature from that which confronts the person who violates a taboo" (p. 72).

Durkheim seems to have preceded Freud in positing a fundamental opposition between sexuality and "civilization," which he referred to as "the eternal antithesis between passion and duty" (p. 112). Sexuality is dangerous and profane; it constantly threatens the family and society. Although Durkheim does not use the term "sublimation," he posited that with the development of humanity, sexuality eventually mingles with social aims: "With time . . . the ideas pertaining to the sexual life became rigorously linked with the development of art, of poetry, and to all the vague dreams and aspirations of the spirit and of the heart, to all the individual or collective manifestations where the imagination plays the largest part" (p. 110). Again, note that Durkheim does not ascribe any human agency to this linkage. Freud had plenty of time to ruminate over such claims until he could offer his own version in 1905 in his *Three Essays on Sexuality*.

This line of reasoning leads Durkheim into the most controversial aspect of his theory, namely, the origins of religion. Society establishes the incest taboo and the rule of exogamy in order to guard against the profaning of the life-force immanent in blood. The family is the prototype of the original clan. The blood of clans and families other than one's own is *not* taboo, hence, no danger is associated with sexuality relative to *their* women. But incest is the most horrible sacrilege because it profanes the sacredness of one's family, which is but an extension of totemism. Durkheim (p. 97) wrote that "It is repugnant to us to admit that a principle of our contemporary morality [incest taboo], one of those most strongly internalized within us, can be traced to a dependence even a long time ago, on absurd prejudices from which humanity has long since freed itself [totemism]."

The import of Durkheim's theory is that the idea of taboo is "the basis of all primitive religions and even, in a sense, of all religions" (p. 70). But we have seen that Durkheim derives the idea of taboo from the phenomenon of blood and associates it especially with sexuality. It is a short leap from these ideas to Freud's killing of the father and the Oedipus Complex. The association of various phenomena with the sacred versus the profane is arbitrary and synthetic. Hence, the irrationality of religion and religious ideas. In the 1897 essay, Durkheim defines taboo as follows (p. 70): "This is the name given to the collection of ritualistic prohibitions which have as their objective to avert the dangerous effects of a magical contagion by preventing all contact between a thing or a category of things, in which a supernatural principle is believed to reside, and others who do not have this same characteristic, or do not have it to the same degree." This is a deceptively simple definition, because it presupposes Durkheim's radical distinction between religion and magic. Religion is collective, while magic is always individualistic, antireligious, and profane. If the taboo is the basis of all religions, then its function is, in part, to avert magic. Freud accepted this Durkheimian distinction, which is the basis of understanding why he regarded neuroses as *magic*, as *private* religions, but not as religion per se. Moreover, Durkheim's definition presupposes the dangerousness of unrestrained desire. These moves require careful elaboration.

Magical Versus Religious Representations

Many social scientists still confound magic with religion, and relegate both to the realm of the primitive. Actually, O'Keefe (1982) is correct in his claims that for Freud and Durkheim there is more magic in industrialized, "civilized" societies than in primitive ones—

magic is essentially a modern phenomenon. Magic develops out of religion and is essentially antisocial and antireligious. O'Keefe (p. 14) summarizes the Freudian-Durkheimian position on magic as follows: "Magic is the expropriation of religious collective representations for individual or subgroup purposes—to enable the individual ego to resist psychic extinction or the subgroup to resist cognitive collapse." O'Keefe reinterprets Freud's claim that neurosis is an attempt at secondary benefits (getting attention, obtaining subtle vengeance, and so on) by calling it "crippled magic." Indeed, in *Totem and Taboo*, Freud likens totemism to religion, but neuroses to magic. Durkheim implied something similar in his 1897 essay, but made the point more explicit in 1912.

In his *Elementary Forms of the Religious Life* Durkheim (1912) differentiates sharply between magic and religion. He cites the works of two of his disciples in this regard, Henri Hubert and Marcel Mauss's *Sacrifice* (1898) and *A General Theory of Magic* (1904). It is important to note that Freud also cites both works by Hubert and Mauss in *Totem and Taboo*. Hubert and Mauss are an important, implicit aspect of both Freud's and Durkheim's works on religion. Hubert and Mauss argue that religion is essentially social, while magic is essentially private and antisocial. Sacrifice is a religious function, but is *not* magical. Hubert and Mauss ([1898] 1964, p. 19) could hardly be more explicit: "Sacrifice is a religious act that can only be carried out in a religious atmosphere and by means of essentially religious agents." Of course, these moves are counterintuitive relative to much modern social theory. But they have important consequences for understanding Freud and Durkheim.

As O'Keefe (1982) put it, all magic is essentially "action." Magic belongs to the realm of human agency, while religion does not. In magic, individuals try to "do something" in relation to religion, which imposes *contrainte* and a passive attitude. Thus both Freud and Durkheim regard the totemic meal as a religious phenomenon. It is essentially a "compulsion to repeat" for Freud, and for Durkheim an instance of "collective effervescence" that imposes itself upon its members. When individuals try to use religion for their own aims, they engage in magic, even though magic and religion share the some collective representations. Magic is the obverse of religion in that it challenges the representations that take on a life of their. To put it another way, religion gives birth to the ideas of *contrainte*, compulsion, and prohibition, all derived from the taboo. But magic recognizes no such vocabulary of submission; it holds to a vocabulary of defiance, rebellion and action. O'Keefe (1982) believes that the very concept of the "individual," since it involve a breaking away from the group, is a magical phenomenon.

In *Elementary Forms,* Durkheim ([1912] 1965, p. 56) expands upon his 1897 essay on incest by defining religious phenomena as those that "always suppose a bipartite division of the whole universe, known and knowable, into two classes which embrace all that exists, but which radically exclude each other," the sacred and the profane. Durkheim notes, however, that: "This definition is not yet complete, for it is equally applicable to two sorts of facts which, while being related to each other, must be distinguished nevertheless: these are magic and religion" (ibid., p. 57).

Both magic and religion involve the sacred and the profane, but they are radically different. "Magic takes a sort of professional pleasure in profaning holy things," Durkheim (ibid., p. 58) writes. Magic is "anti-religious . . . the magician has a clientele and not a Church" (p. 60). Religion binds its members to each other, but individuals who consult a magician are not bound to each other into a moral community. Thus, Durkheim adds to his definition of religion (p. 62): "A religion is a unified system of beliefs and practices relative to sacred things, that is to say, things set apart and forbidden—beliefs and practices which unite into one single moral community called a Church, all those who adhere to them."

Primitive and modern totemisms may be irrational, but for Durkheim, the irrationality of religion is of a different order than the irrationality of the individual neurotic. Collective irrationality is eminently a social phenomenon that holds society together. To be precise, it not only holds society together, but forces, compels, binds and constrains individuals into a group. In fact, society, which is one representation of the sacred, demands "perpetual sacrifices" from individuals and their "natural appetites"—including sexuality (ibid., p. 356). "Society itself is possible only at this price" Durkheim adds. The conclusion of *Elementary Forms* is that the individual is always the enemy of society, and the tension that is the result of this dualism will increase, not decrease, with the growth of civilization. This conclusion was not lost on Freud, who refined and repeated it in his *Civilization and Its Discontents* (1930). It is odd that Durkheim preceded Freud in this gloomy assessment of civilization, but its origin is typically attributed to Freud and has been largely ignored with regard to Durkheim.

In essence, the distinction between religion and magic is another refraction of the object-subject distinction and the distinction between the idea and will, respectively. Religion is social, objective, and consists of representations. Magic is primarily private, subjective, and consists of the individual use of those representations. Yet, religion and magic, while distinct, are a unity. Here is still another original refraction of Schopenhauer's thesis.

This Durkheimian distinction between magic and religion is the heart of Freud's understanding of neurosis relative to society, in *Totem and Taboo* and in general. At the beginning of *Totem and Taboo* Freud points to similarities between totemism and neurosis—he even calls obsessional neurosis "taboo sickness." The similarities have to do with prohibitions against touching, the fear of contagion, and the feeling of necessity inherent in all compulsions. But there is a difference, Freud notes, and in a very Durkheimian fashion: "After all taboo is not a neurosis but a social institution" (Freud [1913] 1950, p. 71). The neuroses are attempts at magic precisely because they are antisocial. Freud continues (p. 73):

> The neuroses exhibit on the one hand striking and far-reaching points of agreement with those great social institutions, art, religion and philosophy. But on the other hand they seem like distortions of them. It might be maintained that a case of hysteria is a caricature of a work of art, that an obsessional neurosis is a caricature of a religion and that a paranoic delusion is a caricature of a philosophical system. The divergence resolves itself ultimately into the fact that the neuroses are *asocial* structures; they endeavour to achieve by *private* means what is effected in society by collective effort [emphasis added].

Freud brings in other Durkheimian observations to support this already Durkheimian assessment. Neuroses are sexual in origin, but "sexual needs are not capable of uniting men" and are instead "private" (p. 74). Durkheim had made this claim in 1897. Freud concludes on this subject (p. 74): "The asocial nature of neuroses has its genetic origin in their most fundamental purpose, which is to take flight from an unsatisfying reality into a more pleasurable world of phantasy. The real world, which is avoided in this way by neurotics, is under the sway of human society and of the institutions collectively created by it. To turn away from reality is at the same time to withdraw from the community of man."

For Freud, as for Durkheim, the essence of neurosis is not its irrationality. Its essence is the privatization of the social. Note that it is by no means obvious that "reality" has to be social. The neurotic's personal problems, his biological urges, the truth of what he is repressing, and so on, may all be regarded as "realities." For Freud, nevertheless, the "real world" seems to be the social world. Humans caricature the social as they attempt to rebel against it. Freud compares neuroses directly with magic in huge, even tedious sections of *Totem and Taboo*. Both magic and neuroses are characterized by what he calls "the omnipotence of thoughts," a belief absent in religion as he understands it. Yet he is careful to regard totemism and its irrationalities as a religion that binds individuals together—in fact, he cites Durkheim in this regard frequently, and always with approval.

Thus, Freud echoes Durkheim when he writes that "Religion in general was an affair of the community and religious duty was a part of social obligation" (p. 134).

Because this sociological, Durkheimian aspect of Freud's thought has not been widely acknowledged, we will pursue it in relation to some of his other works for it requires special emphasis. Note the Durkheimian flavor of Freud's expressions. For example, in "Obsessive Acts and Religious Practices" Freud writes: "An obsessional neurosis furnishes a tragi-comic *travesty* of a private religion. . . . In view of these resemblances and analogies one might venture to regard the obsessional neurosis as a pathological counterpart to the formation of a religion, to describe the neurosis as a *private religious system,* and religion as a universal obsessional neurosis" ([1907] 1963, p. 25, emphasis added).

The depiction of neurosis as a private religion is very much in keeping with Freud's and Durkheim's understanding of the opposition of magic to religion. Freud repeats his argument several years after the publication of *Totem and Taboo* in slightly different form: "It is impossible to escape the conclusion that these patients are, in an *asocial* fashion, making the very attempts at solving their conflicts and appeasing their pressing needs which, when they are carried out in a fashion that has binding force for the majority, go by the names of poetry, religion, and philosophy" (Freud [1919] 1963, p. 225). Two years later he recasts the argument in relation to sexuality and love in his *Group Psychology and the Analysis of the Ego* ([1921] 1959, p. 74):

A neurosis should make its victim asocial and should remove him from the usual group formations. It may be said that a neurosis has the same disintegrating effect upon a group as being in love. . . . Even those who do not regret the disappearance of religious illusions from the civilized world of today will admit that so long as they were in force they offered those who were bound by them the most powerful protection against the danger of neurosis. . . . If he is left to himself, a neurotic is obliged to replace by his own symptom formations the great group formations from which he is excluded. He creates his own world of imagination for himself, *his own religion,* his own system of delusions, and thus recapitulates the institutions of humanity in a distorted way. [emphasis added]

Note that Freud regards religion as protection against neurosis, even though he blasts both phenomena for their irrationality. This thread in his thinking is found especially in *The Future of an Illusion* and *Civilization and Its Discontents.* Having established that Freud accepted the essence of Durkheim's distinction between magic and religion, we are ready to turn to the bloody conclusion of *Totem and Taboo.*

The Killing of the Father and the Sacrifice of the Individual

The Oedipus Complex and the killing of the father emerge suddenly in the conclusion of *Totem and Taboo*. In huge chunks of the book Freud makes tendentious, truly tedious criticisms of theories of totemism and exogamy extant in his time, and then, with abrupt transitions, includes the unexpected tale of the primal murder. In addition to the other similarities between Freud and Durkheim, an extremely important final point of convergence is that both *Totem and Taboo* and *Elementary Forms* end on a note of violence. The emphasis is slightly different—Durkheim emphasizes the religious violence of society's constraint of the individual, and Freud emphasizes the magical violence of the individual lashing out against social authority—but this difference is in emphasis only. Both thinkers acknowledge that there is more to religion than binding its members together in love and solidarity. In fact, Freud liked to repeat the sarcastic observation that religion can bind persons in love only if there are other religions or individuals left over to hate.

Durkheim lays great emphasis on female sexuality and its relationship to totemic blood. In a sense, Freud simply complements Durkheim's study by focusing on male sexuality and its relationship to the totemic sacrifice. This he achieves by noting that in fantasies and dreams, children often substitute "the father for the totem animal in the formula for totemism (in the case of males)" ([1913] 1950, p. 131). Freud had been building up to this step with his analyses of "Little Hans," "The Wolf Man," and other famous cases. Freud's move is as straightforward as Durkheim's, in that both thinkers assume the plasticity of collective representations and their synthetic adhesiveness to other representations. The difference is merely one of emphasis. Women are involved in the "theater of blood" relative to their bodies, for the most part, and men become involved in a different theater of blood, the Oedipus Complex and its bloody violence.

Assuming that the prohibitions relative to the Oedipus Complex and animal phobias in boys are remnants of some ancient explosion of representations, Freud declares that "If the totem animal is the father, then the two principal ordinances of totemism, the two taboo prohibitions which constitute its core—not to kill the totem and not to have sexual relations with a woman of the same totem—coincide in their content with the two crimes of Oedipus, who killed his father and married his mother, as well as with the two primal wishes of [male] children" (ibid., p. 132).

But these prohibitions would not have been established, according to Freud, without the existence of wishes to kill and to engage in lust, in the present and in the primal past. The killing of the father is the action-oriented, magical act of human agency in relation to the prohibitions established by the father. The prohibitions occurred prior to the wishes, along the lines of O'Keefe's insistence that religion precedes magic. After the killing, the totem meal was established, and religion was strengthened, not weakened. This is one way to interpret Freud's brief claim that: "The totem meal, which is perhaps mankind's earliest festival, would thus be a repetition and a commemoration of this memorable and criminal deed, which was the beginning of so many things—of social organization, of moral restrictions and of religion" (p. 142). It is a shame that Freud does not elaborate on this link between the primal crime and the three important phenomena it allegedly produced. (Ernest Jones, 1981, also regrets Freud's failure to develop these thoughts.) Nevertheless, in our reconstruction of Freud's Durkheimian leanings, several aspects of the conclusion of *Totem and Taboo* require special emphasis.

The most important contextual observation is that the framework for Freud's move, above, may be found in Hubert and Mauss's *Sacrifice* (1898). They cite Frazer and hosts of anthropologists to the effect that in many primitive societies, the chief or king is murdered before he reaches old age so that his magical power will be transferred to the murderer. Durkheim touched upon this in his 1897 *Suicide,* when discussing altruistic suicide as a form of sacrifice. Hubert and Mauss observed that "it was often the founder of a cult or the chief priest of the god whose death was related in the myth" that the sacrifice commemorates ([1898] 1964, p. 84). They added: "From this it follows that the sacrifice appears to be a repetition and a commemoration of the original sacrifice of the god" (p. 89). (One wonders, again, to what extent Freud derived his notion of the "compulsion to repeat" from the Durkheimians.) Hubert and Mauss do not trace the original sacrifice back to the primal magical act of murder, at least not as explicitly as Freud does, because that was not their concern in their essay. Freud seems to have simply clarified and followed up the distinction between magic and religion that the Durkheimians began.

Like Hubert and Mauss (1898), Freud insists that the totem meal is a religious, not a magical phenomenon. Freud uses evidence from ethnographies, the Bible, and plays to support his contention. This is probably because he wanted to show that "civilized" people subscribe to myths similar to the ones described by Frazer in *The Golden Bough* (1890). In essence, he regards the dramas of human sacrifice and various Oedipal stories in literature as representations of the original crime, again manifesting his basic Durkheimian belief that representations never die and that they transform themselves. Thus his claim that "the sense of guilt for an action has persisted for many thousands of years and has remained operative in generations which can have had no knowledge of that action" (Freud [1913] 1950, p. 158). Freud's fascination with the various permutations of the father-animal connection as representations is understandable. In various cultures at various periods of history gods are depicted as owning animals, being animals, transforming themselves into animals, being worshipped in the form of animals, and so on—but the animals are sacrificed. The sacrifice is always religious and never magical for Freud, an idea he apparently derived from Hubert and Mauss (1898). Essentially, the sacrifice and resultant totemic meals are collective versions of the individual, magical crime. Thus, religion, which is collective, always "wins" and magic always fails. This is true despite the fact that, in order to "win," religion often absorbs magic (O'Keefe 1982).

At long last one arrives at the essential point of agreement between Freud and Durkheim. It is that beneath the appearance of ancient and modern sacrifices and totemic meals, it is really the individual (considered as the "lower" pole of *homo duplex)* that is being sacrificed to society. Both *Elementary Forms* and *Totem and Taboo* end on the note of the individual's failure to rebel against society. Durkheim's "cult of the individual," what Giddens (1986) calls "moral individualism," is a religious phenomenon that pertain's to the "higher" pole of *homo duplex.* Even so, narcissistic aims must be sacrificed to and contained by this collective indvidualism, this new religion of the future. Secular morality is a refraction of religious morality and its battles with magic; hence, Durkheim's gloomy conclusion concerning civilization and its discontents in 1912 *Elementary Forms* which Freud rephrased in 1930. The logic leading to this conclusion is now clear. If collective representations have a life of their own and exert constraint, then the narcissistic individual is essentially helpless against them. Were it possible for him to rebel against this constraint and get away with it, society and religion would be impossible. This very feeling of helplessness has been institutionalized into a religious feeling, because religion is an affirmation of the superiority of these collective representations (Freud 1927).

Now it is also clear why these two works on religion have been attacked so bitterly, even though their arguments have been obscured and misunderstood. Adherents of either side of the object-subject debate acknowledge the possibility of human action in changing society. For example, Marxists hope to change society by changing the social structure, while pragmatists hope to create society anew through daily interaction. But Freud and Durkheim deny the possibility that individuals can change society. Essentially, they apply Old Testament sentiments concerning submission to modern societies, arguing that life will become more, not less, painful in the future. A gloomy assessment indeed, but one that reflects Schopenhauer's philosophy intimately.

Implications

It is evident that Freud and Durkheim treat religion as a vehicle for a much broader discussion of social issues, not as a topic of interest per se. Consider some of the phenomena they invoke in their discussion: representations, language, the war between the sexes, animal imagery, magic, totemism, psychological and social responses to blood, neuroses, and so on. The application of their insights concerning any of these phenomena, alone or in combination, to contemporary problems in religion, or to the study of social problems in general, would yield volumes. Consider as illustration only the theoretical significance of what might be called Durkheim's sociology of blood. Millions of persons in the Third World still hold to the notion of blood as the primary source of strength and magical power, and its loss as a source of evil. Third World willingness to undergo blood transfusions, taboos concerning menstruation and bleeding, and many other interesting, important medical phenomena are easily explained by Durkheim's theory. The application of this theory could solve some pressing practical problems in Third World medicine. But the truly distinctive aspect of Freud's and Durkheim's treatment of religion lies in their use of the philosophical concept of representations in the context of their independence from the Kantian categories.

Freud and Durkheim applied a novel philosophical move to the problem of religion: the idea that representations are never wholly lost and that they take on a life of their own apart from the human agents who perceive them and the social structure that is their context. It is a move that has enormous consequences for what have come to be known as the sociology and psychology of knowledge, for the object-subject debate—indeed, for the very modern distinction between sociology and psychology. Thus efforts have been made to read Durkheim as a kind of Weberian *and* Marxist, idealist *and* realist. No one can be faulted for reading Freud and Durkheim as he wishes; but, in not reading them as disciples of Schopenhauer, who wanted to transcend the object-subject debate, one perpetuates the current crises in the social sciences that derive from this debate.

Contemporary sociology is beset by epistemological crises that stem from the object-subject debate. "Objectivists"—the structuralists, functionalists, and Marxists—tend to regard society as the central focus of study and as existing prior to the individual. Their basic credo is that if one can change the social structure, one will immediately alter human nature. "Subjectivists"—the symbolic interactionists, Weberians, and phenomenologists—tend to regard society as the outcome of human agency and focus upon the human agent's intentions and reasons for behavior. A host of other theories fall somewhere between these two extremes, but none has transcended the dualism. In fact, the distinction between sociology and psychology is part of this controversy, creating a crisis within a crisis. Sociology tends to be "objectivist," which means that "subjectivism" is seen by some as a relapse into psychology, which subjectivists regard as the only true kind of sociology. Anyone who has taught an introductory course in sociology or psychology has experienced the embarrassed silence that is inevitable when one tries to explain this chaos to neophytes.

Freud and Durkheim consciously and deliberately attempted to transcend the object-subject debate, as did Wundt, their mutual mentor. Wundt's *Volkerpsychologie*, translated into English as social psychology, in reality, recognized the infinite possibilities of representations lying between the individual and the collective. For Wundt, the distinction between sociology and psychology was merely one of choosing which type of representation one chose to study and how one studied it. The notion of a representation is partly objective, partly subjective. It is an "idea," and thus subjective: it holds meaning for individual human agents. But, as Durkheim especially liked to argue, it is also a "thing," as real as any material "stuff." Thus, the traditional object-subject explanations do not apply to representations. They straddle the distinctions and dualisms that have become part of social scientific discourse. It is worth repeating that this unusual stand on the object-subject distinction is what makes Schopenhauer's philosophy distinctive.

Both Freud and Durkheim criticized Marx, the most powerful proponent of the objectivist view in their time, and ignored Weber, the strongest advocate of idealism. They both argued that, contra Marx, if one changes the economic order into any "ism" of one's choosing, one will not eliminate human greed nor other human passions. Their concern with "ideas" was un-Weberian in that they understood these "ideas" as being subject to self-governed alterations, transformations, and vicissitudes. Freud and Durkheim did not adhere to the sharp distinctions between sociology and psychology, which exist today. This is evident especially in Durkheim's *Sociology and Philosophy* (1924) and Freud's *New Introductory Lectures to Psychoanalysis* (1933).

Freud's and Durkheim's epistemology denies the widely held belief among social scientists that individual religious beliefs and behavior can be changed by changing the social structure. For them, the ideas of sacred and profane will attach themselves synthetically to other ideas on their own accord, regardless of what happens to the social structure. These ideas seem to become mutations of the original, and at times very bizarre. The war between the sexes, which is a manifestation of the sacred-profane dichotomy, has survived centuries of revolutions, cultural upheavals, migrations, and other massive social changes across the globe. Various social theories have examined the social position of women in relation to social structure, even as the deliberate outcome of male chauvinism, but few have examined sexuality as a representation that persists regardless of structure or human agency. Freud and Durkheim point out the religiosity of phenomena that one is not used to regarding as religious.

In addition to the phenomena already discussed, Durkheimian disciple Robert Hertz's (1907–1909) study of the right-left dichotomy is an excellent illustration of this trend toward "ideas" and their vicissitudes. The right represents the sacred, while the left represents the profane. This is evident from language (words having to do with the left usually imply something sinister), habits such as greeting and making oaths with the right hand, political symbolism, the fact that women are associated with the left and men with the right, and so on. If Freud and Durkheim are correct, then the left-right dichotomy should persist in diverse cultural settings regardless of social structure. This would be an interesting hypothesis to investigate, yet Hertz's essay remains extremely obscure, as does the Durkheimian theory that informs it.

The list of other representations that Durkheim and the Durkheimians, Freud and Freudians treat as sacred or profane is virtually endless. This is because the idea of sacredness latches onto other phenomena and alters them. Thus Durkheim explains the modern religious respect for the individual, which was unknown in primitive societies; the sacred aura of schools, which were first organized by the Church; the sacrosanct quality of truth, which is degraded by pragmatism, and so on. The social structure does not cause these fantastic permutations of ideas, at least not according to Durkheim.

Without a doubt, Freud and Durkheim also deny the opposite possibility, that the human agent can change society at will and that his behavior should be understood as being primarily purposive, intentional, and rational. The fact that Freud and Durkheim believed in the unconscious, alone negates this possibility. Humans can never account for the full extent of their desires and intentions. All that is truly allowed to the human agent is the possibility of consciousness of his plight. As Durkheim put it: "To be autonomous means, for the human being, to understand the necessities he has to bow to and accept them with full knowledge of the facts. Nothing that we do can make the laws of things other than they are, but we free ourselves of them in thinking them, that is, in making them ours by thought" (Durkheim [1950] 1983, p. 91). Similarly, Freud denied the possibility that neurotics can be cured in any complete sense and offered only the hope that they can become more fully conscious of their compulsions. Again, it may be more than a remarkable coincidence that Freud echoes Durkheim so consistently.

Ultimately, Freud and Durkheim arrive at the conclusion that religion is highly impractical. Its very function is to teach submission, not the possibility of action. A similar conclusion, that the essence of religion is piety and submission, has been the conclusion of artists, theologians, and other thinkers, among them Schleiermacher, Hesse, Kierkegaard, James, Kant, and Augustine. Granted, Freud and Durkheim took a circuitous path to this end, starting with totemism, but for both, the communal totemic meal is victory over independent, individualistic magical action. For them, religion is a collective phenomenon that has to do with the division of everything into sacred and profane representations, which have the power to attach themselves synthetically to other phenomena. These representations make themselves known to humans through the power of constraint and compulsion. Religion is opposed by magic, which is the expropriation of religious representations for individual purposes. Religion and magic are involved in a continual dialectic. Secular morality has not escaped the shadow of this dialectic.

CHAPTER 7

Rethinking Social Integration

IN THEIR INTERPRETATION of Durkheim's theory of suicide, Gibbs and Martin (1964) have maintained that suicide is inversely related to social integration. While it is not clear what they mean by integration, nor that it is the same as what Durkheim meant, it is clear that social integration has something to do with social contacts, resources, and supports. There seems to be something intuitively correct, at least at first glance, about the proposition that the more social integration one has, in this ambiguous sense of social contacts, the better one's mental health will be, the less likely one will be to commit suicide, and in general, the more adjusted one will be. Douglas (1967) had exposed the ambiguity in the concept of social integration, whose meanings range from attachment to a group to properties of groups, but his study has had no appreciable effect upon the use of this concept by sociologists. The idea that social contacts and attachments are an unqualified good, and always beneficial, seems to be firmly rooted in contemporary sociology. Moreover, it is an idea frequently buttressed by citing Durkheim.

But upon closer inspection, this turns out to be a popular misinterpretation of Durkheim's theory. Given that Durkheim's thought was informed in large measure by Schopenhauer's pessimistic philosophy, it is inconceivable that Durkheim would hold that all social attachments and varieties of social integration are beneficial. Moreover, everyone knows from bitter experience that some social interaction can be sources of hurt, disappointment, humiliation, and other negative results. Nevertheless, the optimistic proposition that social support and integration are always beneficial and act as a prophylactic against social and personal problems is frequently invoked with regard to Durkheim. Gibbs and Martin (ibid.) and many others theorists who invoke this proposition claim that Durkheim

117

made it in one fashion or another. Actually, Durkheim consistently held that social contacts are an aggravating factor in suicide.

True, Durkheim ([1897] 1951, p. 209) did write that "suicide varies inversely with the degree of integration of the social groups of which the individual forms a part." But he appears to have been using the concept of integration to refer to a property *of* groups, not the attachment of individuals *to* groups. Suppose for the sake of argument, that Durkheim did intend "integration" to refer to social ties. That would still leave conceptual difficulties. Contemporary sociologists focus on the proposition that suicide varies inversely with integration, and ignore Durkheim's claims that it can also be caused by excessive integration, as in altruistic suicide. Suppose one drops the term "integration" from such discussions because of this problem. That still leaves the fact that Durkheim argued that other versions of social ties, contacts, and "supports" can be pathogenic. For example, he showed that women were shielded from suicide precisely because they participated less than men in society: "If women kill themselves much less than men, it is because they are much less involved than men in collective existence; thus they feel its influence—good or evil—less strongly" ([1897] 1951, p. 299). Furthermore, Durkheim argues that the aged have higher suicide rates than children because the aged have had longer exposure to society, and that suicide rates increase with the lengthening of the day during spring and summer months because longer days enable greater exposure to social interaction. Durkheim goes so far as to claim that "the immunity of an animal has the same causes," namely, the impossibility of human society to penetrate too deeply into animal consciousness (ibid., p. 215).

Durkheim foreshadowed current findings that suicide rates among children and teenagers in "civilized" cultures are increasing (although their rates are still less than those of retired males), but he offers a "total" explanation. Contemporary attempts at explaining youth suicide, among laypersons and professionals alike, assume that the suicide of young people is a unique phenomenon relative to suicide in general. Durkheim implies that any person, young or old, is more likely to kill herself if overexposed—overly integrated in the sense implied by Gibbs and Martin—to a pathogenic society. One should keep in mind that little boys kill themselves more than little girls, and that in general, the suicide patterns of the young reflect overall suicide patterns: suicide among the young is still a predominantly Protestant, urban, affluent, "hyper-civilized" phenomenon. Durkheim writes (ibid., p. 100):

> It must be remembered that the child too is influenced by social causes which may drive him to suicide. Even in this case their influence appears

in the variations of child-suicide according to social environment. They are most numerous in large cities. *Nowhere else does social life commence so early for the child, as is shown by the precocity of the little city-dweller.* Introduced earlier and more completely than others to the current of civilization, he undergoes its effects more completely and earlier. This also causes the number of child-suicides to grow with pitiful regularity in civilized lands. [emphasis added]

Durkheim implies that the "will" of children in modern societies is subjected to the "infinity of desires" earlier than it used to be in traditional societies. But in this as in other cases, social contracts, *not* some alleged lack of social attachment to groups, contribute to suicide. If anything, *social integration is the culprit!*

Those sociologists who wish to maintain the unequivocally benign nature of social integration will no doubt continue to maintain that position. My concern in this chapter is to disengage Durkheim's theory from that position. Durkheim is invoked as a "social support" for this overly optimistic view, despite the fact that his view of civilization and contacts with civilization is profoundly pessimistic. In the remainder of this chapter, I will focus on Durkheim's treatment of the effect of "cosmic factors" upon suicide rates in order to elaborate upon his pessimistic view of the effects of social integration.

Essentially, Durkheim distinguishes sharply between two aspects of social integration, social contacts versus social bonds. The former increase as civilization develops, while the latter decline. Thus, modern man is ripped apart by two antagonistic forces. This dualistic understanding of social integration in Durkheim's thought has been completely missed by his contemporary commentators, yet it is what sets Durkheim's evolutionary scheme apart from other evolutionary theories of society.

The Distinction Between Social Bonds and Social Contacts

In general, in Book 1, Chapter 3, of *Suicide* Durkheim interprets a finding that is still true: "Neither in winter nor in autumn does suicide reach its maximum, but during the fine season when nature is most smiling and the temperature mildest. Man prefers to abandon life when it is least difficult" (ibid., p. 107). In fact, "the seasons come in the following order: summer, spring, autumn, winter" (p. 108). Durkheim also notices that most suicide occurs during the daytime hours, not the night, and combines this finding with the one concerning the seasons. Simply put, the days are longer in spring and summer than winter and autumn.

Durkheim interprets this finding as follows: "Day favors suicide because this is the time of most active existence, when human relations cross and recross, when social life is most intense" (p. 117). There can be no doubt that Durkheim is claiming the very opposite of the received view of the beneficial effects of "integration." Consider some of Durkheim's other statements from this chapter in this regard:

> Thus everything proves that if daytime is the part of the twenty-four hours most favorable to suicide, it is because it is also the time when social life is at its height. Then we have a reason why the number of suicides increases, the longer the sun remains above the horizon. The mere lengthening of the days seems to offer wider latitude to collective life. [p. 119]

> If voluntary deaths increase from January to July, it is not because heat disturbs the organism but because social life is more intense. . . . Of course, we are yet uncertain how collective life can have this effect. But it already appears that if it contains the causes of the variation of the suicide-rate, the latter must increase or decrease as social life becomes more or less active. To determine these causes more exactly will be the purpose of the following book. [p. 122]

In a way, it is a pity that Durkheim does not tip his hand at this point and tell the reader why active social life should be a contributing cause of suicide. The rest of the book is so complex that his answer to this problem has been and continues to be misunderstood. Furthermore, Durkheim's followers had to explain Durkheim's answer in several sequels (Halbwachs [1930] 1978; Mauss [1950] 1979b), because Durkheim's answer is not as clear as it could have been. Durkheim seems to assume that the reader has already filled in many of the steps that he glosses over. I shall make them explicit.

Based upon my reading of Mauss's and Halbwachs's sequels to Durkheim's *Suicide,* I believe that the following is an apt summary of Durkheim's argument concerning the relationship of social integration to suicide:

1. Urban suicide is a fundamentally different phenomenon from rural suicide.
2. Urban life is characterized, in general, by a quantitatively high degree of social contacts but a qualitatively low degree of social bonds.
3. This urban condition of high contacts and low bonds is exacerbated by the lengthening of the day and the seasons of the year; for example, summertime in urban areas is characterized by a high degree of social contact but a low degree of social bonds.

4. Social contacts are generally a source of stress because they multiply the chances for hurt, disappointment, humiliation, and the like, while social bonds can offset this trend. Thus, a condition of high contacts but low bonds is most suicidogenetic.

5. Social bonds are a prophylactic against suicide because they contain human egoism. According to Schopenhauer's philosophy, human egoism is the cause of most social problems.

6. The situation in rural areas is fundamentally different, yet unexplored by the Durkheimans. Thus, rural areas are characterized by low contacts but high bonds; this condition is exacerbated in the winter, because summer is the time for harvest. Thus, suicide is primarily an urban phenomenon, and when it does occur in rural areas, it will follow different social laws from urban areas.

Because I examine Mauss's and Halbwachs's own explication of the above points, it is worth noting that Durkheim, indeed, seems to assume all of the preceding points, but does so with seemingly lightning speed. For example, he cites the receipts for railroad travel in France in his day to illustrate that summer was the "peak season" for travel in his time, and explains: "City life itself is more active during the fine seasons. Communications being easier then, people travel more readily and inter-social relations increase. . . . During this same year, 1887, the number of passengers traveling from one point in Paris to another regularly increased from January (655, 791) to June (848, 831), then decreased as steadily to December (659, 960)" (ibid., p. 120). Another indicator that Durkheim cites is the accident rate in Italy according to the seasons of the year. He shows that accidents are most common in the summer and assumes that this is because of "the increase of social activity during the Summer" (ibid.).

Durkheim does claim that "the forces impelling the farm laborer and the cultivated man of the city to suicide are widely different" (p. 151). He had already made a similar claim in his *Division of Labor in Society* several years earlier: "Civilization is concentrated in the great cities, suicide likewise" ([1893] 1933, p. 247). Durkheim seems to be applying Schopenhauer's and Tönnies's (1887) understanding of the pathogenic effects of civilization to the issue of social integration by dividing integration conceptually into the twin categories social contacts and social bonds. Urbanization multiplies the chances for hurt while lowering social bonds. Durkheim elaborates in *Suicide* ([1897] 1951, p. 120):

If, for reasons just indicated, urban life must be more intense in Summer and in Spring than during the rest of the year, nevertheless the differ-

ence between seasons should be less marked there than in the country.
. . . The greater or lesser length of days especially should have little
effect in great centers, because artificial lighting there restricts darkness
more than elsewhere. If then the monthly and seasonal variations of
suicide depend on the irregular intensity of collective life, they should
be less noticeable in great cities than in the country as a whole.

While Durkheim clearly implies that the effects of the seasons upon
suicide in urban versus rural areas should be vastly different, he does
not spell out these differences. In fact, the phenomenon of rural
suicide is little understood today. Durkheim concentrated on urban
suicide, and his brief remarks on rural suicide have not taken root in
contemporary sociology.

A study of the difference between rural and urban suicide in the
United States by Kowalski, Faupel, and Starr (1987) concludes that
rural suicide is a fundamentally different phenomenon from urban
suicide. This is an essentially Durkheimian conclusion, but the authors make it without invoking Durkheim. The import of this contemporary finding and of Durkheim's statements is that the modern
study of suicide is essentially the study of urban suicide. Urbanism is
the realm of Schopenhauer's unleashed "will," of Tönnies's (1887)
"artificial will" characteristic of *Gesellschaft,* and of Freud's civilization
and its discontents. Social contacts will take on a qualitatively different
significance in this realm compared to rural or "primitive" societies.

But if heightened social interaction can be a positive and beneficial
thing, it can also be a source of pain. Going to the beach, to parties,
and to carnivals can be exhilarating as well as humiliating, disappoint-
ing as well as a source of rejection. It would be interesting to check
whether accident rates in the United States increase during spring
and summer, as they apparently did in Durkheim's time. How many
of these "accidents" are disguised aggression turned toward the self,
as Freud suggests in *The Psychopathology of Everyday Life* (1901), due to
innumerable hurts? Are relationships more likely to be broken off
during the spring and summer than fall and winter? Are there
seasonal variations to "stressful life events?" These important questions have yet to be addressed in suicide research.

Before such research can be undertaken, the theoretical scaffolding
must be set firmly into place. With this aim in mind we turn to the
elaboration of Durkheim's thesis found in Mauss's ([1950] 1979b)
Seasonal Variations of the Eskimo and Halbwachs's ([1930] 1978) *Causes
of Suicide.*

Suffering in Contemporary Social Life

Mauss ([1950] 1979b) turns to a study of the Eskimos for reasons
similar to Durkheim's justification of turning to the study of primitive

Australian aborigines in his *Elementary Forms of the Religious Life*. Both thinkers believe that the study of a primitive people will reveal important insights concerning "civilized" people. This is because the social forces at work in the primitive setting will seem simpler and uncluttered, yet connected to the modern setting (since collective representations are never extinguished, only transformed). Moreover, Mauss, like Durkheim, believes that *one* well-designed experiment is sufficient for establishing scientific laws. In their view, positivistic replication of studies is unnecessary. Mauss ([1950] 1979b, p. 20) is blunt:

> It is wrong to assume that the validity of a scientific proposition is directly dependent on the number of cases that can supposedly confirm it. When a relation has been established in one case, even a unique case but one that has been carefully and systematically studied, the result is as valid as any that can be demonstrated by resorting to numerous facts which are but disparate, curious examples confusingly culled from the most heterogeneous societies, races or cultures. John Stuart Mill states that a well-constructed experiment is sufficient to demonstrate a law; it is certainly infinitely more indicative than numerous badly constructed experiments. Indeed this methodological rule applies just as much to sociology as to the other natural sciences.

Not only does Mauss's passage, above, indicate his anti-positivistic sentiments, it seems to be accurate as well as profoundly relevant. Since Durkheim wrote *Suicide,* sociology has been overwhelmed by mountains of research concerning suicide, and yet it is difficult to point to many scientific laws based upon this research.

Mauss (ibid., p. 56) makes it clear that he is approaching Eskimo social life as a "total phenomenon," as the interaction of geographical, social and psycho-biological phenomena. He concludes that "there is, as it were, a summer religion and a winter religion" (p. 57). This is because in summer the Eskimos live a more individualized, egoistic existence in nuclear families, whereas in winter they live in "a kind of joint-family which resembles that of the Zadruga Slavs, and which constitutes domestic society *par excellence*" (p. 64). Like Durkheim, Mauss distinguishes between qualitative and quantitative aspects of what often passes for undifferentiated "social integration" in contemporary sociology. According to Mauss (p. 76):

> The qualitative differences that distinguish these successive and alternating cultural patterns are directly related to quantitative differences in the relative intensity of social life at these two times of the year. Winter is a season when Eskimo society is highly concentrated and in a state of continual excitement and hyperactivity. Because individuals are

brought into close contact with one another, their social interactions become more frequent, more continuous and more coherent; ideas are exchanged; feelings are mutually revived and reinforced. By its existence and constant activity, the group becomes more aware of itself and assumes a more prominent place in the consciousness of individuals. Conversely, in summer, social bonds are relaxed; fewer relationships are formed, and there are fewer people with whom to make them; and thus, psychologically, life slackens its pace. The difference between these two periods of the year is, in short, as great as can possibly occur between a period of intense social activity and a phase of languid and depressed social life.

Mauss then leaps to contemporary Western life and makes a conceptual link that Durkheim apparently assumes—but does not explicate—in his treatment of the effects of the seasons of the year upon social integration and consequently upon suicide. This theoretical insight is important (ibid., pp. 78–79):

What is more, we have only to observe what goes on around us in our Western societies to discover these same rhythms. About the end of July, there occurs a summer dispersion. Urban life enters that period of sustained languor known as *vacances,* the vacation period, which continues to the end of autumn. Life then tends to revive and goes on to increase steadily until it drops off again in June. Rural life follows the opposite patterns. . . . Statistics reflect these regular variations in social life. Suicides, an urban phenomenon, increase from the end of autumn until June. . . . All this suggests that we have come upon a law that is probably of considerable generality. Social life does not continue at the same level throughout the year; it goes through regular, successive phases of increased and decreased intensity, of activity and repose, of exertion and recuperation. We might almost say that social life does violence to the minds and bodies of individuals which they can sustain only for a time; and there comes a point when they must slow down and partially withdraw from it.

To repeat, Mauss's hypothesis has never been formally tested because it has not yet been formally incorporated into either Durkheimian scholarship or general sociological theories. But it clearly differentiates between urban versus rural suicide; between qualitative and quantitative aspects of social integration; between social bonds and social contacts, respectively; and between society as a system of representations that does violence to something like Schopenhauher's "will" versus its benign, binding aspects, although it treats both as parts of a "total social fact."

Halbwachs ([1930] 1978) not only implies Schopenhauer's philosophy, he mentions Schopenhauer by name to make two key points.

First, Halbwachs (p. 302) agrees with Schopenhauer that the so-called will to die "presupposes that one is still attached to life"—in other words, that the suicide wish is somehow related to the will to live. Halbwachs is quite eloquent, and is worth quoting at some length (ibid.):

> Have these [suicides] in no way consulted society? Should they be said to have separated themselves from society like the dried leaves of a tree whose branches did not even need to be shaken. . . . Shall we assume that they have lost the will to live? But Schopenhauer quite properly remarked that the will to die, seeing that it is a desire, presupposes that one is still attached to life. An unconscious being would be incapable of taking this step. . . . All of the collective sadness and melancholy becomes embodied in him and rises through him to a higher awareness of itself.
>
> "All of us are born to suffer; we know it and we invent the means of deceiving ourselves . . . all is falsehood, all is illusion, deception, all is evil. In the houses, always people upon people, without end, all hating one another" [Leo Tolstoy, *Anna Karenina*].
>
> Not until one is no longer capable of seeing the other aspects of the world are the discouraging ones so plainly uncovered. It is in society, not in himself, that the suffering person best perceives the image of his own destiny.

Second, Halbwachs (p. 314) agrees that this will to life is the source of suffering that in turn leads to suicide, which in turn is related to aspects of social integration:

> It is not enough to know how many people kill themselves or to ascertain that this is, after all, only a limited loss of a substance which may not be healthy. Suicide is also a symptom. What is the extent and the nature of the social trouble it reveals to us?
>
> "If life were in itself a blessing to be prized [wrote Schopenhauer], and decidedly to be preferred to non-existence, the exit from it would not need to be guarded by such fearful sentinels as death and its terrors. But who would continue in life as it is if death were less terrible?"
>
> A man must have reached a rather high degree of suffering for him to decide to pass through these doors. . . . We can assume that the number of suicides is a rather exact indicator of the amount of suffering, malaise, disequilibrium, and sadness which exists or is produced in a group. Its increase is the sign that the sum total of despair, anguish, regret, humiliation, and discontent of every order is multiplying.

Thus, according to Halbwachs (p. 319), suicide increases when social contacts increase pain in the context of weakened social bonds, when "occasions for boredom, humiliation, disappointment, and suffering on account of others are thus multiplied." In this state of affairs, "the weakest or the most unfortunate succumb" to suicide because "society deprives them of support but keeps them in a situation where the chance of injuries and wounds of all kinds are multiplied" (p. 320). Halbwachs is as clear as Mauss concerning the fact that this is in part (p. 327), "because urban societies provide opportunity during a given period for more frequent contacts between people," which can lead to pain, in the context of weakened social bonds. There can be no doubt that the Durkheimians were treating "social integration," at least in part, as the culprit for contemporary human suffering.

Implications

We have established in this chapter that Durkheim's treatment of social integration is more complex than most contemporary versions of this same phenomenon, in that Durkheim distinguishes between its quantitative and qualitative aspects, and conjoins these two dimensions in his discussion. Moreover, Durkheim seems to imply that some versions of this complex understanding of social integration are pathogenic and do *not* always act as a prophylactic against suicide. He certainly does not regard all social integration as being always beneficial. It is evident also that he is adding to his approach to suicide as a "total" phenomenon that entails great socio-psychic-organic pain (discussed in Meštrović 1987). These moves hold far-reaching consequences for contemporary studies that invoke the concept of social integration as well as for contemporary studies of suicide.

What has come to be known as the stressful-life-events school of research, especially, assumes that social integration is an unqualified good that mitigates the effects of stress (Meštrović and Glassner 1983). Durkheim's theory suggests, on the contrary, that certain kinds and quantities of integration are original sources of stress in and of themselves. As a rule, contemporary studies of suicide fail to distinguish between urban and rural suicide. This is most evident in the fact that the Durkheimian understanding of rural suicide should still be applicable to Third World nations, which are still predominantly rural, and yet sociologists have concentrated upon Western, urban suicide rates in a vain effort to give positivistic, universal explanations of all suicide. In both areas of research, the dimension of human suffering is missing. In contemporary research, stress has been linked to symptoms by bypassing the agony of the human agent who experiences both the stress and the symptoms. I have already cited the observation by Alvarez (1970) that contemporary studies of suicide have made the subject unreal by neglecting the role of suffering in suicide.

But beyond these or any other specific areas of research, the greater implication of Durkheim's treatment of social integration is that it exposes the naiveté and felicity of assuming that attachment to society is an unqualified good. Everyone has experienced the harrassment, invasion of privacy, humiliation, and other negative aspects of too many or the wrong kinds of social integration. It is nothing less than incredible that sociological theory has tended to ignore these obvious facts in its unjustified optimism concerning social integration. Durkheim's extreme pessimism in this regard helps to restore a balance.

CHAPTER 8

The Reformation of Individualism

Allan Bloom's (1987) *Closing of the American Mind* takes up the problem that there exist two varieties of individualism in America, one benign and the other cancerous. Cultural relativism is singled out as the culprit in Bloom's attack on destructive individualism, but he seems to offer some variation of ethnocentrism as part of the solution. Similarly, in his thought-provoking *Cultural Contradictions of Capitalism*, Daniel Bell (1976) both attacks and defends individualism, or different versions of individualism. On the one hand, individualism seems to be so modern, even so American. It would be difficult to imagine returning to more traditional times in which individualism, in both its benign and malignant aspects, was less developed than in the modern era. On the other hand, it is difficult to distinguish individualism from narcissism, in theory or in practice.

It is curious that Durkheim's theoretical stand on individualism is hardly ever invoked in such discussions. Bloom and Bell, to cite only two of the many commentators on this problem, focus instead on Marx, Nietzsche, Freud, and other classical thinkers. This is probably because Durkheim has been depicted as being against individualism and as being conservative in his stance on social solidarity. In fact, his ponderous position on the object-subject debate led him to a unique stand on these topics. In this regard, Durkheim's affinities with John Calvin are most evident. Calvin also stood for individualism, but was against egoism. This distinction between two radically distinct forms of individualism is what sets Durkheim's stand apart from many other thinkers, past and present.

The problem of individualism has been a thorn in sociology's side for many years. This problem, too, has polarized sociologists. On

128

the one hand are the theorists who argue for social consensus and social order. They have been accused of promoting the oversocialized view of man (Wrong 1961). On the other hand are the theorists who argue that society is the outcome of human agency (Giddens 1976). They have been accused of leftist ideology. Meanwhile, individualism has been developing at a rapid pace throughout the world, even though sociologists have not yet been able to reconcile their differences. David Riesman attempted to correct the bias against individualism in his *Individualism Reconsidered* (1954) but the pendulum at present has swung to the other extreme without much progress in distinguishing the benign from the destructive variety of individualism.

Durkheim referred to individualism in two diametrically opposed ways that are nevertheless a unity. One is individualism as a collective representation, and the other is individualism as the subjective will. Schopenhauer's formula for *homo duplex* and its reconciliation, which we have been following throughout this book, informs his resolution of the problems that have to do with individualism. Durkheim's concept of political anomie also follows this formula. It occurs when the "will of the people," which is as subject to the infinity of desires in political life as it is in any other aspect of social life, predominates. But because the individual's will is the source of anomie does not mean that Durkheim was against individualism. This is because Durkheim distinguished between two radically distinct varieties of individualism, whereas many contemporary discussions, within sociology and among laypersons alike, confound narcissism with individualism. For Durkheim, it is not that there is a destructive side to individualism, but that individualism is based on the "higher" side of *homo duplex* and narcissism on the "lower" pole.

Political Anomie as Tyranny by "The Will of the People"

In *Professional Ethics*, Durkheim links his discussion of political anomie with a discussion of economic anomie ([1950] 1983, p. 96), which comes first in the presentation. Durkheim apparently believes that the causes of economic anomie lie in socialist *and* classical capitalist theories, because both imply that human desires will regulate themselves of their own accord. The view that Durkheim attacks is apparently still the staple of much contemporary economic theory. But Durkheim writes (ibid.), in contradistinction to these theories:

To the extent the individual is left to his own devices and freed from all social constraint, he is unfettered too by all moral constraint. [p. 7]

> It is not possible for a social function to exist without moral discipline. Otherwise, nothing remains but individual appetites, and since they are by nature boundless and insatiable, if there is nothing to control them they will not be able to control themselves. [p. 11]

> The unleashing of economic interests has been accompanied by a debasing of public morality. We find that the manufacturer, the merchant . . . is aware of no influence set above him to check his egoism. He is subject to no moral discipline. [p. 12]

Durkheim concludes, "There is no form of social activity which can do without the appropriate moral discipline" (p. 14). The shadow of Schopenhauer's thought is evident in Durkheim's argument: society is the system of representations that must restrain man's will, which is by nature insatiable. If society fails to restrain man's desires and aims, "it is inevitable that these aims will become anti-social" (p. 15). It is also easy to spot here Freud's dictum that when conceived as the narcissistic bundle of id, the individual is the enemy of civilization.

We can begin to comprehend Durkheim's scattered discussion of political anomie that immediately follows the discussion above by noting the following: Durkheim treats the State strictly as a system of "representations," never as will, and the people, the nation it rules, as a bundle of chaotic desires, as "will." The formula for *homo duplex* is reproduced here with the State representing the "higher" aims and the nation representing the "lower." The State is the "organ of social thought" (p. 79) whose "responsibility it is to work out certain representations which hold good for the collectivity" (p. 50). Durkheim's vocabulary in describing the State includes the following words: deliberation, reflection, conscious, clarity, organized, and ego. "The people," on the other hand, he depicts in terms of what is obscure, unconsidered, automatic, blind, prejudiced, diffuse, subconscious, unconscious, and indefinite. Again, one can scarcely avoid summing Durkheim's characterization of the State and the people in Freud's terms of "ego" and "id," respectively, and, to some extent, even consciousness versus unconsciousness. But this Freudian terminology is also a refraction of Schopenhauer's opposition between idea and will, mind and heart. Durkheim reflects Schopenhauer's thought even to the extent of claiming that the State is the weak force and "the people" are the strong force in this dualistic scheme of things (p. 95). Political anomie occurs when the people's will rules the State.

It follows that Durkheim does not regard the role of the State as administrative, as one of action. On the contrary, its role should be one of "consciousness and reflection" (p. 50). Moreover, Durkheim disagrees with the popular view of democracy as society governing itself. He writes (p. 91): "It is often said that under a democratic system the *will* and thought of those governing are identical and merge with the *will* and thought of those governed" (emphasis added). He attributes this erroneous view to Rousseau (p. 99), and proceeds to attack it. If everyone is to govern, in Durkheim's view, then in fact no one governs, because the will of the masses in the political arena is as insatiable and unstable as it is in the economic arena: "it is collective sentiments, diffused, vague and obscure as they may be, that sway the people" (p. 83). Democracies ruled by the will of the people are "pseudo-democracies" characterized by chaos, stormy changes in politics, instability, even "evil" (pp. 95–100 passim).

The will is inherently unstable. Durkheim writes: "How does the fact of having willed a certain law make it worthy of my own particular respect? What my will has done, my will can undo. Mutable as it is in its nature, it cannot serve as a foundation for anything stable" (p. 107).

Rather than follow in the wake of the will of the masses, the State must superimpose reflective thought on their desires. Democracy is not rule by the people, but effective "communication" between the State and the people: "The more that deliberation and reflection and a critical spirit play a considerable part in the course of public affairs, the more democratic the nation. It is the less democratic when lack of consciousness, uncharted customs, the obscure sentiments and prejudices that evade investigation, predominate" (p. 89).

It is no surprise, therefore, that Durkheim puts little faith in mandate theory or universal suffrage: the voting behavior of the masses is subject to the instability of the will. Moreover, a good share of the population does not vote. Nor does he see any great difference among various forms of government, monarchies or elective. In fact, he believes that France was more authentically democratic when it was ruled by seventeenth century monarchs than in the aftermath of Rousseau's "narrowly individualistic" democratic theory. The essential thing is for the State to rule by thought, discussion, and elaboration of the will of the people. Freud's maxim that the ego should rule where the id dominates applies to Durkheim's thought.

Durkheim (p. 109) concludes his discussion of political anomie as follows: "Instead of offering this absence of organization, wrongly called democracy, as an ideal, a limit should be set to that condition. Instead of clinging to a jealous preserving of these rights and privileges, a cure has to be applied to the evil that makes them inevitable for the time being. In other words, the primary duty is to work out something that can relieve us by degrees of a role for which the individual is not cast." It is not clear what this "something" is in Durkheim's mind. "It" still has to be worked out. But this does not mean that Durkheim's thought is "oversocialized," as Wrong (1961) has charged with regard to Parsonian functionalism as well as Durkheimian thought. We turn next to Durkheim's conceptions of justice and individualism, respectively, to clarify the deeper implications of Durkheim's concept of political anomie.

Justice in Relation to Political Anomie

The theme of justice is among the most neglected in Durkheimian scholarship. Durkheim continues to be read from the perspectives of "social control" (Park and Burgess 1921) and "social order" (Parsons 1937). These perspectives seem to be rough approximations of what Durkheim meant but upon closer inspection, they turn out to be ambiguous and inconsistent with the thrust of Durkheim's thought. And it is important to note that Durkheim preferred the French word "réglementation"—notoriously difficult to translate—in discussions of how the will should be maintained, not "order" or "control." The problem is this: societies characterized by social control and social order, evidenced by a high degree of normative consensus, can, nevertheless, be unjust. Normative consensus does not solve the problem of the tyrannical will in any case. Just because individuals agree intellectually on a common set of norms, it does not follow that their desires will automatically fall in line with their intellects. Durkheim understood these problems and therefore focused on justice, not normative consensus. Moreover, justice implies a certain respect for human dignity that the seemingly more authoritarian social order does not.

Sirianni (1984) and Filloux (1977) are among the few contemporary sociologists who have focused, to some extent, on Durkheim's notion of justice. Sirianni claims correctly that justice, not social order, is the major theme of Durkheim's *Division of Labor*, but she does not investigate its importance for his thought in general, nor does she explore its context. Filloux is correct to observe a superficial affinity between justice as used by Durkheim and as a rallying cry for socialism. But one must account for the fact that Durkheim was highly critical of socialism, especially in his *Socialism and Saint-Simon* (1928). Durkheim sympathized with socialism's own pity for human suffering, but he would not grant it any scientific status, and he blamed Saint-Simonianism, in part, for the economic and political anomie it tried to address. In any case, Durkheim ([1893] 1933, p. 388) concludes his *Division of Labor in Society* with the claim that "The task of the most advanced societies is, then, a work of justice. . . . Just as ancient peoples needed, above all, a common faith to live by, so we need justice." More important, he implies that justice constitutes part of the solution to anomie: "What we must do to relieve this anomy is to discover the means for . . . introducing . . . more justice by more and more extenuating the external inequalities which are the source of the evil" (ibid., p. 409).

For the purposes of this discussion, it is important to note that Durkheim regarded the State as the organ whose duty is the maintenance of justice: "The State is the civil organ of justice" ([1897] 1986, p. 49). And he elaborates: "Justice becomes ever more important. Indeed the progress of justice is measured by the degree of respect accorded to the rights of the individual, because to be just is to grant to everyone what he has the right to demand."

This passage is reminiscent of *Division of Labor* in which Durkheim claims that "the collective conscience is becoming more of a cult of the individual" ([1893] 1933, p. 407). But if the individual's will is the source of anomie, how can justice address the question of individual rights?

Schopenhauer emphasizes that egoism—the unrestrained will not cognizant of the will of others—is the root of all evil and all conflict ([1818] 1977, pp. 430–50 passim). Left on its own, the will is destructive, so it must be restrained; but any restraint does harm to the will and therefore is evil. Schopenhauer only hints at a solution, that justice consists in a contractual order in which men willingly restrain their egoisms for their own good and for the good of society. One wonders if the following lines by Schopenhauer were not the seeds for much of Durkheim's political sociology: "Thus we have come to recognize in the state the means by which egoism endowed with reason seeks to escape from its own evil consequences which turn against itself, and now each promotes the well-being of all because he sees that his own well-being is involved in it. . . . But as yet the state has always remained very far from this goal" (Schopenhauer [1818] 1977, vol. 1, p. 451). Schopenhauer implies that justice is a kind of covenant between the individual and society, a contractual order, which ensures that the will is neither harmed nor allowed to reign unrestrained.

In his review of Tönnies ([1887] 1963), Durkheim agrees that in modern times, "individual wills are no longer absorbed in the collective will, but are, so to speak, encamped face to face with one another in the fullness of their independence" (Durkheim [1889] 1978, p. 119). This situation necessitates the contract. Almost the entire conclusion of *Professional Ethics* and a good portion of *Division of Labor* are devoted to the question of how the social contract emerged. For Durkheim, this is not a simple question. He understands the contract as an "agreement of two wills bent upon a common aim" that is binding upon both ([1950] 1983, p. 179). But since the will is inherently unruly (p. 127), how did the contract ever develop?

Durkheim's reply is long and tedious. In summary, he claims that the contract developed at a late date in social evolution (p. 176), that it was not derived from the social structure to fulfill a perceived need, and that it is not the result of the utilitarian calculation of individals (pp. 127–184 passim; [1893] 1933, pp. 417–24 passim). Along the way he attacks Kant, Spencer, Rousseau, and the utilitarian tradition, apparently on the grounds that the will is too strong for men to choose subjectively to subdue it. Rather, Durkheim argues, the sacredness of society's collective representations gradually attached itself to the oath and the covenant, so that failure to keep one's word came to be regarded as sacrilege, to "the profaning" of a sacred thing, and the commission of an act forbidden by religion ([1950] 1983, p. 193). Society—representation, thought, the incarnation of the sacred—is the only force capable of subduing the will.

We are now in a position to give a reply to the problem Durkheim posed in the opening pages of *Division of Labor* that is consistent with the thrust of his thought: "Why does the individual, while becoming more autonomous, depend more upon society? How can he be at once more individual and more solidary?" (Durkheim [1893] 1933, p. 37). The more autonomous modern man is more dependent upon society, because without it, he would annihilate himself and other individuals due to his emancipated will. And he is simultaneously more individual and bound to others because modern societies are held together by justice—not by normative consensus—which mediates between the individual will and society as a system of collective representations. Thus the division of labor fosters individualism at the same time that it restrains it. We turn next to this seeming paradox.

Individualism Reconsidered

It is well known that Durkheim's thought is typically understood as being anti-individualist and "oversocialized." Nevertheless, a few dissenting voices have noted his references to and defense of "the cult of the individual," which seems to contradict, at least in part, the oversocialized view. For example, Giddens (1986, p. 13) writes that Durkheim's "individualism must not be identified with the utilitarian egoism of Spencer and of the economists." This is only partly true because at times, Durkheim does treat individualism as egoism. Durkheim's friend and follower Paul Fauconnet offers ([1922] 1958, pp. 31–32) this startling assessment of Durkheim's thought in this regard: "People are so accustomed to opposing society to the individual, that every theory that makes frequent use of the word society seems to sacrifice the individual. Here, again, they are mistaken. If any man has been an individual, a person, in every sense that this term implies of creative originality and resistance to collective influences, it is Durkheim. And his moral theory corresponds so well to his own character, that one would not be proposing a paradox by giving this theory the name of individualism." It certainly seems to be a paradox. Fauconnet's remark points to a more fundamental role for individualism in Durkheim's thought than is commonly supposed. How can Durkheim be simultaneously for and against individualism?

The problem begins to resolve itself once we realize that Durkheim uses the concept of individualism in two diametrically opposed ways. One kind refers to the will, and the other to a collective representation. For Durkheim, there is the merely egoistic individualism "rooted in our bodies" ([1914] 1973, p. 157), but there is also the individualism that will become the collective religion of the future. Thus in *Suicide* he claims that in modern times "man has become a god for men" but that "this cult of man is something accordingly very different from the egoistic individualism above referred to, which leads to suicide" ([1897] 1951, p. 336). Durkheim elaborates upon the way in which individualism can be thought of as a collective phenomenon (p. 337):

> Originally society is everything, the individual nothing. . . . man is considered only an instrument in its hands. . . . But gradually things change. As societies become greater in volume and density, they increase in complexity, work is divided, individual differences multiply, and the moment approaches when the only remaining bond among the members of a single human group will be that they are all men. Under such conditions the body of *collective sentiments* inevitably attaches itself with all its strength to its single remaining object, communicating to this object an incomparable value by so doing. . . . For man, as thus suggested to *collective affection* and respect, is not the sensual, experiential individual . . . but man in general, ideal humanity as *conceived* by each people at each moment of its history. None of us wholly incarnates this ideal, though none is wholly a stranger to it. . . . Such an aim draws him beyond himself; *impersonal* and disinterested, it is above all individual personalities; like every ideal, it can be conceived of only as superior to and dominating reality. This ideal even dominates societies, being the aim on which all social activity depends. . . . Our dignity as moral beings is therefore no longer the property of the city-state; but it has not for that reason become our property. [emphasis added]

It is becoming apparent why Fauconnet characterized Durkheim's sociology as individualism. This collective individualism, this new cult and religion, is the guiding star of modern societies.

But this thesis in *Suicide* is but a refraction of a similar argument in *Division of Labor*. The cult of the individual replaces the collective conscience. Thus, "the individual becomes the object of a sort of religion," such that this cult "is common in so far as the community partakes of it," and "it turns all *wills* towards the same end" (Durkheim [1893] 1933, p. 172, emphasis added). Durkheim adds that "it is still from society that [the cult of the individual] takes all its force." The division of labor is thus simultaneously a social and individual phenomenon.

Durkheim expresses the distinction between collective and narcissistic individualism with the greatest clarity in his essay "Individualism and the Intellectuals" ([1898] 1975). Most of the points he raises are still applicable today, to contemporary sociology as well as to society. He laments that individualism "has been confused with the narrow utilitarianism and utilitarian egoism of Spencer and the economists" (ibid., p. 60). And he notes (p. 70) that

> A verbal similarity has made it possible to believe that *individualism* necessarily resulted from *individual*, and thus egoistic, sentiments. In reality, the religion of the individual is a social institution like all known religions. It is society which assigns us this ideal as the sole common end which is today capable of providing a a focus for men's wills. To remove this ideal, without putting any other in its place, is therefore to plunge us into that very moral anarchy which it is sought to avoid.

But in contradistinction to this trend, Durkheim (p. 66) asserts that "not only is individualism distinct from anarchy; but it is henceforth the only system of beliefs which can ensure the moral unity of the country." When society is threatened with the "non-religion of the future," as Guyau (1887) put it, something must fill the vacuum. According to Durkheim ([1898] 1975, p. 67), "all the evidence points to the conclusion that the only possible candidate is precisely this religion of humanity whose rational expression is the individualist morality." This collective individualism, the new religion of the future, cannot be held back from its inevitable progress. The real problem is to distinguish it clearly from narcissism, which is still a problem today.

One reason why sociologists in general—although there have been exceptions—have not developed Durkheim's notion of the religion of humanity is that it does not seem to be an "empirically observable" religion. Where are the churches of this new religion? Where is the dogma? Durkheim's answer might have been that the churches and the dogma are hidden behind a veil. As I have pointed out earlier, religious society for Durkheim, as any other society, is a system of representations, and some of these are unconscious. There can be no doubt that individualism animates many of the churches and dogmas that can be "observed." No one today disputes that the faithful across many denominations are demanding more autonomy, freedom, opportunity, and privacy at the same time that they are rebelling against dogmatism, authoritarianism, and tradition. Even the fundamentalist movement leaves the final interpretation of dogma up to the individual conscience.

Durkheim's *Moral Education* ([1925] 1961, p. 6) begins with a discussion of this shift in focus from duties of man toward his gods in primitive religions to duties of man to man in modern religions:

> The principal obligations [in primitive religions] are not to respect one's neighbor, to help him, to assist him; but to accomplish meticulously prescribed rites, to give to the Gods what is their due, and even, if need be, to sacrifice one's self to their glory. . . . But gradually things change. Gradually, human duties are multiplied, become more precise, and pass to the first rank of importance; while others, on the contrary, tend to become attenuated. One might say that Christianity itself has contributed most to the acceleration of this result. An essentially human religion since its God dies for the salvation of humanity, Christianity teaches that the principal duty of man toward God is to love his neighbor. Although there are religious duties—rites addresssed only to divinity—the place they occupy and the importance attributed to them continue to diminish.

Durkheim (p. 7) adds that "with Protestantism, the autonomy of morality is still more accentuated by the fact that ritual itself diminishes." Rationalism and individualism develop in parallel, and both have to be renovated to avoid dogmatism and narcissism.

Durkheim (p. 75) believes that "morality continuously disengages itself from particular ethnic groups or geographical areas," and no arbitrary limit can be set to this progress. Thus, "there is nothing to justify the supposition that there will never emerge a state embracing the whole of humanity" (p. 76). This new religion of the future will have as its object "the general interests of humanity—that is to say, committing itself to an access of justice, to a higher morality" (p. 77). It is curious that sociologists of religion have not regarded the spread of Christianity in the so-called Third World today as one of the stages in Durkheim's developmental theory of religion. Durkheim clearly believed that Protestantism will develop, not into a religious vacuum, but into the new religion of humanity, the "cult" of the individual.

The key point is that egoistic individualism pertains to the will, while collective individualism is an abstraction, an ideal, a representation. Thus Durkheim reproduces his formula for *homo duplex* in still another form, by pitting one kind of individualism against another. We have followed Durkheim's references to egoistic individualism as the source of anomie in *Professional Ethics,* but he also refers to the other type: "It is not this or that individual the State seeks to develop, it is the individual *in genere*, who is not to be confused with any single one of us" ([1950] 1983, p. 69). This collective individualism is not antagonistic to the State; rather, "it is the State that sets it free" (ibid.). Collective individualism, the State, and democracy develop in parallel, not in opposition nor mutual antagonism: "There is nothing negative in the part played by the State. Its tendency is to ensure the most complete individuation that the state of society will allow of. Far from its tyrannizing over the individual, it is the State that reedems the the individual from the society" (ibid.).

Durkheim brings together many of the themes that concern this discussion in the following intriguing passage:

> The fundamental duty of the State is laid down in this very fact: it is to persevere in calling the individual to a moral way of life. . . . If the cult of the human person is to be the only one destined to survive, as it seems, it must be observed by the State as by the individual equally. This cult, moreover, has all that is required to take the place of the religious cults of former times. It serves quite as well as they to bring about that communion of minds and *wills* which is a first condition of any social life. [ibid]

Durkheim understood that Guyau's (1887) "non-religion of the future" would unleash the will that had been restrained by former religions. But he was not against individualism for that reason. He recognized that there was no way to stop individualism; yet he recognized also that individualism can be thought of as a collective phenomenon. Thus, when the State restrains the individual, it simultaneously enhances the individual. We should keep distinct the two types of individualism that informed Durkheim's thought. For Durkheim, the expansion of the State, the progress of democracy, and the progress of collective individualism are, ideally, in a state of evolution such that "progress is always going on and it is not possible to set any bounds to its course" (ibid., p. 68). As the State develops, it makes possible more—not less—democracy and individualism. Democracy is ensured when the egoistic individual's obscure will is refined by the State's more reflective thought. The individual is truly free when his desiring will is restrained, not when he gives in to its tyranny. This ideal state of affairs is marred by periods of political anomie in which something is awry in the relationship among the State, the individual, and democratic theory. Durkheim believed that such periods were temporary and could be repaired. But he also believed that "democracy is not a discovery or a revival in our own century" (ibid., p. 89). The steady tide of progress, despite its setbacks, has been evolving since the beginning of civilization, because it is intimately linked to the development of collective individualism and the division of labor.

The connection of rationalism with these other developments in democracy, individualism, and justice has been mentioned several times. Durkheim makes the conceptual link somewhat more clear in *Moral Education* ([1925] 1961, p. 12):

> Rationalism is only one of the aspects of individualism: it is the intellectual aspect of it. We are not dealing here with two different states of mind; each is the converse of the other. When one feels the need of liberating individual thought, it is because in a general way one feels the need of liberating the individual. Intellectual servitude is only one of the servitudes that individualism combats. All development of individualism has the effect of opening moral consciousness to new ideas and rendering it more demanding. Since every advance that it makes results in a higher conception, a more delicate sense of the dignity of man, individualism cannot be developed without making apparent to us as contrary to human dignity, as unjust, social relations that at one time did not seem unjust at all. . . . For injustice is unreasonable and absurd, and, consequently, we are the more sensitive to it as we are more sensitive to the rights of reason. Consequently, a given advance in moral education in the direction of greater rationality cannot occur without also bringing to light new moral tendencies, without inducing a greater thirst for justice, without stirring the public conscience by latent aspirations.

It is clear that the depiction of Durkheim as the enemy of individualism is as false as it is unfair.

We have resolved what seemed to be a paradox. Contrary to Merton and Parsons, anomie is caused by man's biological, imperious will being unrestrained. But Durkheim has not abandoned the sociological perspective by adopting the position of *homo duplex*. This is because genuine, collective individualism is maintained by the State's and other collective elaborations and "réglementation" of egoistic will. In this way, too, Durkheim's thought has escaped Wrong's (1961) searing critique of the oversocialized man. For Durkheim, socialized man is actually most free of society because he can be an individual only when his will is restrained. Even if Lacroix (1981) is correct in claiming that, following Durkheim's self-reported "discovery" of the importance of religion in 1895, he began to envision all phenomena in religious terms, it does not follow that a hiatus exists between Durkheim's political and religious thought. This is because both are informed by the thesis that man is a *homo duplex*, torn by the division of everything into the opposing categories of representations and the body—and the attendant dualisms of this dualism, including epistemological dualisms—ultimately, the sacred versus the profane. Durkheim, the "son of a rabbi" (Filloux 1977), the philosopher, the socialist sympathizer, and the "pope of sociology" was always Durkheim the scientific moralist, the social reformer. In approaching Durkheim from the perspective of Schopenhauer, we have restored Durkheim's thought to the unifying principle that informed it, not fragmented it.

Implications

Nowadays one frequently hears and reads that Americans are searching for some sort of consensus, something to offset the fragmentation and evil effects of what is often called cancerous individualism. But phrased in this imprecise way, the problem—which is hardly new, given that Durkheim foreshadowed it at the turn of the century—leads only to unsatisfactory solutions. Thus, as I have already indicated, in *Closing of the American Mind,* Bloom (1987) seems to advocate a return to a kind of ethnocentrism to offset what he sees as the evil effects of cultural relativism. Ethnocentrism is hardly an encouraging option. "Consensus" has definitely been overused and overadmired. Moreover, consensus—as used by Parsons (1937)—clashes with the healthy kind of individualism that most everyone seems to admire, especially in America. Diversity and diversification are with us to stay, and they will progress further. There can be no going back, but something must be done to relieve society of the malignant forms of individualism. The first step is to recognize that there exist these two distinct, mutually antagonistic forms of individualism, one healthy and the other evil. This recognition has been an important aim of this chapter.

Durkheim's sociology teaches us that a *kind of* "consensus" actually exists all around us, that we need not search high and far for some remnant from the past. That paradoxical "consensus" is individualism. It is paradoxical because it fosters efforts to distinguish one's self from the crowd and the average, even though that seems to be the new average trend. For example, even businesses no longer target an average middle class taste for any commodity, but target a myriad of individual tastes under the rubrics of being individual and unique. Americans especially but, for that matter, Westerners in general guard jealously the rights that accompany individualism and demand more rights. The right to privacy, the rights of various minority groups, the rights demanded by children that children of previous generations could not imagine, even the right to hold opinions—among many others—are sweeping contemporary Western social life. David Riesman has remarked that a generation ago, the average American *began* to feel that he had a right to an opinion on virtually everything, and that this is a more surprising finding than the opinions that are actually held. Individualism as a set of collective representations that bestow dignity upon the human person is here to stay, and it is something most persons in Western societies will probably agree upon. It is difficult to escape Durkheim's conclusion that, indeed, man has become a god for men in modern times.

But this individualism is still intertwined with narcissism, which makes it difficult to know how one should deal with either phenomenon. This confounding of two separate phenomena applies to public opinion as well to contemporary sociological theory. Bloom (1987) demonstrates that Americans, in particular, do not know if they should be proud or ashamed of individualism. This is understandable given that there are two distinct forms of individualism under discussion, often confounded as one. Daniel Bell (1976) distinguishes between a seemingly healthy Weberian individualism required in our worklives from the narcissism that is encouraged after five o'clock. He rightfully makes much of this contradiction in modern life. Yet, the Durkheimian interpretation offered here suggests that both the healthy and malignant forms of individualism can and do invade both work *and* leisure. Sociology itself is split between the "old guard," which still invokes Parsons and the themes of social order, normative consensus, and social control, and the new sociology of "human agency," the "actor's point of view," and subjectivism. Clinging to Parsons as the totem for the social order paradigm is bound to be perceived as being offensive to a society moving further toward the new religion of individualism. At the very least, it is old-fashioned. Yet on the other extreme, the preoccupation with Weber and subjectivism is an invitation to anomie in still another disguise. Where can unrestrained subjectivism lead except to anomie?

This reading of Durkheim offers a fresh alternative: Collective and moral individualism should be accepted as inevitable and as phenomenona that will increase, not decrease, in the future. At the same time, this "higher" type of individualism must be distinguished clearly from egoism and narcissism, which must be restrained. If these two antagonistic phenomena continue to be confounded, public opinion as well as social theory will find itself mired in a conceptual wilderness that will make it difficult to embrace the future, understand the present, or appreciate the past. This reading of Durkheim began with very old starting-points, such as Schopenhauer's philosophy and the identification of Durkheim with the image of John Calvin as one of the first moral individualists, but it led to and illuminates contemporary problems.

References

Alexander, Jeffrey C. 1982. *The Antinomies of Classical Thought: Marx and Durkheim.* Berkeley: University of California Press.

Alpert, Harry. 1961. *Emile Durkheim and His Sociology.* New York: Columbia University Press.

Alvarez, A. 1970. *The Savage God.* New York: Bantam Books.

Angeles, P. A. 1981. *A Dictionary of Philosophy.* New York: Barnes & Noble.

Archie, Lee C. 1977. "Hume, Kant, and Contemporary Analyses of Causation." Ph.D. dissertation, University of Arkansas.

Augustine. 1971. *Confessions and Enchiridion.* Philadelphia: Westminster Press.

Baillot, A. 1927. *Influence de la philosophie de Schopenhauer en France (1860–1900).* Paris: J. Vrin.

Bauer, Jules. 1929. *L'école rabbinique de France.* Paris: Presses Universitaires de France.

Bell, Daniel. 1976. *The Cultural Contradictions of Capitalism.* New York: Basic Books.

Bellah, Robert N. 1973. *Emile Durkheim on Morality and Society.* Chicago: University of Chicago Press.

Benjamin, Walter. 1968. "The Work of Art in the Age of Mechanical Reproduction." Pp. 219–66 in *Illuminations,* edited by Hannah Arendt. New York: Harcourt, Brace & World.

Bergson, Henri. 1944. *Creative Evolution.* New York: Modern Library.

———. 1970. *Ouevres.* Paris: Presses Universitaires de France.

Bernard, Claude [1865] 1957. *An Introduction to the Study of Experimental Medicine.* New York: Dover Books.

———. [1865] 1966. *Introduction à l'étude de la medecine experimentale.* Paris: Garnier-Flammarion.

———. [1866] 1974. *Lectures on the Phenomena of Life Common to Animals and Plants.* Springfield: Charles Thomas.

———. 1878. *La Science experimentale.* Paris: Bailliere.

Besnard, Philippe. 1982. "L'anomie dans la biographie intellectuelle de Durkheim." *Sociologie et Sociétés* 14: 45–53.

———. 1983. *The Sociological Domain: The Durkheimians and the Founding of French Sociology.* Cambridge: Cambridge University Press.

———. 1985. "Un conflit au sein du groupe Durkheimien." *Revue française de sociologie* 26: 247–55.

143

————. 1987. *L'anomie.* Paris: Presses Universitaires de France.

Bloom, Allan. 1987. *The Closing of the American Mind.* New York: Simon & Schuster.

Blumenkranz, Bernhard. 1972. *Histoire des juifs en France.* Toulouise: Edouard Privat.

Bossu, Jean. 1967. "Silhouettes d'autrefois." *La liberté de l'est.* February 14, 1967.

————. 1982. *Chronique des rues d'Epinal.* Vol. 2. Epinal: Jeune chambre économique d'Epinal.

Bossuet, Jacques. [1731] 1836. *Traite de la concupiscence.* Paris: Editeurs des Portes de France.

Bouchard, Marie. 1983. "Henri Bouchard, Paul Landowski et le Monument de la Réformation (1908–1917) à Genève." *Bulletin de la Société de l'Histoire de l'Art français.* 76: 263–75.

Bouglé, Célestin. [1908] 1971. *Essays on the Caste System.* Cambridge: Cambridge University Press.

————. 1918. *Chez les prophètes socialistes.* Paris: Alcan.

————. 1921. *Les démocraties modernes.* Paris: Flammarion.

————. 1922. *Lecons de sociologie sur l'évolution des valeurs.* Paris: Armand Colin.

————. [1924] 1974. "Preface to the Original Edition." Pp. xxxv–xli in *Sociology and Philosophy,* by E. Durkheim. New York: Free Press.

————. 1925. *Les idées égalitaires: Etude sociologique.* Paris: Alcan.

————. 1930. "Introduction." Pp. 1–11 in *Proudhon,* edited by C. Bouglé. Paris: Alcan.

————. 1938. *The French Conception of "Culture Générale" and Its Influences Upon Instruction.* New York: Columbia University Press.

Bourgin, Hubert. [1938] 1970. *L'Ecole normale et la politique de Juares à Leon Blum.* Paris: Gordon & Breach.

Brand, Myles. 1982. "A Course Module on the Nature of Events." *Teaching Philosophy* 5: 221–25.

Calvin, John. 1975. *Institutes of the Christian Religion.* Vols. 1 and 2. Philadelphia: Westminster Press.

Camus, Albert. 1955. *The Myth of Sisyphus and Other Essays.* New York: Random House.

Charle, Christophe. 1984. "Le beau mariage d'émile durkheim." *Actes de la recherches en sciences socialies* 55: 45–49.

Chastenet, Jacques. 1949. *La France de m. Fallières.* Paris: Brouty.

Cuvillier, Armand. 1961. *Précis de philosophie.* Vol. 2. Paris: Armand Colin.

Czarnowski, Stefan. [1919] 1975. *Le culte des héros et ses conditions sociales: Saint Patrick, héros national de l'Irlande.* New York: Arno Press.

Davy, Georges. 1911. *Emile Durkheim.* Paris: Louis-Michaud.

————. 1922. *Le droit, l'idéalisme et l'expérience.* Paris: Alcan.

————. 1941. "Célestin Bouglé, sociologue." *Revue de Métaphysique et de Morale* 14:24–47.

————. 1949. *Sociologues d'hier et d'aujourdhui.* Paris: J. Vrin.

————. 1950. *Eléments de sociologie.* Paris: J. Vrin.

————. [1950] 1983. "Introduction." Pp. xii–xliv in *Professional Ethics and Civic Morals,* by E. Durkheim. Wesport, Conn.: Greenwood Press.

Deploige, Simon. 1912. *Le conflit de la morale et de la sociologie.* Paris: Nouvelle Librairie Nationale.

Douglas, Jack. 1967. *The Social Meanings of Suicide.* Princeton: Princeton University Press.

Durant, Will. 1961. *The Story of Philosophy*. New York: Simon & Schuster.

Durkheim, Emile. [1885] 1978. Review of Albert Schaeffle's *Bau und Leben des Sozialen Körpers*. Pp. 93–114 in *Emile Durkheim on Institutional Analysis*, edited by M. Traugott. Chicago: University of Chicago Press.

——. [1887] 1975. Review of Guyau's *L'irréligion de l'avenir*. Pp. 24–38 in *Durkheim on Religion*, edited by W. Pickering. London: Routledge & Kegan Paul.

——. [1887] 1976a. "La Science positive de la morale en Allemagne." Pp. 267–343 in *Textes*, edited by V. Karady, Vol. 1. Paris: Les Editions de Minuit.

——. [1887] 1976b. "L'avenir de la religion." Pp. 149–65 in *Textes*, edited by V. Karady. Vol. 2. Paris: Les Editions de Minuit.

——. [1887] 1976c. "La Philosophie dans les universites allemandes." Pp. 437–86 in *Textes*, edited by V. Karady. Vol. 3. Paris: Les Editions de Minuit.

——. [1888] 1976. "Introduction à la sociologie de la famille." Pp. 13–34 in *Textes*, edited by V. Karady. Vol. 3 Paris: Les Editions de Minuit.

——. [1889] 1978. Review of Tönnies' *Community and Society*. Pp. 115–22 in *Emile Durkheim on Institutional Analysis*, edited by M. Traugott. Chicago: University of Chicago Press.

——. [1892] 1965. *Montesquieu and Rousseau: Forerunners of Sociology*, translated by Ralph Manheim. Ann Arbor: University of Michigan Press.

——. [1893] 1933. *The Division of Labor in Society*, translated by George Simpson. New York: Free Press.

——. [1893] 1984. *The Division of Labour in Society*, translated by W. D. Halls. New York: Free Press.

——. [1893] 1967. *De la Division du travail social*. Paris: Presses Universitaires de France.

——. [1893] 1976. "Définition du fait moral." Pp. 257–87 in *Textes*, edited by V. Karady. Volume 2. Paris: Les Editions de Minuit.

——. [1895] 1982. "The Rules of Sociological Method." Pp. 31–163 in *Durkheim: The Rules of Sociological Method and Selected Texts on Sociology and Its Method*, edited by S. Lukes. New York: Free Press.

——. [1895] 1983. *Les Règles de la méthode sociologique*. Paris: Presses Universitaires de France.

——. [1897] 1951. *Suicide: A Study in Sociology*, translated by John A. Spaulding and George Simpson. New York: Free Press.

——. [1897] 1963. *Incest: The Nature and Origin of the Taboo*, translated by Edward Sagarin. New York: Lyle Stuart.

——. [1897] 1982. "Marxism and Sociology: The Materialist Conception of History." Pp. 167–74 in *Durkheim: The Rules of Sociological Method and Selected Texts on Sociology and its Method*, edited by S. Lukes. New York: Free Press.

——. [1897] 1983. *Le Suicide: Etude de sociologie*. Paris: Presses Universitaires de France.

——. [1897] 1986. "Socialism and Marxism: Critical Commentaries." Pp. 121–45 in *Durkheim on Politics and the State*, edited by A. Giddens. London: Polity Press.

——. [1898] 1974. "Individual and Collective Representations." Pp. 1–34 in *Sociology and Philosophy*, by E. Durkheim. New York: Free Press.

——. [1898] 1975. "Individualism and the Intellectuals." Pp. 59–73 in

Durkheim on Religion, edited by W. Pickering. London: Routledge & Kegan Paul.

————. [1900] 1973. "Sociology in France in the Nineteenth Century." Pp. 3–24 in *Emile Durkheim on Morality and Society*, edited by R. Bellah. Chicago: University of Chicago Press.

————. [1902] 1933. "Preface to the Second Edition." Pp. 1–31 in *The Division of Labor in Society*, edited by George Simpson. New York: Free Press.

————. [1902] 1967. "Préface de la seconde edition." Pp. i–xxxvi in *De la Division du travail social*. Paris: Presses Universitaires de France.

————. [1904] 1980. Review of Lambert's *La Fonction du droit civil comparé*. Pp. 124–27 in *Emile Durkheim: Contributions to L'Année Sociologique*, edited by Y. Nandan. New York: Free Press.

————. 1908. Remarks in "L'inconnu et l'inconscient en histoire." *Bulletin de la Société Française de Philosophie* 8:217–47.

————. [1909] 1976. "Leçons sur la morale." Pp. 292–312 in *Textes*, edited by V. Karady. Vol. 2. Paris: Les Editions de Minuit.

————. [1909] 1978. "Sociology and the Social Sciences." Pp. 71–87 in *Emile Durkheim on Institutional Analysis*, edited by M. Traugott. Chicago: University of Chicago Press.

————. [1912] 1965. *The Elementary Forms of the Religious Life*, translated by Joseph Ward Swain. New York: Free Press.

————. [1912] 1969. "Review of Wilhelm Wundt's *Elemente der Voelkerpsychologie*." Pp. 685–96 in *Journal Sociologique*, edited by J. Duvignaud. Paris: Presses Universitaires de France.

————. [1912] 1979. *Les Formes élémentaires de la vie religieuse: Le système totémique en Australie*. Paris: Presses Universitaires de France.

————. [1914] 1973. "The Dualism of Human Nature and Its Social Conditions." Pp. 149–66 in *Emile Durkheim on Morality and Society*, edited by R. Bellah. Chicago: University of Chicago Press.

————. 1915. *L'Allemagne au-dessus de tout: la mentalité et la querre*. Paris: Librairie Armand Colin.

————. [1920] 1976. "Introduction à la morale." Pp. 313–31 in *Textes*, edited by V. Karady. Vol. 2. Paris: Les Editions de Minuit.

————. [1920] 1978. Introduction to *Morality*. Pp. 191–202 in *Emile Durkheim on Institutional Analysis*, edited by M. Traugott. Chicago: University of Chicago Press.

————. 1921. "Préface de la premiere edition." Pp. v–xi in *Le Système de Decartes*, by O. Hamelin. Paris: Alcan.

————. [1922] 1958. *Education and Sociology*, translated by Sherwood Fox. Glencoe, Ill.: Free Press.

————. 1924. *Sociologie et philosophie*. Paris: Alcan.

————. [1924] 1974. *Sociology and Philosophy*, translated by D. F. Pocock. New York: Free Press.

————. [1925] 1961. *Moral Education*, translated by Everett K. Wilson and Herman Schnurer. Glencoe, Ill.: Free Press.

————. [1925] 1963. *L'éducation morale*. Paris: Presses Universitaires de France.

————. [1928] 1958. *Socialism and Saint-Simon*, translated by Charlotte Sattler. Yellow Springs, Ohio: Antioch Press.

————. [1928] 1978. *Le Socialisme*. Paris: Retz.

————. 1938. *L'évolution pédagogique en France*. Paris: Alcan.

————. [1938] 1977. *The Evolution of Educational Thought*, translated by Peter Collins. London: Routledge & Kegan Paul.

———. 1950. *Leçons de sociologie: Physique des moeurs et du droit.* Paris: Presses Universitaires de France.

———. [1950] 1983. *Professional Ethics and Civic Morals,* translated by Cornelia Brookfield. Westport, Conn.: Greenwood Press.

———. [1955] 1983. *Pragmatism and Sociology,* translated by J. C. Whitehouse. Cambridge: Cambridge University Press.

Duvignaud, Jean. 1965. *Durkheim, sa vie, son ouevre.* Paris: Presses Universitaires de France.

Ellenberger, Henri. 1970. *The Discovery of the Unconscious.* New York: Basic Books.

Espinas, Alfred. [1882] 1977. *Des sociétés animales.* New York: Arno Press.

———. 1925. *Descartes et la morale.* Paris: Editions Bossard.

Fauconnet, Paul. 1920. *La Responsabilité: Etude sociologique.* Paris: Alcan.

———. [1922] 1958. "Introduction to the Original Edition." Pp. 27–57 in *Education and Sociology,* by E. Durkheim. Glencoe, Ill.: Free Press.

Filloux, Jean-Claude. 1976. "Il ne faut pas oublier que je suis fils de rabbin." *Revue française de sociologie* 17:259–66.

———. 1977. *Durkheim et le socialisme.* Paris: Droz.

Fisher, Seymour, and Roger Greenberg. 1977. *The Scientific Credibility of Freud's Theories and Therapy.* New York: Basic Books.

Flew, Anthony. 1985. *Thinking About Social Thinking: The Philosophy of the Social Sciences.* New York: Basil Blackwell.

Fodor, Jerry. 1981. *Representations.* Cambridge, Mass.: MIT Press.

Foulquié, Paul. 1978. *Dictionnaire de la lanque philosophique.* Paris: Presses Universitaires de France.

Frazer, James G. [1890] 1981. *The Golden Bough: The Roots of Religion and Folklore.* New York: Avenel.

Freud, Sigmund. [1900] 1965. *The Interpretation of Dreams.* New York: Avon Books.

———. [1901] 1965. *The Psychopathology of Everyday Life.* New York: W. W. Norton.

———. [1905] 1974. "Three Essays on the Theory of Sexuality." Pp. 125–243 in *The Standard Edition of the Complete Psychological Works of Sigmund Freud,* edited by J. Strachey, Vol. 7. London: Hogarth Press.

———. [1907] 1963. "Obsessive Acts and Religious Practices." Pp. 17–26 in *Freud: Character and Culture,* edited by P. Rieff. New York: Collier Books.

———. [1913] 1950. *Totem and Taboo.* New York: W. W. Norton.

———. [1919] 1963. "Preface to Reik's *Ritual: Psychoanalytic Studies.*" Pp. 222–27 in *Freud: Character and Culture,* edited by P. Rieff. New York: Collier Books.

———. [1921] 1959. *Group Psychology and the Analysis of the Ego.* New York: W. W. Norton.

———. [1925] 1959. *An Autobiographical Study.* New York: W. W. Norton.

———. [1927] 1967. *The Future of an Illusion.* New York: W. W. Norton.

———. [1930] 1961. *Civilization and Its Discontents.* New York: W. W. Norton.

———. [1933] 1965. *New Introductory Lectures on Psychoanalysis.* New York: W. W. Norton.

Fromm, Erich. 1955. *The Sane Society.* Greenwich: Fawcett.

———. 1962. *Beyond the Chains of Illusion.* New York: Simon & Schuster.

Gernet, Louis. 1981. *The Anthropology of Ancient Greece.* Baltimore: Johns Hopkins University Press.

Gibbs, Jack P. 1982. "Testing the Theory of Status Integration and Suicide Rates." *American Sociological Review* 47:227–37.

Gibbs, Jack P., and Walter T. Martin. 1964. *Status Integration and Suicide: A Sociological Study.* Eugene: University of Oregon Press.

Giddens, Anthony. 1971. "Durkheim's Political Sociology." *Sociological Review* 19:477–519.

———. 1976. *New Rules of Sociological Method.* New York: Basic Books.

———. 1977. *Studies in Social and Political Theory.* New York: Basic Books.

———. 1986. *Durkheim on Politics and the State.* London: Polity Press.

Goodwin, Patrick. 1967. "Schopenhauer." Pp. 325–32 in *The Encyclopedia of Philosophy,* edited by P. Edwards. Vol. 7. New York: The Macmillan Co.

Greenberg, Louis M. 1976. "Bergson and Durkheim as Sons and Assimilators: The Early Years." *French Historical Studies* 9:619–34.

Guyau, Jean-Marie. [1885] 1907. *Esquisse d'une morale sans obligation ni sanction.* Paris: Alcan.

———. [1887] 1909. *L'irréligion de l'avenir.* Paris: Alcan.

———. [1887] 1962. *The Non-religion of the Future.* New York: Shocken Books.

Halbwachs, Maurice. [1912] 1974. *La Classe ouvrière et les niveaux.* London: Gordon & Breach.

———. 1918. "La doctrine d'Emile Durkheim." *Revue philosophique* 85:353–411.

———. 1925. "Les Origines puritaines du capitalisme." *Revue d'histoire et de philosophie religieuses* 5:132–57.

———. [1930] 1978. *The Causes of Suicide.* London: Routledge & Kegan Paul.

———. [1938] 1964. *Esquisse d'une psychologie des classes sociales.* Paris: Colin.

———. [1938] 1970. *Morphologie sociale.* Paris: Colin.

———. [1950] 1980. *The Collective Memory.* New York: Harper & Row.

Halphen, Etienne. 1987. "Préface Affective." Pp. 5–10 in *Durkheim: 100 ans de sociologie a Bordeaux.* Bordeaux: Socio-Diffusion.

Hamelin, O. 1921. *Le Systeme de Descartes.* Paris: Librairie Felix Alcan.

———. 1927. *Le Système de Renouvier.* Paris: J. Vrin.

———. 1952. *Essai sur les elements principaux de la représentations.* Paris: Presses Universitaires de France.

Hamlyn, David. 1980. *Schopenhauer.* London: Routledge & Kegan Paul.

Herbart, Johann. [1816] 1904. *A Textbook in Psychology: An Attempt to Found the Science of Psychology on Experience, Metaphysics, and Mathematics.* New York: D. Appleton.

Hertz, Robert. [1907–1909] 1960. *Death and the Right Hand.* Aberdeen: Cohen & West.

———. 1922. "Le péché et l'expiation dans les sociétés primitives." *Revue de l'Histoire des Religions* 86:5–60.

———. 1928. *Mélanges de sociologie religieuse et folklore.* Paris: Alcan.

Hertzberg, Arthur. 1968. *The French Enlightenment and the Jews.* New York: Columbia University Press.

Hilbert, Richard A. 1986. "Anomie and the Moral Regulation of Reality: The Durkheimian Tradition in Modern Relief." *Sociological Theory* 4:1–19.

Hirst, P. Q. 1975. *Durkheim, Bernard and Epistemology.* London: Routledge & Kegan Paul.

Horkheimer, Max. 1947. *The Eclipse of Reason.* New York: Oxford University Press.

Horowitz, Irving L. 1987. "Disenthralling Sociology." *Society* 24:48–55.

Hubert, Henri. [1925] 1934. *The Rise of the Celts.* New York: Alfred A. Knopf.

Hubert, Henri, and Marcel Mauss. [1899] 1964. *Sacrifice: Its Nature and Function.* Chicago: University of Chicago Press.

———. [1904] 1972. *A General Theory of Magic.* New York: W. W. Norton

Isay, Raymond. 1946. *Paul Landowski.* Paris: Librairie de France.

James, William. [1896] 1931. *The Will to Believe, and Other Essays in Popular Philosophy.* New York: Longman Inc.

———. [1879–1907] 1948. *Essays in Pragmatism.* New York: Hafner Publishing.

Janik, A., and Stephen Toulmin. 1973. *Wittgenstein's Vienna.* New York: Simon & Schuster.

Javelet, Robert. 1969. *Epinal à la belle époque.* Mulhouse: Presses des Etablissements Braun et cie.

Joas, Hans. 1985. *G. H. Mead.* Cambridge, Mass.: MIT Press.

Johnson, Samuel. 1755. *A Dictionary of the English Language.* Oxford: Clarendon Press.

Jones, Ernest. 1981. *The Life and Work of Sigmund Freud.* Vols. 1–3. New York: Basic Books.

Jones, Robert A. 1986. *Emile Durkheim.* Beverly Hills: Sage Publications.

Kant, Immanuel. [1788] 1956. *Critique of Practical Reason.* Indianapolis: Bobbs-Merrill.

Karady, Victor. 1972. *Maurice Halbwachs: Classes sociales et morphologie.* Paris: Les Editions de Minuit.

———. 1976. *Durkheim: Textes.* Vols. 1–3. Paris: Les Editions de Minuit.

Kowalski, Gregory S., Charles E. Faupel, and Paul D. Starr, 1987. "Urbanism and Suicide: A Study of American Counties." *Social Forces* 66:85–101.

Knapp, Peter. 1985. "The Question of Hegelian Influence Upon Durkheim's Sociology." *Sociological Inquiry* 55:1–15.

La Capra, Dominick. 1972. *Emile Durkheim: Sociologist and Philosopher.* Ithaca: Cornell University Press.

Lacroix, Bernard. 1981. *Durkheim et le politique.* Paris: Presses de la Fondation Nationale des Sciences Politiques.

Lalande, André. [1926] 1980. *Vocabulaire technique et critique de la philosophie.* Paris: Presses Universitaires de France.

———. 1960. "Allocution." Pp. 20–23 in *Centenaire de la naissance d'Emile Durkheim.* Paris: Annales de l'Université de Paris.

Landowski, Paul. 1943. *Peut-on enseigner les beaux arts?* Paris: Editions Baudiniere.

Laplanche, Jean, and J. B Pontalis. 1974. *The Language of Psychoanalysis.* New York: W. W. Norton.

Lèvy, Albert. 1904. *Stirner et Nietzsche.* Paris: Société Nouvelle.

Levy-Bruhl, Lucien. 1885. *L'idée de responsabilité.* Paris: Hachette.

———. 1899. *The History of Modern Philosophy in France.* Chicago: Open Court Publishing.

———. 1903. *La morale et la science des moeurs.* Paris: Alcan.

———. 1922. "Conference sur Emile Durkheim et son oeuvre." Paper presented in Paris to the Faculté de Droit.

———. [1922] 1966. *The Soul of the Primitive.* Chicago: Henry Regnery.

Littré, Emile. [1863] 1963. *Dictionnaire de la langue française.* Vols. 1–9. Paris: Gallimard.

Logue, William. 1983. *From Philosophy to Sociology: The Evolution of French Liberalism, 1870–1914.* De Kalb: Northern Illinois University Press.

Lukes, Steven 1982. *Durkehim: The Rules of Sociological Method and Selected Texts on Sociology and Its Method.* New York: Free Press.

———. 1985. *Emile Durkheim: His Life and Work.* Stanford, Calif.: Stanford University Press.

Lyonnet, Stanislas, and Leopold Sabourin. 1970. *Sin, Redemption and Sacrifice: A Biblical and Patristic Study.* Rome: Biblical Institute Press.

Magee, Bryan. 1983. *The Philosophy of Schopenhauer.* New York: Oxford University Press.

Mann, Thomas. [1939] 1955. "Introduction." Pp. iii–xxiii in *The Works of Schopenhauer,* edited by W. Durant and T. Mann, New York: Frederick Ungar.

Marrus, Michael R. 1971. *The Politics of Assimilation: A Study of the French Jewish Community at the Time of the Dreyfus Affair.* Oxford: Clarendon Press.

Mauss, Marcel. [1950] 1979a. *Sociology and Psychology.* London: Routledge & Kegan Paul.

———. [1950 1979b. *Seasonal Variations of the Eskimo: A Study in Social Morphology.* London: Routledge & Kegan Paul.

———. 1969. *Oeuvres.* Vols. 1–3. Paris: Les Editions de Minuit.

———. 1983. *Sociologie et anthropologie.* Paris: Presses Universitaires de France.

Meillet, A. 1906. "Comment les mots changent de sens." *L'Année sociologique* 9:1–39.

Merton, Robert K. 1957. *Social Theory and Social Structure.* New York: Free Press.

Meštrović, Stjepan G. 1982. "In the Shadow of Plato: Durkheim and Freud on Suicide and Society." Ph.D., dissertation, Syracuse University.

———. 1984. "Durkheim's Concept of the Unconscious." *Current Perspectives in Social Theory* 5:267–88.

———. 1985a. "Anomia and Sin in Durkheim's Thought." *Journal for the Scientific Study of Religion* 24:119–36.

———. 1985b. "A Sociological Conceptualization of Trauma." *Social Science and Medicine* 21:835–48.

———. 1985c. "Durkheim's Renovated Rationalism and the Idea That 'Collective Life Is Only Made of Representations.'" *Current Perspectives in Social Theory* 6:199–218.

———. 1986. "Magic and Psychiatric Commitment in India." *International Journal of Law and Psychiatry* 9:431–49.

———. 1987. "Durkheim's Concept of Anomie Considered as a 'Total' Social Fact." *British Journal of Sociology* 38:567–83.

———. 1988a. "Durkheim's Conceptualization of Political Anomie." *Research in Political Sociology* 6:1–24.

———. 1988b. "Review of Philippe Besnard's *L'anomie.*" *Contemporary Sociology* 17:836–38.

Meštrović, Stjepan G., and Hélène M. Brown. 1985. "Durkheim's Concept of Anomie as Dérèglement." *Social Problems* 33:81–99.

Meštrović, Stjepan G., and Barry Glassner. 1983. "A Durkheimian Hypothesis on Stress." *Social Science and Medicine* 17:1315–27.

Mizruchi, Ephraim H. 1983. *Regulating Society.* Chicago: University of Chicago Press.

Montgomery, Robert L. 1984. "Bias in Interpreting Social Facts: Is It a Sin?" *Journal for the Scientific Study of Religion* 23:278–91.

Niebuhr, Reinhold. 1976. *Love and Justice.* Gloucester, Mass.: Peter Smith Publishers.

Nietzsche, Friedrich. [1901] 1968. *The Will to Power*. New York: Random House.

Ochs, Peter. 1986. "Scriptural Pragmatism: Jewish Philosophy's Conception of Truth." *International Philosophical Quarterly* 26:131–40.

O'Keefe, Daniel. 1982. *Stolen Lightning: The Social Theory of Magic*. New York: Random House.

Orru, Marco. 1983. "The Ethics of Anomie: Jean Marie Guyau and Emile Durkheim." *British Journal of Sociology* 34:499–518.

————. 1987. *Anomie: History and Meanings*. London: Allen & Unwin.

Oxford English Dictionary. 1972. *The Compact Edition of the Oxford English Dictionary*. 2 Vols. Oxford: Clarendon Press.

Park, Robert E., and Ernest W. Burgess. 1921. *Introduction to the Science of Sociology*. Chicago: University of Chicago Press.

Parsons, Talcott. 1937. *The Structure of Social Action*. Glencoe, Ill.: Free Press.

Pickering, W.S.F. 1975. *Durkheim on Religion*. London: Routledge & Kegan Paul.

————. 1979. *Durkheim: Essays on Morals and Education*. London: Routledge & Kegan Paul.

————. 1984. *Durkheim's Sociology of Religion: Themes and Theories*. London: Routledge & Kegan Paul.

Raphael, Freddy, and R. Weyl. 1980. *Regards nouveaux sur les juifs d'Alsace*. Strasbourg: Editions d'Alsace.

Renouvier, Charles. 1892. "Schopenhauer et la metaphysique du pessimisme." *L'Année philosophique* 3:1–61.

Ribot, Theodule. 1874. *La Philosophie de Schopenhauer*. Paris: Librairie Gerner Bailliere.

————. 1896. *The Psychology of Attention*. Chicago: Open Court.

Riesman, David. [1950] 1977. *The Lonely Crowd*. New Haven: Yale University Press.

————. 1954. *Individualism Reconsidered and Other Essays*. Glencoe, Ill.: Free Press.

Riesman, Paul. 1977. *Freedom in Fulani Social Life: An Introspective Ethnography* Chicago: University of Chicago Press.

Rochberg-Halton, Eugene. 1986. *Meaning and Modernity: Social Theory in the Pragmatic Attitude*. Chicago: University of Chicago Press.

Scharf, B. R. 1970. "Durkheimian and Freudian Theories of Religion: The Case for Judaism." *British Journal of Sociology* 21:151–63.

Schopenhauer, Arthur. [1813] 1899. *On the Fourfold Root of the Principle of Sufficient Reason and On the Will in Nature*, translated by Mme. Karl Hillebrand. London: G. Bell & Sons.

————. [1818] 1977. *The World as Will and Idea*, translated by R. Haldane and J. Kemp. Vols. 1–3 New York: AMS Press.

Schwarzfuchs, Simon. 1982. *Breve histoire des juifs de France*. Paris: Editions Polyglottes.

Simmel, Georg. [1907] 1986. *Schopenhauer and Nietzsche*, translated by Helmut Loiskandl, Deena Weinstein and Michael Weinstein. Amherst: University of Massachusetts Press.

Simpson, George. 1963. *Emile Durkheim*. New York: Thomas Y. Crowell.

Sirianni, Carmen J. 1984. "Justice and the Division of Labour." *Sociological Review* 32:449–70.

Stauben, Daniel. 1860. *Scenes de la vie juive en Alsace*. Paris: Levy.

Strikwerda, Robert A. 1982. "Emile Durkheim's Philosophy of Science:

Framework for a New Social Science." Ph.D. dissertation, University of Notre Dame.

Sylvan, David, and Barry Glassner. 1985. *A Rationalist Methodology for the Social Sciences*. New York: Basil Blackwell.

Tönnies, Ferdinand. [1887] 1963. *Community and Society,* translated by Charles Loomis. New York: Harper & Row.

Torrance, T. F. 1977. *Calvin's Doctrine of Man*. Wesport, Conn.: Greenwood Press.

Traugott, Mark. 1978. *Emile Durkheim on Institutional Analysis*. Chicago: University of Chicago Press.

Trigg, Roger, 1985. *Understanding Social Science*. New York: Basil Blackwell.

Turner, Stephen. 1986. *The Search for a Methodology of Social Science: Durkheim, Weber, and the Nineteenth Century Problem of Cause, Probability, and Action*. Dordrecht: D. Reidel.

———. 1988. "Durkheim Fra i Statistici." *Quaderni di Sociologia* (forthcoming).

Verneaux, Roger. 1945. *Renouvier: Disciple et critique de Kant*. Paris: Vrin.

Wallwork, Ernest. 1972. *Durkheim: Morality and Milieu*. Cambridge: Harvard University Press.

Weymuller, François. 1985. *Histoire d'Epinal: Des origines à nos jours*. Le Coteau: Editions Horvath.

White, Allan R. 1970. *Truth*. New York: Doubleday.

Wistrich, Robert S. 1982. *Socialism and the Jews*. Rutherford, N.J.: Farleigh Dickinson University Press.

Wrong, Dennis. 1961. "The Over-socialized Conception of Man in Modern Sociology." *American Sociological Review* 26:183–93.

Wundt, Wilhelm. [1874] 1910. *Principles of Physiological Psychology*. New York: The Macmillan Co.

———. [1886] 1902. *Ethics: An Investigation of the Facts and Laws of the Moral Life*. New York: The Macmillan Co.

———. [1887] 1916. *Elements of Folk Psychology: Outlines of Psychological History of the Development of Mankind*. London: Allen & Unwin.

———. 1907. *The Principles of Morality and the Departments of the Moral Life*. New York: The Macmillan Co.

———. [1912] 1973. *An Introduction to Psychology*. New York: Arno Press.

Index